Branch Rickey

BOOKS BY ARTHUR MANN

THE JACKIE ROBINSON STORY
BASEBALL CONFIDENTIAL
THE REAL McGRAW (*edited*)
HOW TO PLAY WINNING BASEBALL
BRANCH RICKEY: AMERICAN IN ACTION

Branch Rickey

American in Action

BY

ARTHUR MANN

1 9 5 7

The Riverside Press Cambridge

HOUGHTON MIFFLIN COMPANY BOSTON

The Riverside Press

CAMBRIDGE · MASSACHUSETTS

PRINTED IN THE U.S.A.

Branch Rickey

1

FROM THE DAY he entered the world in December, 1881, Branch Rickey has been close to the core of controversy. An experience in his seventy-fifth year, when he applied for a birth certificate, illustrates the unbelievable scope of the difficulties he can encounter without even trying. He needed the certificate to obtain a passport to travel in Mexico where he planned to scout baseball players for his Pittsburgh Pirates. The custodian of vital records at the Scioto County Court House in Portsmouth, Ohio, insisted he was born on December 6, 1881.

"That's possible but ridiculous!" Rickey argued. "My mother ought to know, and my father, too. They observed my birthday on December twentieth, and so have I over seventy times."

"But see the record for yourself. It says here — "

"I don't care what it says," Rickey interrupted. "Just pencil a line through the six and add a twenty. That's my official birthday, because it always has been. Now, my certificate, please."

The record was corrected. A careless clerk had listed Branch and his older cousin, Ephraim Rickey, now a Portsmouth realtor, as born in Madison Township on the same day.

Except for the birth-date error, responsibility for Branch Rickey's personal and professional complications can be charged to his pioneering thoughts and perpetual action and a stubborn refusal to compromise basic teachings and beliefs. That the complications in his life were a by-product of it and never an end in themselves may be questioned in many quarters. Some sports writers commercialize their conviction that the man and his methods are steeped in gall or guile. Some former associates agree with them, for they have doubted Rickey's sincerity on the basis of a presumed affront. He is conscious of his shortcomings, but seldom attempts an explanation — on the grounds that "friends need none, and explaining to enemies does no good."

Friendship with Rickey is an unforgettable experience with many rewards, but remaining a friend calls for the sublime patience and fortitude displayed by his busy employer in Pittsburgh, John Galbreath. After arriving in New York for an important dinner conference on baseball matters, Galbreath left town without meal or meeting. While he waited, Rickey, oblivious to the appointment, was window shopping on Fifth Avenue with Mrs. Rickey. Always properly remorseful after such catastrophes, Rickey's apparent helplessness arouses enough compassion in his victims to win forgiveness.

Branch Rickey's relatives, of course, have more of an emotional strain than his friends, for there is no escape or retreat for them. Anger and reprisal do no good. Rickey invariably pleads *nolo contendere* and throws himself on the mercy of the offended.

"Turn around. We should have stopped at Dayton!" he called one day to the driver of his automobile speeding across Ohio. The driver made no secret of his impatience at having to return thirty miles until Rickey explained, "I was supposed to stop and pick up Mrs. Rickey. She's waiting for me in a drugstore there . . . I hope."

Ordinarily such oversights indicate a wretched memory,

but Branch Rickey is blessed with a most retentive one. It simply backfires when he burdens it with last-minute items, particularly promises of favors. But very often necessary rearrangement of tight schedules, aided by his constant foe, the clock, push some appointments or promises into the future. Of course, he catches up on everything eventually, sometimes to the surprise and remorse of those who have "given up" on him.

Many years ago Rickey hired an assistant who plunged into work with the zeal characteristic of all his employees. After two hectic months, the uncomplaining worker handed Rickey a memorandum for his signature. Rickey stared in disbelief at an order for the auditor to put the assistant on the payroll retroactive to his first day on the job. He insisted it must be a joke. "No salary for two months! Why didn't you say something, boy? How on earth did you live?"

While scrawling his signature, Rickey murmured that he was truly sorry, that a thing like this should never be, that he was guilty of carelessness, neglect and allied shortcomings.

Rickey has provided sports writers with "live copy" throughout his professional life. With no effort at all, he has caused an eddy of dispute one day and been engulfed the next when it returned as a wave of eight-column indignation. Some writers sincerely believe he has planned his provocations. He never has, though he has always known the value of headlines to sports, and was the first in baseball to employ a team publicity man.

One sports writer emerged from an early Rickey press conference in Brooklyn cursing him for giving out seven or eight stories, each worthy of an individual headline. Asked if he could spread them over several days, the writer said, "No, because we can't trust each other. I've got to run them all in one story."

News and comment about Rickey is never neutral. He is

constantly pictured as either a saint or a rogue, but he is neither. When on Sunday, August 28, 1904, he absented himself from the Cincinnati baseball park and was therefore fired from the Reds and his first big-league job, the manager did not understand why, nor did any of the writers, who garbled the story unfairly for the next fifty years. The truth was simply that he had secretly vowed never to play baseball on Sunday in tribute to his mother for voicing no objection to his entering a profession that was held in low esteem. Rickey has made no particular effort to correct distorted explanations for his absence from ball parks on Sundays — religious bigotry, strait-lacing, hard-shell Methodism, and so on — or repetitious insistence that he was insincere. One writer made the preposterous claim that Rickey rented a special room in the Railroad Y.M.C.A. overlooking the St. Louis ball park in order to watch the game without actually breaking the "pledge."

Yet, had critics known the facts, it is doubtful that they would have believed or understood the simplicity of Rickey's nature. For instance, he boycotted his own St. Louis ball park on a weekday in the early 1920's. An old Ohio Wesleyan University friend and football teammate had dropped into the Dodier Street office. The visitor, Dr. Charles Thomas, a St. Louis dentist, was a Negro. Since Negroes were not permitted in the Sportsman's Park grandstand, Rickey, vice-president and field manager of the Cardinals, remained in his office throughout the game in order to chat with his old friend.

"Tommy," he whispered, gesturing toward the adjacent ball park, "some day we'll have all that changed."

While this might easily be construed as a prophecy, in view of Rickey's integration of the Negro into organized baseball some twenty-odd years later, he was merely expressing a logical belief that the refusal to sell tickets to Negroes had to end one day.

There have been many times over the years when Branch Rickey preferred not to be understood. During the progress of complicated baseball deals, for example, the truth in print could upset well-laid plans in this highly competitive business. Truth-telling is a fetish with Rickey and, in these cases, to sidestep the costly pitfall of disclosure, he has discouraged inquisition with a skill at circumlocution that has driven many an exasperated newsman to drink, perhaps, but not before he typed out an angry reprisal for the next edition.

Except for wincing from an occasional low blow, Rickey has risen above the infamy. Once at the peak of a long and vicious attack in print when he was carefully assembling evidence to support a whopping action for civil libel against a sports writer and his paper, he was offered a lethal weapon — a vicious letter over the sports writer's signature, reeking with racial hatred and naming prominent names. It was the ideal instrument to silence his tormentor, but he tossed it aside with, "I thought this fellow was a responsible person. We never should have taken him seriously. Now we can forget him."

Even Rickey's staff, quietly indignant at being denied sweet revenge, failed to realize that sinking so low as to use the sports writer's tactics in reprisal was more odious to him than the prolonged attack in print. His meticulous observance of moral codes, temperance and ethics is disarmingly unobtrusive to those around him. His rigid principles of self-discipline are simple, rather than narrow. He despises the use of alcohol, yet he can associate with drinkers and respect them. His approach to spiritual observance in living is more nonsectarian than his supposed Methodism would indicate. In a world of shifting spiritual values, Rickey's stout anchorage to simple precepts makes him something of an anachronism.

Perhaps the greatest shock of his life came after his seventieth year when a leading churchman declared as they lunched
togther, "Hardly anybody really believes in the divinity of
Jesus any more," and that the Apostles' Creed couldn't be
applied to modern thinking and spiritual philosophy.
Stunned and hurt, Rickey listened to the observation in
silence. He returned to his office unable to work. He went
home thoroughly upset by the startling pronouncement. For
several days he remained depressed, sinking deeper in bewilderment. Early assimilation of a few indestructible truths
had shaped his mature spiritual philosophy like an inverted
pyramid. By tearing away the foundation stones in a single,
sweeping generality, the liberal-minded prelate knocked the
whole structure askew.

But the observation, so foreign to his lifelong acceptance
of the Christian ritual, left him struggling alone to assemble
the pieces of a shattered belief. He was unable to pray or
even give customary thanks before his meals. "I feel like
a stranger in my own house," he reflected bitterly.

Eventually he developed a refusal to reconcile the declaration with his deep-rooted credo. He composed a strong letter
to his church pastor, who had also heard the statement
without protest. Phrasing the Apostles' Creed pointedly,
Rickey expressed doubt that any responsible cleric could
preach and teach the Bible and Methodism without literal
acceptance of the Creed. He then resigned his membership.

At this writing, nearly five years later, he had not mailed
the letter, though the problem continued to badger him.
He could think and work, but not with the same peace and
spiritual security he knew all his life. But his dilemma did
not limit his enthusiasm when a new and worthy approach
to Christian teaching and living sought his helping hand.
He almost forgot the unposted letter to the pastor.

Pioneers in the Fellowship of Christian Athletes needed funds. The movement had interested an impressive number of "name" athletes in many sports: Otto Graham, Doak Walker, Robin Roberts, Alvin Dark and Carl Erskine are a few of the 150 top athletes now actively spreading the idea of applying Christian principles in daily thought, living and sports competition.

Branch Rickey quickly assembled a group of prominent Pittsburghers as his luncheon guests and prevailed upon them to join him in establishing a treasury for the Fellowship. The two-hour meeting produced $25,000. Rickey was keynote speaker at the organization's first national conference. He termed the mushrooming movement an unparalleled opportunity for outstanding athletes. In a nation of hero-worshiping youth, the Fellowship could be the most "effective witnesses for a faith to the youngsters over whom all great athletes exercise a unique and priceless influence."

The roots of such spiritual solidity are necessarily deep and, in Branch Rickey's case, go back to the hills of Southern Ohio. There both paternal and maternal forebears, New England born, pioneered in the early nineteenth century. Great-grandfather Jacob Rickey broke the soil in Madison Township and preached the gospel of Baptist fundamentalism. Grandfather Ephraim Wanser Rickey was equally devout, but he concentrated on farming and became one of the largest landowners in the township. He married Annie Rockwell and had two daughters, Rosetta and Telina; and three sons, James Silas, Jacob Franklin and Nathan Thompson. He observed the marriage of each with a gift of a house, two hundred acres and stock.

Jacob Franklin married Emily Brown on March 12, 1874. Their first-born, Orla Edwin, lived, but the next two children died in infancy. When Wesley Branch was eighteen months old, they sold the farm and left the tragic memories of

Madison Township. They crossed the Scioto and settled in hilly Rush Township on the rugged and less esteemed "west side" of the river. Frank had bought a piece of distressed property, a small house and one hundred acres, for $330.

A generous meadow of the acreage was watered by Duck Run, a rivulet with fingers reaching up into the 1000-foot hills of Morgan Township. This was the scene of Branch Rickey's early awareness. He doesn't remember the flood of 1884 that inundated Duck Run and the McDaniel-Owens store at nearby Owensville Fork, but he well recalls the bounty it yielded. From Reilly's bookstore in Portsmouth, ruined by flood and fire, Branch's father brought home a dozen damaged books. He still treasures the pictorial Bible with Gustave Doré's magnificent steel-engraved illustrations.

Branch couldn't read, but he learned much of his mother's skill at answering questions by personal parallel and colorful anecdote. The Doré book became the foundation of his education. Each glorious engraving came to life as Emily Rickey narrated the story behind the picture.

Branch Rickey knew the Bible before he could say the words. With teen-aged Orla at school and doing man-sized farm chores, Emily was Branch's only playmate for nearly seven years. She taught him to read before letting Minnie English take him to grade school at Rushtown. Her fifth child, Frank, appeared in 1888. That year Jacob Franklin was elected Scioto County Commissioner for the second time. He had prospered in Duck Run, though not in terms of hard cash. He built the soil and added to his acreage, set out peach orchards and, during his first term as Commissioner, helped get a 312-foot all-purpose bridge across Brush Creek at a cost of $495. When his brother Jim's wife died, he took the oldest of the three boys, Lewis Denver, called "Dude," and young Branch lived the most unforgettable summer of his boyhood.

At sixteen, Dude was gay, good-looking and had the easy manner of a confidence man. He could dance, sing, play musical instruments, tell jokes, and, wonder of wonders, execute a perfect backflip. He even had a short cut to the backflip, "soople oil," to make uncooperative muscles more "soople." Branch, with eagerness equaled only by his gullibility, followed Dude's directions. He dug enough earthworms to pack a quart canning jar three quarters full, filled it with water from a nearby sulphur spring and "cured" it in the hot sun for two weeks. Fortunately Branch's father discovered the nauseating mess on a fence post the day before his acrobatic-minded son was to rub the "soople oil" on his muscles.

The Gay Nineties began for Branch Rickey with the discovery of baseball. He had learned to backflip without benefit of lotion, but tumbling gave way to his new interest. Orla, six years older, bigger, and left-handed, could throw hard enough to pitch regularly for local teams and Branch could hold the speed. His throwing arm had unusual power and only his size kept him from the pitching mound.

A climax of Branch's earliest baseball efforts came in the big game between Duck Run and Dry Run on a midsummer Saturday. He had risen at dawn and joined Warren Lauterbach with baskets of peaches to sell in Portsmouth. At fifty cents a basket, he could gross between twelve and eighteen dollars for the family pocketbook. The game began at 2 P.M. in a bottom meadow near Dry Run and drew a partisan crowd of Dry Runners. Branch's piercing cry of encouragement to Orla from behind the plate and through a catcher's mask matched the shouts of derision through nine exciting innings. Duck Run was only a couple of putouts from victory when Branch yelled:

"Come on, Orlie! Make this the big one!"

Orla cut loose with one of his speediest pitches. The ball

sailed up and over Branch's arms and three base runners circled happily as the catcher raced back for the ball. Fortunately the roar of the crowd drowned whatever young Rickey had to say about the wild pitch. He recovered the ball and continued on home, for the game was over.

"We'd have played baseball anyway," Rickey once said in explaining the irrepressible urge, "but we renewed our enthusiasm daily by devouring the news in the Cincinnati *Enquirer*. It was our contact with the paradise of big-league baseball. Cincinnati was my team, of course, but I had no particular hero. We'd read about the new plays and rules in the *Enquirer* and then check the rules in the new *Spalding's Guide*. You had to study these changes to meet challenges. When some kid yelled, 'Look it up in the book!' you had to yell back, 'I already did.'

"The *Guides* also carried pages of ads that tantalized kids always hungry for good equipment. Everything was cheaper compared with today's prices, but we never had enough money. In the early nineties baseballs were priced at five cents for the 'Nickel Rocket' to a dollar and a quarter for the official National League ball. You could get a kid's bat for a nickel, and a 'Wagon Tongue' for a dollar. The cheapest catcher's mask was fifty cents, but a hard foul bent the wire. The good ones were four dollars."

Sunday in the Rickey home was devoted to worship and rest. After washing at the large stone table just outside the kitchen door, the family gathered for a substantial breakfast. Later, while Emily was finishing the dishes, J. Frank hitched "Old May" to a small surrey. The five Rickeys, with little Frank on Emily's lap, rode to church and sang hymns in four-part harmony en route. Most of Duck Run knew when the Rickeys were on their way to service. Few humans, Branch Rickey believes, had a firmer faith than his mother.

"I was as cruel and as thoughtless a boy as the worst," he

recalled with a heavy sigh. "I once heard my mother say in my presence that she thought 'Branch could step over a hoe handle easier' than anyone she had ever known. Yet, there was no lashing from tongue or whip, or corporal punishment of any kind. What she did on one occasion had a deeper effect. She took me into her bedroom, reviewed what I had done and asked me to kneel with her at the bedside.

"There I heard her ask God's forgiveness, not for me, but for herself as a mother who had not done her duty. In return, she promised to be a better mother and not commit the sin of letting me misbehave. It was a solemn and unforgettable moment. I felt as though I had hit her, and I was thoroughly chastised."

The fall of 1892 brought a major milestone in Branch Rickey's life. He had completed academic classes at the Rushtown school and was eligible to attend a more advanced school. The nearest was in Lucasville, a distance of four miles by short cut through Buck Knob. After a winter of watching Branch and Orla battle the elements, J. Frank Rickey rented a six-room house in Lucasville on the Valley Pike, diagonally across from Chandler J. Moulton's general store.

The school at Lucasville consisted of three large rooms in a two-story frame building, with plenty of play yard in the rear. Branch began classes there in fifth-sixth grade work with George Bricker as a teacher. He served under the local Superintendent of Schools, Frank Appel. Frank was only twenty-three and still an undergraduate at Ohio Wesleyan University in Delaware. His brother, Edgar, was in Branch's class, and a great friend from the start. The Appels were special, and when Frank was appointed superintendent of schools at Wheelersburg, Ohio, upriver from Portsmouth, it was no ordinary loss.

The new school head was James H. Finney. He had a

force and firmness that belied his apparent good nature and soon Branch Rickey suffered the first major scholastic crisis of his life. Sensitive and conscious of his rural "west side-ness" — his father still operated the Duck Run farm — Branch felt that "Professor" Finney was too critical of his stacatto, almost stuttering speech. His classmates compounded his errors and he resented the ridicule. Without warning one spring day he quit school and returned to Duck Run "where he belonged." His forebears were farmers, and he could be one, too, without an education.

"It was an adolescent flare-up," Rickey explains. "I was about fourteen at the time and unhappy about everything, particularly about some recent grades I had made. They, as much as the imagined hostility from Mr. Finney, were responsible for my retreat to Duck Run. I told my father I wanted to quit and work on the farm. He consented and took me over on Sunday night. After a private discussion with the hired man, Gus Massie, I was turned over to Gus and worked like the dickens from Monday through Friday.

"I was drilling wheat on Friday, and, thinking about my acrobatic cousin, Dude Rickey, I decided to try a back somersault off the forward moving drill. I stood with my face toward the horses and did the flip off the top of the drill, and landed on my head. I spent Saturday pulling beans over across the run. We pulled beans all morning until I thought I'd die of exhaustion and the hurt in my neck from my fall and I was wondering how in the name of common sense I could get back to school. Well, Gus knew the signs and he got me back into Lucasville. Mr. Finney and I never had words, or any real difficulty. He became an idol of mine."

One reason could have been Finney's interest in baseball. He organized teams and played first base on them. Ed Appel remembered it well.

"One of Jim's first teams was the Lucasville Giants," Appel said. "I was a pretty good hitter, and got the catching post. I was doing a fair job this day, but Finney hadn't put 'Rick' on the team. From the start of the game Rick sat or stood behind third base like a fish out of water. He plunked his catcher's mitt, twirled his wire mask, plunked the glove again, and paced back and forth. It was like somebody peering over my shoulder, breathing down my neck. It made me nervous and made me tired.

"Around the middle of the game, I called him to spell me. In doing so, I knew I was losing my catching job on the Giants. Right away he took over as though he owned the whole team. He put new life into it and was always catcher after that."

For Branch, a new interest soon challenged baseball for supremacy. Jennie Moulton, fourth of the six Moulton children, lived next to the general store. Branch says he was first impressed by her unusual speed afoot. She was small, but she could outrun any boy or girl in the school yard. She never seemed to get caught, and she had a saucy way of tossing her head at the kids who failed to catch her. However, she was just another girl to Branch until the February morning he found a folded paper addressed to him under the door.

"Among the many things I didn't know," Rickey recalled later, "were the exact requirements and responsibilities of being somebody's Valentine. But I didn't care. Nothing could have stopped me from accepting the honor from such a nice girl. My blissful ignorance included the fact that Jennie Moulton had spent most of the previous evening making six, or maybe a dozen, similar Valentines and slipping them under the doors of as many homes. All I knew was that a nice girl had asked me to be her Valentine. Oh, boy, would I!"

2

SOME DESIGNS for living and growing can have the casual symmetry of a winding stream, but not Branch Rickey's. To him the stark realities of maturing were harsh. The unpredictable demands of teen-aged body and spirit, not to mention pocketbook, distilled a desperation that sometimes left him hopelessly confused, fighting blindly, head down in a bullish charge, against opposition that struck without warning and knew no rules.

Most husky boys of the area pedaled their bicycles in fair imitation of the professional racers, so popular at the time, but Rickey rode his with his head down into the darkness of a covered bridge at Rushtown. Failing to see a team and wagon enter the other end, he pedaled into the shaft, and wrecked his precious Sterling bike.

Countless millions of adolescent male voices have changed without incident, but Branch Rickey's tenor slid for the first time to a froglike growl when he was performing in the Lucasville Methodist Church. He broke up a quartet that included Jennie Moulton, and sent the audience into uncontrollable laughter.

His growing-up difficulties were varied and complex. To give his mother freedom for her endless home chores and neighborly obligations, he took charge of little Frank, seven years his junior. His early supervision of his brother developed into a lifelong paternalism toward him. He worried about him even when Frank was old enough to care for himself.

Branch's schooling had such a patchwork quality that he always faced extra classes to make up lost ground. He nurtured a growing devotion to baseball in which his fame was spreading as a player, but he was upset about it because ball players as a whole had a poor reputation in the society of the time. Jennie was responding to his attention and he wondered whether she and her family would ever "accept" him if he continued to play ball.

The Rickeys now lived in a Lucasville house of their own, but Branch taunted himself with the fact that he was a "west sider" and had no skill for earning pocket money. He tried to relieve this latter shortcoming by taking a sales agency for *Dr. Chase's Third, Last and Complete Receipt Book and Home Physician*. Starting out on his bicycle on a would-be triumph in itinerant merchandising, he stopped first at the nearby home of the Widow Crow. She gave him an order for the $2.90 volume and paid the fifty cents down. But guilt assailed him before he had reached his bicycle, for he knew Mrs. Crow couldn't afford the book. He returned immediately, handed her the money and ended his sales career.

When Branch Rickey was nearing seventeen he lacked a high school education and the chance of getting one. Students came out of the Lucasville school with a smattering of knowledge, but no diploma. Jennie Moulton's brothers were going to college. So were Clyde Brant and Ed Appel. It pinked Branch's pride and heightened his desperation. How could a person get into college with insufficient credits and no money?

Professor Finney offered a solution. If Branch kept up his good work in his final year at Lucasville, Finney would help him bone up on the requirements to be a teacher. If he passed the examinations, the school board might give him a teaching certificate and an appointment. Finney had had one at eighteen and earned $30 a month. The lowest pay now was $35!

Except for farm chores, Branch's only "work" had been playing baseball. He played a lot of it, because he was better than many bigger and older boys. He could run well, hold his own as a left-handed batter and outthrow any catcher he had seen. He could play on any town team in the county.

Branch played no baseball in the spring of 1899. He studied instead. When June ended the school year, he was ready for the County Board. He took the examinations in July, passed and was awarded a certificate to teach.

His assignment was the two-room Friendship school in the Turkey Creek area, known as the very worst in the west side of Scioto County. Near Turkey Creek flourished many of the most active moonshine stills north of Kentucky's notorious Beauty Ridge. It was a political roost ruled by Daddy Clifford, who boasted he never broke the law by selling moonshine on Election Day. It was free. And there were Mershons in the vicinity!

George Beedle Mershon had given this border a legend that was unforgettable to all but decent folk. In '53, Mershon fought Larkin Hammond, of Kentucky, for $100 at the old Stone House. A bloodthirsty crowd of three hundred looked on as the two brutes nearly killed each other.

They stripped to the waist and greased their torsos with butter. They fought bare-handed with no holds barred. Mershon was the winner, but Hammond gouged his left eye until it fell out on his cheek. Mershon chewed off all of Hammond's fingers and also tore his left eye out.

The fate of previous teachers at the Turkey Creek school had been miserable. Just before Christmas in John Shepard's second year a pupil hit him over the head with a piece of stovewood and it took seventeen stitches to close the wound. Big Fred Wilson took it over the next year. Wilson resigned in January, unable to take the constant stream of tobacco juice spat beneath the table-desk upon his shoes. Small wonder Branch and his family were apprehensive about the appointment.

A wave of stark responsibility swept over Branch Rickey as more than thirty students, some older than he, paraded into his room to open the school year. He envied Jack Hood in the next room with only the lower grades to deal with. He called for quiet and began the tasks of name-taking and separating the children into classes from the Fourth Reader up, and arranging for each class to take the front row of deskless seats for recitals.

Trouble was not long in appearing. It came from the belligerent person of Gordon Tatman, son of the local blacksmith. He was nearly eighteen and slovenly. He wore a built-in sneer. His greasy hair, uncut for months, hung down to his shoulders. He carried a copy of *Black Beauty*, but had no intention of using it, or any other book. He had come for the sole purpose of running this Republican appointee out of school. He sprawled in a chair near the drum stove in which Branch had made a coal fire. He created waves of half-suppressed laughter by spitting into the near-empty scuttle, producing a sound like the peal of a bell. The ring punctuated Branch's sentences, and fueled his temper, because now Pat Clifford, son of the local Democratic leader, flatly refused to write on the blackboard.

Branch ignored the noise and the laughter, for he knew that Tatman wanted a fight. The boy who "beat up the teacher" earned a measure of local fame. Branch's only fear was of losing his temper and charging the offender. He kept reminding himself not to teach with his fists. Still talking to the class, he left his desk. He grabbed Tatman by the shoulder and dug his fingers into the hollow just below the collarbone. Branch asked Tatman if he worked, and the boy said he did, piling ties, a dollar ten a day.

"That's just about what I make here," Branch said, digging his fingers into the shoulder. "What would you do if I came up to the tie piles and took your job?"

"I'd kill you," Tatman muttered.

"Do you want to run me out of my job?"

Tatman didn't reply. His body trembled and his tobacco-stained lips tightened as Branch pinched his fingers into the shoulder with all his might. "Well, I need this job," he said, "and you're not going to run me out of it, and nobody in this district will, either!"

A gasping sigh escaped Tatman's throat when Branch suddenly released the painful grip and went for the scuttle. Tatman ducked. Branch kicked open the stove door, heaved with the scuttle and scattered coal everywhere but in the fire. Then he almost broke the bell rope ringing to announce the first recess.

Hostility continued through that first week of teaching. The disgruntled Daddy Clifford element doubled their efforts to discourage the new teacher with threats of whippings and even of arrest for alleged "beatings" administered to pupils. Branch was defied, challenged and driven to wonder if he really could stick it out when Doc Hopkins, the local physician intervened. Doc Hopkins proved to be a physician of the spirit as well as of the flesh by leading Branch into the hills to have dinner in the Clifford homestead with the political patriarch.

Daddy Clifford, grizzled, bearded and shaggy gray, regarded Branch with narrow-eyed suspicion through much of the meal until he learned of the boy's sound religious background and beliefs.

"Then you don't tell our children," he exclaimed, "that we all come from monkeys. Y'don't teach that, do you?"

"No, sir," Branch replied truthfully.

"Tell me this, Rickey," he continued, clutching his knife

and fork as he whacked the table. "You teach that the sun an' moon go round the world, don't you?"

"Why, I —" Branch stammered. "The state books —"

"Well, d'you teach it, or don't you?"

Doc Hopkins saved the evening and Branch's job with the nearest thing to what, fifty years later, was called double talk. Branch sat back with a sigh of relief. At the end of the visit, Daddy Clifford said good night with a hearty handshake. His smile indicated that all was right in his stationary world.

On Friday, the fifth day of school, Gordon Tatman remained in his seat after classes. When the last of the students had straggled out, he shuffled to Rickey's desk and confessed that his original intention had been to run him out of the school. Now he wondered if it would be possible to make up for lost time.

"He became a real student," Rickey recalled, "and he was my great defender throughout my term and a half at Turkey Creek. He even beat up a fellow at Ross's store after overhearing him say I couldn't play checkers."

Branch Rickey was old enough to know that youth can be reached through a common denominator. Unfortunately he knew of only one, baseball. Many weeks and much heavy weather would have to pass before the game could be played.

"Not long after Branch came to teach at Friendship," Elsey, oldest of three Tatman brothers, revealed more than a half-century later, "we were playing 'black man' in the school yard. I saw him standing at the window, watching us have a lot of fun. He looked awful lonesome. I know I'd have been lonesome, and I was a year older than Branch. Suddenly he left the window, came into the yard and started dodging, grabbing, running and having as much fun as anybody. First time he grabbed and swung, I thought I'd fly clear across the road and into Turkey Creek. After that, he was just one of us boys."

Rickey's Saturdays in the fall were devoted to football. It was the day of the flying tackle and the flying wedge, and flying teeth. His love of competitive sports may be gauged by the number of times he suffered injury in these contests and returned for more. Scarcity of manpower prevented quitting for any reason except total incapacitation.

One Saturday Branch sustained a broken jaw. He broke a collarbone, and he suffered a caved-in chest which mended poorly. A bony knot developed which puzzled X-ray examiners for the rest of his life.

Shortly after school closed, Branch was in Wheelersburg, studying six days a week with Frank Appel. His objective was a chance for an appointment to West Point. He was the youngest of thirty-five who took the examination and finished third.

"Winning guaranteed a college education and a career and I was very unhappy about the result," Rickey said many years later, "but my father and Mr. Finney were always congratulating me on my finish. I made almost nothing in history — didn't know what the thing was about."

His disappointment was eased considerably by a chance to teach school in Pike County. The pay would be $65 monthly, nearly double his Turkey Creek salary. Branch had decided in his mind to try for it when he was asked to return to the school at Friendship with a salary rise to $40.

"Had the choice been left entirely to me," Rickey once said, "I might not have returned. My father said it was a job undone. At that time I was not disposed to dispute his very set opinions. My father's directions were pretty compelling to me as long as he lived. Besides, Mr. Cole produced an unforgettable letter.

"It was a resolution from Friendship people with three or four 'whereases' and said, 'We most respectfully ask that you return to teach our school.' It was signed by just about everybody in the Turkey Creek area who could write, and at least two who couldn't. They made X's. I told Mr. Cole I'd take the school again."

Branch made the second year at Turkey Creek more difficult for himself with a self-teaching program. He spent much of his free time poring over Caesar and Cicero and a fifty-cent Latin grammar that Frank Appel had given him. During the Christmas holidays the combined force of several factors crystallized his plans to attend college. Ed Appel and Clyde Brant extolled the advantages of their alma mater, Ohio Wesleyan.

"They knew all the ropes," Rickey recalled later, "what extra classes I needed, and convinced me I had enough money to swing it. Of course, both were good baseball players and wanted me for the team. That was an influence. Jennie Moulton's presence at the same college was not a deterrent. At the same time, I felt that I had to make good in some direction or other in order to win this girl. In fact, I knew I had to do it. I wanted to go to college more than anything else in the world and I didn't care how I got there."

Early in March, Branch turned over his classes at Turkey Creek to a substitute and packed a well-worn telescope bag. Before dawn a few days later, he descended the stairs at home, ready for the hot breakfast his mother was preparing. After he had eaten, Emily Rickey rolled some newspapers, tied a string around one end and shredded the other.

"Be careful of the wind when you light it," she warned.

He gave her a final embrace, picked up his bag and hurried to the tracks. At the proper moment, he carefully lighted the shredded end of the homemade torch, flagged his train to a halt and was on his way to higher education at Ohio Wesleyan.

3

MICHAEL AVENUE in Delaware bordered the Delaware Run, a sluggish creek, sometimes redolent of a nearby sulphur spring that emptied into the Olentangy River a half mile away. Number 4 was a small two-story frame house operated as sleeping quarters for a few students by Mrs. Luckenbell. Branch got a room — actually a clothespress containing only a cot — at the head of the stairs for fifty cents a week. The cot prevented the door from opening all the way, and to enter the cubicle at all was a tight squeeze.

Members of the Delta Tau Delta fraternity took Branch in tow from the start. "Prep" Barnes, a senior, let him use his large front room for study. "Buzz" Martin introduced him to his mother's cooking. Mrs. Martin fed eight or ten boys and divided the cost among them.

As he felt his way through this strange and perplexing world, each move brought challenges and evidence of his insufficient preparation for what lay ahead. He was fortunate, however, in finding sympathetic understanding, beginning with Professor Grove in his very first class.

Branch responded to the order, " . . . will you take up the text at this point?" with a unique translation of Virgil. Using an audible Duck Run inflection, he bridged difficulties with an English word here and there and charged through a literal interpretation with scarcely a pause for breath. Professor Grove finally managed to halt him, asked a few questions and then, removing his glasses, inquired, "Just what Latin grammar did you study?"

"Yours, sir," Branch replied bluntly. *"Grove's Latin Lessons for Beginners."*

The amphitheater-like classroom rocked with laughter at "Johnny" Grove's expense. The teacher's face reddened and Branch felt his own take on the fire of deepest embarrassment, shame, chagrin and anger. His throat tightened against a rising tide of tears that spilled down his cheeks. Only then did he realize the full meaning of his father's warning that he "might make a fool of himself." He had no business being in college, and vowed then and there to board a southbound Hocking Valley train for home.

As Principal of the Preparatory Department, Professor Grove recognized familiar signs. After class, he called Branch to his desk.

"Professor Grove devoted forty minutes daily from his own time," Rickey said in recalling that first term. "Took time from his own family and lavished it on me every school-day morning for two months. I got a furnace-tending job and, as soon as my firing and ash-removing was done, I rushed over to his office at seven-twenty, and there he was ahead of me. With rare patience and understanding, he explained the words and the work in *Harkness' Latin Grammar.* I never could have stayed in college a minute, had it not been for Johnny Grove."

During those two months, Branch was never called on in class. One morning near the term end, Grove asked if he thought he was ready. Branch said he was, and then studied all that night. He waited expectantly through class, in vain. He studied through a second night and, on the following day, the students heard, "Mr. Rickey, will you take up the text at this point?"

Mr. Rickey rose. Translating quickly and accurately, he paused only for quick intakes of breath. He read through the lines, oblivious to everything but his task, until he heard, "That will do, that will do. Mr. Rickey! That will do!"

Professor Grove closed his book and placed it on top of his desk. "Many people come to college who ought not to," he said solemnly. "They should be out with their hands on plow handles, adding to the material wealth of the nation. But they have a right to come here, and when that right is coupled with deep desire . . ."

Though Professor Grove was lauding Branch's accomplishment, it was more embarrassing to him than the first day's shambles.

"He became my great friend," Rickey recalled later, "but the fact is, I never had a teacher, at grade school or at college, who didn't encourage and help me. I have a very high regard for the teaching profession, and I owe them so much. It is the most underpaid group of professionals in the world."

College life took on an occasional glow of hope for Rickey because of the imposing University Hall and peaceful Gray Chapel, the thousands of books in the library — and Monnet Hall. Jennie Moulton lived there. The rules made dates difficult and, for Branch, who lacked funds and wardrobe, to see her was almost impossible. His struggle, both academic and financial, was so apparent that few classmates expected to see him the next year.

Rickey not only returned to Ohio Wesleyan in the fall of 1901; he signed up for extra hours, determined to meet the challenges. He occupied the same room, fired the furnace again and waited on tables. He cut his cash needs to a minimum, but a wholly unexpected obstacle to his success arose.

All Delt members were supposed to further fraternity prestige. Rickey kept to himself and wasn't "seen." After the

Christmas vacation, Russ Foster grew bold enough to say that Rick wasn't doing his share for the Delts. Branch protested. Foster didn't stop there. He guessed aloud that Rickey might be anti-social. He sat with the "nondescript" groups in Gray Chapel. He never went to dances and never dated any of the important girls. Actually, he was harming the Delts by going around "with the cockleburs still in your hair and on the seat of your pants — "

Branch Rickey had never thought of himself, his family or any of his relatives as poor for the simple reason that they were not. Families were poverty-stricken, he had been taught, because they lacked the very things he was rich in — food, shelter, health, clean clothes, decent living standards, domestic tranquillity and affection, and an unshakable belief in God's will. Branch's people were "cash poor," but this was common in nearly all pioneering communities. Nobody felt poor who had plenty of creature comforts, and a desire to work hard and worship God.

"Mother sensed my predicament and tried to relieve it," Rickey explained in recalling the trying period. "She sent me small sums in her regular letters, usually a dollar bill. I took great pride in returning it, except when my expectation of odd jobs failed to materialize and I really had need of the dollar. My wants, though, were quite simple during that first term-and-a-half. I attended only entertainments or lectures that were free, and many were.

"I suppose my clothes were more than insufficient, since I had only one pair of pants. But at the time, I was completely unconscious of my personal appearance. I didn't think it mattered very much. I probably retain the same indifference to this day. As I look back, it was a pretty tough year, but I didn't realize many hardships then. I was having a whale of a time, busy and happy every minute."

Later the entire Delta Tau Delta chapter did some mature soul-searching and collectively realized their mistake. When Rickey talked of leaving college at the term end, they moved, without his knowledge, to ease his distress. Branch never knew why he was asked to leave the meeting on the night of February 14, 1902, but the secretary's graphic report read:

Adelphus Rickey was asked to retire. Discussion concerning means of raising money to keep Rickey in school in the Spring term. Motion made to subscribe a dollar per each member for the baseball fund, provided Rickey stays in school during the Spring term.

— W. J. King, Gr.

Early in his first term at OWU, Rickey found that baseball was far from the paradise promised by Appel and Brant. The stony field resembled a swamp when the bordering Olentangy overflowed, but it was still better than the pastures he had used a home. And he brought a new skill and spirit that was recognized by the Delaware *Gazette* when, in an early game, he batted leadoff, hit a single and stole a base:

Rickey is playing a star game as catcher, making many brilliant stops and only a few men have been able to steal second.

Branch gave no thought to football when he returned in the fall of 1901 until Coach Charlie Boyle pleaded for his running speed in the backfield. By then the limited equipment had been distributed. Outfitted in a leftover sweater to which he sewed his own elbow pads, and odds and ends, he was conspicuous before playing his first game, and more so afterward, because his first college touchdown produced a controversy.

Trailing Ohio University 6–5, he spilled a ball carrier into fumbling. OWU recovered and, a few plays later, Branch plunged across the goal line to make it 10–6. Umpire Edmondson blew his whistle, canceled the play and ordered the ball back.

This was certainly rank work [said the newspaper account of the game], as the only way in which the ball could be legally returned would be on a foul by someone. Edmondson gave no penalty and therefore conceded there was no foul. Referee Hough decided later that the touchdown counted and that Ohio Wesleyan had won by a score of 10–6.

Rickey played every game, despite his increased hours of study. A new baseball coach was hired in the spring, Danny Daub, a former big-league pitcher. Rickey became the workhorse of his squad. With cousin "Eph" playing first base, the two Rickeys gave the 1902 team a distinctive Scioto County flavor, for Ed Appel was at shortstop and Clyde Brant played third base. The Bishops, as they were called, put together one of OWU's greatest baseball seasons by losing only two of thirteen games. Ten victories in twelve games against Ohio college teams gave them a percentage of .833 and the state championship.

Playing under the rules of the newly formed Ohio College Conference, Ohio Wesleyan had begun the 1902 football season with victories over Wittenberg and Kenyon when the squad was summoned by Professor Rice, biology instructor and faculty adviser. He assembled them to explain the new Articles of Agreement, signed by the six Conference members. He handed out individual applications, a formality, except for one requirement of eligibility. Branch returned his.

"I can't sign this," he said to Dr. Rice. "It requires the

applicant to swear he has never received compensation for his athletic ability. Last July I played baseball on a pickup team called the Portsmouth Navies. 'Maje' Anders paid me twenty-five dollars a week."

"Of course, that was expenses," Rice suggested hopefully.

"Not to me," Branch replied. "I managed to save out of it for clothes I needed badly, and I used some to pay term bills here."

Professor Rice sighed and shook his head. "The rules were only adopted a few weeks ago. Even so, under the code, I guess that makes you . . . well, a professional. You can't play on any teams."

News of Rickey's "professionalism" shocked the campus next day. It made headlines in Cincinnati and Cleveland. Within a few days Branch hurried to answer a summons from the office of President James Bashford, wondering what he had done. The college head handed him a penciled letter, written on cheap lined paper, that said in part, "My Dear President, Whoever called Branch Rickey a professional is a God-damned liar. I never paid that boy a damned cent. — Maje Anders."

"That isn't true, is it?" Dr. Bashford said, taking the letter back.

"No, sir, it isn't true," Branch murmured.

More was made of the news than the facts merited, Rickey always felt.

"My teachers regarded it as praiseworthy, but I didn't," Rickey added many years later. "I knew nothing about the code when I joined the Navies, but it probably wouldn't have made any difference. I was then seeking a so-called education, and the money provided a way of getting back to school respectably. I think I would have played, even had I known about the rule, or if it had been in existence. What's more, I think any other player in my predicament would have reported as I did."

Athletic ineligibility provided time for expansion of courses to a point where Rickey carried twenty-two hours to make up needed credits. Then the college decided he should coach baseball, and though only twenty-one, he was named Director of Athletics at $250 for the 1903 spring term.

The new role was like a tight shoe at first, and then felt comfortable as it fused with Branch's unbridled personality. His speech became even more clipped and he never lacked for words to demonstrate and prove his points. He had a way of giving emphasis a pictorial quality with his large and strong fists and a shake of his head. He was far too opinionated and egotistical at twenty-one, but the depth of his sincerity and purpose enabled him to get away with it.

"He didn't change exactly," said Ed Appel in recalling Rickey's first weeks as baseball coach. "He simply acted like a catcher all the time, giving orders, directing or changing things, shifting people, and he never stopped scheming and trying. Even I chafed at first under his autocratic methods, but he soon won everybody over by helping them see things they never thought of before.

"Charlie Thomas was a fine hitter. He was a great outfielder, running down extra-base hits and holding runners with that great arm. Not to Rick. He said the arm had more value behind the plate cutting down extra bases, stolen bases and bunts. So Thomas became a catcher. Our pitching wasn't the best that year. We lost too many one-run games, but the pitchers looked good because of Thomas."

Unless you followed professional baseball, as Branch Rickey did, you couldn't understand a young player's belief in the game as a respectable means of livelihood. The entire structure had been reorganized during the winter of 1902–3.

Two eight-club major leagues flourished again, the old National and the new American. Opportunities had been doubled at the top, causing a rush to organize small or minor leagues. Players were needed.

A few days after the term closed, Rickey was catching a game in Terre Haute, Indiana, despite a splint on one broken finger. Three days later he had grasped a new opportunity and $150 a month by catching for LeMars, Iowa. It was before the uniform player-contract in minor-league baseball. You were hired or fired or could quit without warning. Branch played through nearly two months, catching 41 games and hitting .265. And LeMars won the 1903 pennant.

Fall brought another source of income, and Rickey tapped it as soon as he had laid out his program for the final year. Football stars were offered fantastic sums for single games, and Rickey had enough reputation as an athlete to seek a high fee.

"When I found I could get up to a hundred and fifty dollars a game, I grabbed it," he explained. "I weighed nearly one-seventy. I was strong, fast and healthy. A sheet tube company at Shelby, about fifty miles north of Delaware, sponsored the team. I rode up by train in the evenings to practice. But it had the drawback common to all pleasures, and even life itself: it didn't last long."

In October Branch was spilled by a pair of flying tackles. He came down on buckling legs, breaking the bones in his right leg, above the ankle. He convalesced at Lucasville.

The Chandler Moultons were not openly antagonistic to Branch because of his obvious intentions toward Jennie. They were just silently hostile. They liked him. Few could help responding to his sincerity, his effervescence, his unflagging enthusiasm and constant wonder and joy in living. Like parents the world over, however, they wanted security, a good home, and an ordered and dignified life for their child. The life of a professional baseball player in the early 1900's was still the antithesis of respectability, and the wife of a player — No, unless Branch showed interest in an honorable career, they would do nothing to encourage the courtship.

Rickey's final term as a student coach was filled with big moments. The first came in March, 1904, when he sat with the graduating class as an accredited senior. Another came in early May when his father sat in the wooden grandstand at Selby Field and watched his team of speedy Bishops beat Ohio State.

Then came the news that the faculty had moved in his behalf again. Since he was certain of graduating, George Ellison initiated the request for him to teach. He was tended an offer to teach history and English and coach football at Allegheny College. The salary would be $1400.

In the last game of this most successful season [said the June 15, 1904, issue of the Ohio Wesleyan *Bijou*] OWU defeated Kenyon by 10–2. Without doubt Coach Rickey has the fastest team that the Delaware people have ever called their own.

OWU hailed the college baseball champions of Ohio, and said goodbye to Branch Rickey, Bachelor of Literature. He reached Duck Run with his hard-earned diploma in one hand and a telegram in the other. A catcher was needed in Texas.

It was 3.30 A.M. in Dallas when Fred Hunter, who had sent the telegram, responded to a pounding on the door of his hotel room. He opened it as the caller answered "Branch Rickey," but the sight of the grimy, disheveled figure sent him reeling back in momentary fright.

"What'd you do," Hunter gasped, "ride the rods from Ohio?"

Certainly not, he was told. Branch had made a vow never

to hop freights after doing it once. In addition to the dirt and cindery landings, his conscience resented taking something free that he should pay for.

"He didn't have a dime," Hunter remembered later. "Actually he was beginning a way of life. He never kept track of finances. You're always more liable to meet him without money than with it."

Over the years few friends or associates have escaped the Rickey "touch." It is usually their favorite recollection of him. A fraternity brother tells of how Branch awakened near dawn one day with the realization that he was to leave within two hours for a speaking engagement and had forgotten to get $25 for expenses. He rushed through the Delta house, arousing first one and then another to borrow small amounts until he had the necessary total. He stuffed it into his pants pocket only to discover — yes, he had remembered to get the money before going to bed. Now he had $50.

"So he woke up everybody all over again returning the money — everybody, because he had forgotten who had made the loans."

"Rick was also hungry when he reached Texas," Hunter added. "After being my guest, he made me take him to a newspaper office so he could study the North Texas League records. Then he reported to Joe Gardner, the Dallas owner, then to Charlie Moran, our catcher-pitcher-manager, worked out, signed a contract saying he wasn't to play on Sundays, and that night made one of the greatest speeches I ever heard before a crowd of young men at the Dallas Y.M.C.A. Quite a first day."

Playing conditions in the Texas league were poor. Trips were made in hot and dusty daycoaches. Most hotels were third class, providing fifty-cent rooms with mosquitoes, and mass feeding in their dining rooms. But it was a baseball opportunity and twenty-two-year-old Branch Rickey asked nothing else. Moreover, it paid $175 a month.

He played in forty-one games with impressive results. He survived a free-for-all and a riot on the field in Fort Worth. He made many friends and he began storing memories of faces, techniques, idiosyncrasies, character and intelligence of players. He batted .261 and scored 25 runs. He stole 14 bases, and his forty-one assists as a catcher proved that few runners stole on him. Most impressive was his hustle and "take charge" type of catching. Cincinnati was alerted by a dispatch in the *Enquirer*:

Dallas, Aug. 22 — Cincinnati has purchased catcher N. B. [sic] Rickey of the Dallas Club. He was the star catcher of the Texas League, best ever seen down here. Rickey is a college player and came to Texas from Lucasville, Ohio, having previously played with the University team at Delaware in that state.

And the next day's edition published a two-column portrait photograph of "Branch Rickey, the Reds' new catcher."

4

An ambitious baseball player asks no more than a foot in the door of the big leagues. From that point, he will gladly accept whatever fate deals out because, once inside, there is no limit to the heights he can reach with his skill and hustle, especially financially. Merely reaching the threshold is an achievement, but to have your contract purchased by a major-league club is the full answer to a ball player's hopes and dreams.

It meant all that to Branch Rickey, but also, with his teaching-coaching salary, enough money to support a wife. He reported to Manager Joe Kelley, one of the Baltimore Orioles he had revered ten years before. After a lively workout on Thursday, Kelley used him as catcher in an exhibition game at Rushville, Indiana, on Friday. Anxious and weary from his long trip, and visibly nervous, the rookie catcher permitted two stolen bases, and made an error, but he also made a base hit and a good impression.

"He has a splendid whip and knows how to use it," wrote Ren Mulford in the *Enquirer*. "His cheery voice was heard all through the contest."

Branch Rickey sat in the Cincinnati dugout the next day, Saturday, and watched the Reds defeat Boston by a score of 7-1. In the locker room he handed the padded "body protector" of which he, as junior catcher, was custodian, to the veteran Heinie Peitz and said, "You better take this. I won't be here tomorrow —"

"You what?" roared Manager Kelley.

He was dressing a few feet away. Branch started to remind him that the Dallas contract, which the Reds had assumed, excused him from Sunday play, and, since tomorrow was Sunday, he would visit his home. But Kelley stormed on.

"You'll be here tomorrow! If you're not here, you can go see Mr. Herrmann and pick up your pay!"

Rickey went home for the weekend.

Branch Rickey, the Red recruit [said Monday morning's *Enquirer*], has never played Sunday ball and he was not in uniform yesterday. Three of the Bostons are also in the non-Sabbath playing clan. Fred Tenney and Charley Pittinger will not go to the diamond on Sunday, but they helped out on the gate yesterday and Irving Wilhelm, another of the Sabbatarians, enjoyed the game [Boston, Wilhelm's team, lost again, 10–6] from the Palace of the Fans.

The prospect of seeing August Herrmann was not a pleasant one, and Branch briefly considered not seeing him at all. As Chairman of the Waterworks Commission, he was part of a ruthless political machine, long headed by "Big Boy" Cox, who dominated the baseball club from behind the scenes. After deciding to visit Herrmann at his spacious City Hall office, he expected a curt hello and goodbye and received a most pleasant surprise. Herrmann, a bright-eyed, soft-spoken German, was most curious about the reluctance to play baseball on Sundays. Branch insisted that he didn't belong in the game, that he had come down on orders from Joe Kelley and that he was going home, and then to teach college. Herrmann knew all that. What about the Sunday business?

Branch's face grew warm. He stammered that it wasn't something you talked about. Word would get out. He would be mocked. Herrmann edged his big leather chair closer, and leaned forward until his bulbous nose almost touched Rickey's.

"I'd really like to have you tell me," he pleaded. "Certainly I'd never tell anybody."

Branch struggled for coherence in a battle with deepest reluctance, an unwarranted feeling of shame and a sort of nakedness for baring his secret vow which a stubborn nature wouldn't let him break. He told Herrmann of his deep-rooted admiration for his uncomplaining mother, of her simple reverence for the Sabbath and of her tenet of passive obedience. His playing professional baseball had caused her worry and suffering. Though she had overheard many words of censure and ridicule of her sports-minded son, she had never uttered one of her own. He had felt obliged to reward her or pay tribute, and the only way possible, in his mind, was to set aside Sunday. Thus, he didn't play on Sunday, but never because it was or wasn't morally wrong, legal or illegal. And to make sure he kept the vow, he remained away from baseball parks.

"And she doesn't know this?" Herrmann murmured.

Branch's lowered head moved from side to side.

Decades later, when his continued observance had, in the public's mind, become equal to the mark of Cain, Branch Rickey sat at her grave at Rushtown and wept for the blasphemy of her name and memory he had caused. He plagued himself with the thought of her own horror upon discovering she was the reason for such an unnecessary situation. Actually he went to the ball park on Sundays in Brooklyn, once to help a War Bond drive, again to help the Red Cross blood bank drive, and again to calm down a player mutiny. But the stigma "he promised his old lady" never died.

The whole business must be wrong, he concluded aloud, to come out like this. He didn't belong in baseball.

Herrmann patted his shoulder and ordered gently, "You go back to the team. Tell Kelley I sent you. Report every day . . . except Sundays."

The troubled rookie did as directed, but it was an ordeal.

"Kelley didn't use me and scarcely spoke to me," Rickey recalled in later years. "I tried to be useful by hitting fungoes in practice, but I was never good at that. Some older players, taking a cue from Kelley's attitude, crowded me out of batting practice and I wouldn't have hit at all if Fred Odwell hadn't stepped aside and let me go in ahead of him. We beat Boston again on Monday, then lost two in a row to John McGraw's great team of Giants. Mathewson and McGinnity had already pitched and won more than sixty games before Labor Day."

Rickey followed the team as they left for Pittsburgh by way of Niles, Ohio. There he caught Tom Walker and Win Kellum the full nine innings in an exhibition victory. He singled in the eighth and scored the Red's sixth run. Ren Mulford wrote, "It was the opinion of the fans that Kelley has picked a good one in getting Rickey."

But the young catcher suspected the worst. Confirmation came in the Pittsburgh clubhouse after the game had been rained out. While the Reds returned to Cincinnati for a Sunday game with the Pirates, he would stop off at Lucasville and spend Sunday with his family. Kelly repeated the ultimatum.

During the return to Cincinnati on Monday morning, Labor Day, Branch bought an *Enquirer* at a way-station stop. He turned to page 3. The Reds had played a 4–4 tie on Sunday. Then he read:

"Won't do" was the sign hung on the back of Branch Rickey yesterday and the young fellow was let go. As he had not yet signed a contract it was unnecessary to give him his release and the O W U boy can now sign anywhere he chooses.

Branch Rickey's two-year tenure at Allegheny started pleasantly enough, but mainly because of a Cincinnati check. Garry Herrmann paid him more than $400 when he left the Reds. Fifty years later Rickey was still trying to figure out how he was entitled to so much. In his new college post, he taught English, freshman history and Shakespeare. He had a poor memory for Shakespeare and plagued himself nightly trying to keep up with the students.

He committed a significant indiscretion at the President's reception for the faculty. While engaged in an enthusiastic talk about the football team with Dr. William H. Crawford, the college head, he used the word "fight." The sudden chill that blanketed the gathering indicated that such a word simply wasn't used at Allegheny College.

"Fight" seemed to be missing every other week on the football field, too. They won five of their ten games that first year, but their five defeats in a later day would have been characterized as "clobberings." Said Rickey in recollection:

"It was never easy. Only seventeen reported for football, which wasn't too bad from a student body of three hundred and fifty potential ministers. We were very handicapped in practice. I had to join the scrimmages to have seven men against the offense on runthroughs. We used eleven for defense plays, and I'd make the seventh man on the offense. I became the sixth man when one boy suffered a broken leg.

"The work was frustrating. I became impatient, and I'm afraid I lost my temper more than once. I certainly regretted chewing up one boy when he developed what I thought was a dislike for running into people. I called him 'yellow' and threw him off the squad, though I couldn't spare him. We met again after he graduated. I'm sure he forgave me."

Early spring of 1905 brought the best of news: Dallas had sold his contract to the Chicago White Sox which, in turn, had sold it to the St. Louis Browns. Rickey reported when his work at Allegheny was finished in June, and he immediately made a lasting friend.

"Manager Jimmy McAleer was a native of Ohio," Rickey said. "He had been a fine outfielder and a graceful athlete in Cleveland during the National League days. He was forty when I first met him, but he never fought it. He had faith in his future through intelligence and baseball brains.

"He called me 'kid' from the very start. I sat as near as I could to him on the bench, watching him give orders and signs and matching them with what was happening on the field. It was another new world, and the best yet."

His first opportunity to play in the major leagues came on June 16 during a game in Philadelphia at the old Athletic Park. Connie Mack's team had mistreated the Brown's starter. When Rube Waddell, the A's pitcher, doubled in the second, McAleer replaced him with Cy Morgan, a spitball pitcher. After another inning Morgan had fared no better and the Athletics led, 8–1.

"Kid, warm up and I'll put you in."

Branch Rickey grabbed his mitt. The Brown's catcher, thirty-five-year-old Joe Sugden, protested: "No, no, Jim! Not the kid. Start him with Barney, or somebody. Cy'll break his wrist with that spitter!"

Branch gulped and looked somewhat hopefully from Sugden to McAleer. The manager nodded for him to warm up. By the time Waddell had retired the Browns in the fourth, the rookie catcher was ready. He huddled briefly with Morgan on signs.

"One finger spitter, two for curve," the pitcher said.

Danny Murphy . . . Lave Cross . . . Harry Davis . . . Topsy Hartsel . . . Ossee Schreckengost . . . the great Rube Waddell

. . . and over on the bench a tall, black-haired, bushy-browed manager named Connie Mack.

"They meant little to me as names at that moment," Rickey said of his first big-league ball game. "The spitball was on my mind. It was a wicked delivery, not because of the saliva, but because it broke unpredictably at the plate from lack of spin. I had to call for it and, when I did, there was trouble. It didn't break my wrist, but it did knock off my glove. I called time to recover it.

"Before I got down again, the catcher I had relieved, Joe Sugdon, waddled over from our bench. He had a look of sorrow and pity on his face and tobacco juice spotted his lips, but he had the kindest gray eyes I ever saw. He held out his own mitt, well-broken-in and with a big pocket. He said, 'Here, kid, use mine before you get killed.' It was a gesture of compassionate understanding that I could never forget."

Rickey caught a hustling ball game that Jimmy McAleer never forgot. While Cy Morgan's control wasn't the best, he gave up only one hit in the five innings that Rickey worked. The hit followed a couple of passes for two runs. Branch threw the ball around with accuracy and a speed that stung palms through the tiny finger gloves of the period. He stopped the A's base stealing, and, batting left-handed three times against Waddell, Rickey flied out once and added two strikeouts to the speedy southpaw's total of 286 for the year.

He was summoned to the telephone that night at the hotel.

"It's Mother," Orla called unsteadily. "It's bad, Branch. She's very sick. We don't know what to do."

"What does the doctor say?"

"That's just it. We haven't had one yet. They can't decide between Warwick or Beard. You know that business. Can you come home?"

Jimmy McAleer understood. "You're only allowed one mother, kid," he said. "Go on home. Stay as long as you're needed. Come back when you can."

Emily Rickey was a very sick woman. J. Frank was beside himself and somewhat helpless. Fortunately Orla and his wife Winifred were spending the summer at Duck Run. Branch straightened out the dispute about doctors. He and "Win" then set up a twenty-four-hour nursing program for his mother. The crisis was passed several weeks later.

He called McAleer, who said the Browns couldn't get anywhere and did not need him and that he was free to report again to Dallas and should do so because there he would have a chance to play every day.

Branch Rickey made up for lost time by sparking a poor Dallas team through five exciting weeks to a break-even record. By Labor Day he had proved himself a professional ball player with a great future. Some thirty base runners had stolen on him, but his powerful arm cut down thirty-seven would-be stealers in thirty-seven games. As a batter he had eight doubles and a home run among his thirty-nine base hits, and he led his team with an average of .295.

He returned to Allegheny on September 10, confident that he'd be back with some big-league team in the spring. McAleer soon confirmed it, notifying him to report to the Browns in March to discuss spring training.

During his mother's illness, Branch had borrowed law books to study by lamplight in a little room at the top of the stairs at home. Now he tackled Blackstone in earnest. An all-summer baseball job, with his Allegheny post, assured him of a year-round income and the right to plan a marriage. Jennie Moulton hadn't actually said yes to a formal proposal, but that was a mere technicality, for he had asked her in one way or another countless times. She admitted that her folks would not object to his playing professional baseball, if he used the income to get a law degree. And he agreed to play for only one year.

Next to marrying his girl, his greatest wish was to convince her family that he would make good. Thus far, his life had lacked direction. There was no doubt that he could do things, but he did them very much as he used words: too many at one time. He could leave people shaking their heads in bewilderment over what he had meant, said, or was going to do.

This very penchant produced a happy difference of opinion as to whether he had actually proposed marriage when Jennie, thinking this was "it," said, "Oh, my soul, yes!" Branch claims he was amazed when he should have been delighted, because he hadn't actually proposed.

"He proposed, all right," Jane Rickey always maintained. "After all, I had heard him skirt it enough times."

"That is true," Rickey admitted, "It was a hundred times. I kept count. And most of the time I had no right to mention marriage. But on this occasion we happened to be visitors in May Armstrong's house at Delaware, sitting on the sofa, and I was talking and talking. About what I surely don't remember. True, marriage may have been mentioned, because I was always thinking or talking about it, but that doesn't give any girl the right to take words out of context, arrange them satisfactorily to her immediate pleasure, call it a proposal of marriage and gasp, 'Oh, my soul, yes!' "

Branch Rickey watched his first opening of a major-league season in 1906 from the Browns' bench. The game was a good one but the 3-1 defeat by Cleveland was hard to swallow.

With the schedule out, Jennie named the day — June first, right at the end of the first eastern trip. Branch found rooms on Bell Avenue, not far from the ball park. Everything was set by the time he started the eastern trip.

Before the eastern swing started, Rickey had hit safely in all but one of the games he caught. McAleer batted him sixth. No world ever looked rosier than Branch Rickey's a month later. He had caught 19 of the 34 games played by the Browns who were in third place. His batting average was encouraging, .277, and he had made only four errors behind the plate. Jimmy McAleer not only tolerated his hundreds of questions on the bench but, as they rode together on street-cars, McAleer answered even more questions — always about baseball, the smart thing to do, the dumb thing to do, the dumb thing that the other team did, how best to balance batting strength for your lineup, how to play for hitters, how to make opposing batters hit where you want them to.

McAleer was all in favor of the marriage. "Just give me the Cleveland series," he said. "Kid, your first marriage comes only once. After Cleveland, take all the time you want."

Unfortunately Branch and his roommate dined rather well in Philadelphia on Monday night, the twenty-eighth of May, which has no "R" in it, and they dined on oysters that would have been inedible in February.

During the night he became deathly sick on the train. There was no doubt about it being ptomaine poisoning and that he should be in a hospital.

"No I . . . I can't," Rickey gasped. "They won't let me out. I've got to get downstate."

The nausea and retching continued through the night. Morning found him weak and feverish and his pounding head ready to split. But he fought hospitalization. They carried him to a carriage and then through the hotel lobby to a room. A doctor said there was nothing a hospital could give him.

"Doctor, he gave me everything but the Cleveland series," McAleer said with a wry smile. He turned to Branch. "Don't worry about us, kid. Just make sure you reach Lucasville by Friday."

Branch was almost too weak to reply. Through his pounding head there raced only one thought.

"If . . . if I miss this," he murmured, "it might never come off. I'll get down there Friday if I have to crawl."

And he almost did. He got an Allegheny College friend, Bill Cappean, to escort him home.

As the train was flagged to a halt at Lucasville, he complained to Cappean about a noise inside his head, a booming and shrill —

"It's not your head, Branch," his companion laughed. "They've got a band here!"

Cappean was right. More than one hundred cheering friends were not enough to drown it out. To the music of the band, the entire asemblage paraded from the station to the brightly lighted Moulton home. With Branch safely inside, the band exhausted their repertoire and themselves with three more pieces and the crowd dispersed.

Jane and Branch were married the next day, June 1, 1906, in the Moulton home.

5

BRANCH WAS HUSTLED into the Browns' lineup when the regular catcher, "Rowdy" O'Connor, was tossed out of a ball game. He caught Ed Smith in a 9–5 victory over the league-leading New York Highlanders, thanks to fifteen hits, one of which was his. The next day he caught "Handsome" Harry Howell in a brilliant shutout. Of the Browns fourteen hits and five runs, a Rickey base hit drove in a run.

Base hits and a bride will make any player happy, but there were other reasons in his life for rejoicing. One was best expressed in the final issue of the Ohio Wesleyan *Transcript* for the 1906 term:

> OWU is fortunate in securing the services of Branch Rickey as Director of Athletics for next year . . . At present Rickey is catcher for the St. Louis Browns and his good work and strict adherence to the principle never to play on Sunday are bringing him considerable notoriety.

A high spot of the summer came in mid-July when, after a stopover visit in Lucasville, Jane Rickey reached New York City.

Branch had just sweated through a 4–2 defeat in the first game of a double-header at the old New York American League Park when a young man tapped his shoulder and handled him a note. It read, "I am up in the stands." He quickly scribbled on the back, "Just stay right where you are."

He had made arrangements for Jane on arriving to wait for him at the Fifth Avenue Hotel, then on the northwest corner of Fifth Avenue and Twenty-third Street. Reaching the ball park would be a hazardous excursion to a Lucasville girl, and was still something of a safari to Rickey himself. He usually played it safe by trailing players to 165th Street and Broadway.

The subway had been in operation less than two years and construction to 242nd Street was in progress, but trains ran only to 137th Street where, to continue uptown, you had to board a horsecar or hire one of the seldom available carriages.

That Jane had made the trip alone confounded Rickey for years. Nearly a half century later he couldn't successfully negotiate a direct route from New York's Grand Central Station to a newly rented home in nearby Westchester County. But he could explain it.

"I actually envied those commuters hurrying through the gates," he said, "but I had to choose from four or five Pelhams, a few Larchmonts, Scar-this and Scar-that. I knew only one place, Mount Vernon, so I got off there and telephoned for somebody to come and get me."

After a few weeks of this, Mrs. Rickey gave up and moved to suburban Forest Hills, not entirely convinced that it may have been his way of expressing displeasure at the selection of a house.

The St. Louis Browns had a good year in 1906.

Branch began to hit well in August. He batted at a .370 clip for the last nine weeks. For the final four weeks he swung the hottest bat in the league, hitting at .421. He hit safely in his final seven games, totaling fourteen hits in twenty-seven times at bat for .513. He had a double and three singles — four for four — against the White Sox on September 15. Against New York on September 18 and 20, he hit Manager Clark Griffith's pitchers so freely that Griffith himself, then thirty-seven, went in, and Rickey hit his deliveries.

He was having another big day in St. Louis on September 27 against the immortal Cy Young and the Boston Red Sox. His two hits in three times at bat had driven in two of the Browns' nine runs. While catching Jacobson in the late innings, a foul tip dislocated and jammed his right thumb, finishing him for the season. His batting average for sixty-four games was a strong .284, and only one other teammate's figures were higher. George Stone's .358 won the American League batting championship.

At the season's end, Rickey assumed his duties as football coach at OWU. The president of Ohio Wesleyan, Dr. Herbert Welch, failed to join the alarmists when college football hit an all-time low in public esteem. His remedy for the low-scholastic standing of players, the brutality and short-cut ethics was not a multiplication of the rules, but leadership by responsible coaches "with a sincere belief in high competitive principles and enough influence over players to incorporate that belief into their teaching."

Coach Rickey highlighted a disappointing season in 1906, that began with the loss of his star end through a heart attack in practice, by raising morale with his own influence and oratory. Just before the final game, against Western Reserve at Cleveland, all his skill and technique of elocution were poured into a Niagara of persuasion. "When we left his room for the game," said one player, "all we could hear was Rickey's speech that sent us on the field to give better than our best."

"They left with more than the sound of my voice," Rickey

laughed in recollection. "They had concrete methods of expressing themselves on the field: we had worked some surprise plays, as had almost all coaches that year, the first of the forward-pass legislation. Reserve outweighed us sixteen pounds to the man, but I made sure the plays had the benefit of a high-spirited team to offset the disadvantage."

The inspired Bishops raced like mavericks to a wild and woolly victory, 22–11, insuring Ohio Wesleyan a tie with Wooster for second in the Ohio College Conference behind Ohio State.

The season closed with a gathering of the team and coaches at the home of Dr. and Mrs. Welch on Oak Hill. To Branch Rickey the year couldn't have been better in a material way. In mid-October he had received a surprise check for $320 from Robert Lee Hedges, owner of the Browns, and a note saying that the players had voted him a full share of their City-Series victory over the Cardinals. In addition he took an appointment at a modest fee as temporary secretary of the OWU branch of the Y.M.C.A. Finally, he had taken extra courses in the fall and acquired enough hours and credits for a baccalaureate degree in Arts, which was conferred. It was a merry Christmas indeed at Lucasville that year.

Clark Griffith, manager of the New York Highlanders, impressed by Rickey's late-season finish with the Browns, obtained him in an exchange of contracts during the winter.

"Branch looked like the answer to anybody's need, but especially ours," Griffith said later. "We had one of the greatest spitball pitchers, Jack Chesbro. He had won more than a hundred games for me in four years. Rick could catch a spitball as well as anybody."

Rickey's 1907 contract called for $2700 and no Sunday baseball (then illegal in New York), and permission to skip spring training because of coaching commitments. Work with his OWU team figured to train him as well as would a few weeks in the South.

Branch Rickey never knew exactly when or how his arm got sore. No victim of a sore arm ever does, though everyone tries to pinpoint with hindsight. Since he had done considerable throwing in the indoor baseball practice at Edwards Gymnasium, he always believed that it resulted from snap throws. At any rate, pain beneath the right shoulder blade persisted after heavy workouts. The University excused him in early April. He turned the baseball team over to an assistant and reported to the Highlanders in New York, unable to throw at all.

Rickey got into his first game on his first wedding anniversary and grounded out in the eighth inning of a 2-0 defeat.

The only things bright about June 28 were the woolen undershirts worn by Rickey and "King" Brockett, called the Red Shirt Battery. Otherwise it was the blackest of Fridays. Washington hit Brockett freely. The record shows that thirteen bases were stolen and the catcher also made an error.

"The error came early in the game," Rickey recalled. "I tried to throw a runner out at second and Keeler trapped the ball in rightfield. That's how erratic the arm was. Actually I never made another throw to second base. They all ran down as soon as they got on. Kleinow was hurt and Mr. Griffith had especially asked me to catch. He knew about my arm, but that made no difference."

Branch tried again three days later, but there was no longer fear of the once-powerful Rickey arm. After that he was a leftfielder, and, when Hal Chase suffered a spiked arm in early August, Rickey took over at first base for several games.

But the days were uniformly dismal. The strain and frustration might have beaten down anyone less cushioned to setbacks than Branch Rickey. The cushioning came from his ability to stem the tide of emotional upheaval by mental preoccupation. In later years he turned to the chessboard, always set up for play in his home, frequently with Mrs. Rickey. Or he would commandeer help to start a quick game of bridge, hearts or cribbage.

Back in 1907 his escape was through playing checkers, which he had learned the hard way as a youngster. He was taught by cracker-barrel experts in the McDaniel-Owens store at the Owensville Fork, and at Ross's store in Turkey Creek.

The Eden Musée was just around the corner from the Fifth Avenue Hotel, on the north side of Twenty-third Street. It was interesting as a museum for one or two visits, but Ajeeb, the automatic checker marvel, was a perpetual challenge. Large, grotesque, leering, it sat before a board dressed in a musty East Indian costume. The lifeless, clawlike hands actually moved, picked up the checker pieces and won games. That was the trouble. It always won. At ten cents a game, even for a draw, this was annoying. Beat Ajeeb and you could play him free.

Rickey's repeated jousts with Ajeeb developed a small following. They were two other rookies, big Ira Thomas, a native New Yorker, who shared the catching with Kleinow, and Judd Bruce Doyle, a pitcher called "Slow Joe" because his speediest running was no more than a trot. Joe alone comprised the cheering section one morning as Branch sat before the leering East Indian and no happier person ever lived than Doyle when the big beast refused to move. Rick had looked up and winked.

"We got the bastard beat!" Slow Joe shouted.

"Come on, Ajeeb, move," Branch directed.

The jeweled head moved from side to side.

"You're beaten, Ajeeb," Rickey said, but the head only wagged. "You can't move without running into a double-jump. You're beaten!"

"Why, the dirty no-good — " Slow Joe Doyle lost patience and dropped to the floor. He crawled beneath the table, lifted the skirts and started to pull at control wires.

Rickey dragged the loyal Doyle from the table. Joe kicked and fought to get back and "tear that damned brute apart!"

"Don't touch a thing," Rickey ordered. "I'll get the manager. Watch out that Ajeeb doesn't move any pieces."

"He better not," Doyle threatened, "or I'll knock his teeth in."

Rickey rushed to the ticket taker with the news that Ajeeb was beaten and wouldn't move. The ticket taker got the manager who accompanied Rickey to the automaton. The pieces were as he had left them.

"Move, Ajeeb!" Rickey ordered angrily. "Move and you lose!"

Only Ajeeb's turbaned head moved, from side to side. The harassed manager offered a free game, but Rickey only wanted his victory and Ajeeb couldn't be beaten until he moved. The manager finally prevailed upon the impatient patrons to calm down and return the next day to meet the operator. Everything would be straightened out. It was, when Branch returned alone.

Ajeeb was cleverly controlled from a room about eight by ten feet directly above the board. Every move and face was visible through a screen. The operator, a small, pale and emaciated man, entered.

"You play a good game, Mr. Rickey," he said after the manager had presented the plaintiff. "I've watched you coming here. I have to keep track of repeaters. You see, Ajeeb has never been beaten — "

"Until yesterday," Rickey interrupted.

The operator wouldn't concede. They reconstructed the play and discussed the variations. Asked what books he had read, Rickey named several of the more popular, adding that his favorite was Mitchell's.

"That's my book," the operator said. Then, "I don't know what I did to get into that position, but I can't afford to lose. We have too much invested in Ajeeb. If you can understand our situation here, I'd appreciate your forgetting what happened. You can come in and play any time without charge."

Rickey was pleased and flattered. He shook hands and reached the hotel just in time to placate Slow Joe who had almost convinced Thomas that they should go over and tear Ajeeb apart.

Branch Rickey caught his last major-league baseball game on September 5, 1907, in the first of a double header against the Athletics in Philadelphia. He singled as a pinch hitter on Friday the thirteenth. Shortly afterward he packed his things in the Hilltop clubhouse and said goodbyes. He expressed profound thanks to Manager Clark Griffith for his kindness and understanding. Griff refused to be pessimistic about the arm condition, and tried to exact a promise from him to return in the spring. Rickey declined with more thanks and expressed a belief that this was his farewell to big-league baseball of any kind.

"I'm going to study law in earnest," he confided. "I've got a chance I'll never have again."

Far more than coaching and law studies were involved. In February of 1908 he would be a father. He had saved money to start a home. Now he belonged in a business that wouldn't cause long absences from his wife and child, as baseball did.

The Christmas vacation in Lucasville began happily enough. Branch announced that he was no longer a baseball player, but a law student. It was the best news to the Moultons since hearing that another Ohio son, Cincinnati's Bill Taft, was being groomed by President Roosevelt as his successor next year. And then came the worst of news. Janie did not feel well. Branch called a doctor over mild protests and she was ordered to bed.

Two days later she was delivered of a premature baby girl that struggled gallantly through the night and part of the next day when the little life ended.

They returned to Delaware for a busy and most taxing year. It began with a course of law at Ohio State University in personal property. Branch made daily round trips by electric railway from Delaware to Columbus. He coached baseball at OWU and he got into the long campaign in behalf of prohibitionists backing the Rose Local Option Law. He traveled up and down the state, speaking at all hours, under the worst possible conditions and sleeping anywhere he could. At Chillicothe one night the crowd was hostile and the hotels more so. He found sanctuary with Fred Hunter and slept in Fred's room over his place of business, a saloon. Hunter was a bartender, and also a lifelong teetotaler.

By August Rickey had also begun speaking in behalf of William Howard Taft and he introduced James S. Sherman at Gray Chapel. In September he took over the class in elementary law and taught Blackstone. As the Christmas holiday approached, he was really tired. A numbing weariness trailed him to Lucasville. The heavy year of work and travel, study and pressure, had cost him weight, appetite and energy.

April seemed colder than it really was, and he should have been cheered by the best and fastest starts of all his teams. But now, for the first time in his life, baseball was secondary. He could scarcely get up in the morning. He couldn't eat. And his muscular body, once an elastic one hundred seventy-five pounds, had thinned so much as to make him fearful of stepping onto the gymnasium scale. Jane finally found his resistance low enough to get him down to Dr. Seamans. He weighed barely one hundred forty-five pounds. He admitted suffering regular night sweats, but knew nothing of any fever. Yet there it was, almost constant, the doctor said, at 100°, 101° . . .

He had tuberculosis.

Consumption was the word for it in 1909. That you had it was a quiet pronouncement of impending death. There was no cure, and very little relief. At best, you could delay the inevitable, but not for long. Branch and Jane Rickey made the sorrowful trip to Trudeau Sanitarium, at Saranac Lake, New York, plagued through the day-long ride by their thoughts. He was weak from weariness and worry over his interrupted plans and the uncertainty of ever returning. He asked himself silently, over and over, for an answer to what had happened and why it had happened. And how bad was it?

There followed ten of the grimmest possible days. Hope was a fickle and transient thing, often no more than a brief reflection of morning sun that scurried away when Rickey's harried mind reviewed the immediate past.

"My physical pain," Rickey said in recounting the experience, "was considerably less than the mental strain, which was largely self-imposed. Determination of degree was still a major problem. Roentgen ray equipment was crude and not to be relied upon, for the science of X-ray was comparatively new, less than ten years old.

"Dr. Lawrason Brown, head of the Sanitarium at that time, was a pioneer in the field of tuberculin test, and supervised my exposure to five steps. If you failed to react on all five, you were negative. I reacted on the third, indicating incipiency, and calling for strict bedrest, stepped-up diet and no exercise until my fever had subsided. Regaining weight was the big problem. I couldn't do it. I force-fed myself — raw eggs with orange juice in the morning, and again at night, if I hadn't eaten anything else. After ten days, I was still skinny, but well enough to be moved into the Jacob Schiff cottage, near the entrance gate to the grounds.

"It was quite a while, about August, before I was given what was known as 'two-hour exercise,' which meant walking very slowly for two hours in the morning and two in the afternoon. When I got that allowance, I was able to go to the workshop where Mr. Schofield was in charge of what is now known as occupational therapy. I made leather wallets and hand-tooled them. I read every available book on tuberculosis. I did some fine picture-framing. Then they made me a paid assistant to Mr. Schofield, which helped my fast depleting finances. And I also won the croquet championship of the Sanitarium."

Finally, he could reach Dr. Wynn's, outside the grounds, where Jane was living, and walk slowly through the wooded paths of Mount Pisgah and plan again. Once a week he hired a spirited team and a topless phaeton from Pop Hutchens at $3.75 for the day. Jane and he drove through the lush countryside, enjoyed picnic lunches and were able to laugh once more. At summer's end he left Saranac conditionally, still tethered by probation and promises of rest and check-ups.

Branch Rickey reached the University of Michigan campus at Ann Arbor on the day before classes began in the fall of 1909. Jane was back in Lucasville again with her family. He took a small room at Mrs. Ruby's boardinghouse and budgeted his capital, depleted to $200, to carry him through the first semester at the law school. After making good grades, he petitioned for extra hours, and was granted them after standing examination on the elementary law course, the one he had taught for Professor Grove a year before. He carried as many as twenty hours and, because of previous credits, laid out a program for completing the three-year course in two.

Undergraduate Rickey was under full scholastic speed when he saw a news item in the Michigan *Daily* saying that the baseball coach, Lew McAllister, had resigned and that Phil Bartelme, Director of Athletics, was seeking a successor. Branch lost no time asking for the post through a written application, setting forth his experience and qualifications. He rushed to the Athletic office and dropped it on a desk.

"When the interview was finally held," Rickey laughed in recollection, "Phil made the 'mistake' of asking for references. He underestimated my need of a job. I wanted it desperately for more than economic reasons. It meant working at something I knew and loved. He said it was wide open. I asked if it would be all right to have the personal references mailed directly to him, and he said yes. So I returned to Mrs. Ruby's and began a sort of chain-letter campaign, the biggest I ever tackled."

He wrote about sixty letters to individuals in high places, setting forth his problem and asking, if they could say something good, would they please write to Bartelme. He also respectfully requested that they mail the letter on a specific day. By staggering the dates of the replies, he was assured of Bartelme receiving an average of two a day.

Nearly a month passed before Mrs. Ruby brought the glad tidings. "Mr. Bartelme of the Athletic Association is calling." It was lunch time and Branch promised to be there right after classes. Bartelme, who was only thirty-seven, appeared to have lost some of his ruddy color. He looked like anything but a happy employer-to-be, hunched at his oaken rolltop desk in the chilly, bare-floored office.

"The job is yours," he said, "on one condition."

It was agreed.

"Stop sending me those darned letters!"

The contrast in Michigan baseball coaches between 1909 and 1910 was as sharp as the difference in playing personnel. Lewis "Sport" McAllister was of the old tobacco-chewing school, a down-to-earth-with-spikes-flying type. He was one of a few listed who played every position at one time or another in big-league games. His college coaching technique reflected this rugged background, according to one Michigan player of 1909 who remembered McAllister calling upon a pinch hitter.

"What'll I do, Coach?" the boy asked as he grabbed a bat.

McAllister spat and said, "Strike out, you sonofabitch, you never done anything else."

Yet he pushed his players to win eighteen games while losing only three and tieing one in his final season at Ann Arbor.

Rickey's method from the beginning was weighted with sympathy and understanding. A little fellow came out for the Michigan varsity with the sole distinction of having been mascot for his high school team. He was really too small to be considered seriously. Rickey watched him run and then timed his speed, which was very fast. Naturally right-handed, he was taught to bat left-handed for a faster start to first base. Hours were spent showing him how to bunt, wait for the good pitches and utilize his one asset: speed. The boy batted well over .300, what with bases on balls, beating out bunts, and hitting safely now and then when the pitcher had to "come in" with the ball. He was a good fielder and played a very acceptable third base for the varsity.

From the start Rickey drilled the new and green Michigan squad daily on cutoff plays, bunt squeezes, fast getaways from the bases, sliding into sand pits and teaching catchers to get the mask off and out of the way automatically on foul flies.

His unique efforts to correct long-striders and foot-in-the-bucket batters failed on two counts. He tried constriction of the offending foot with a strip of rubber for two days. On the second day he also used the wooden arc employed at the front edge of the shot-putter's circle. Those who didn't lose their balance were too conscious of the constriction to swing.

"A few of the fellows nearly got killed," Rickey recalled. "I became convinced and believed then, as I do now, that it is an uncorrectable fault. Mr. McGraw and Mr. Mack, in fact all the intelligent baseball men with whom I ever talked about the subject, agreed with me. Nothing has ever cured a definite overstrider at the plate. There isn't a great batsman today in either major league, so far as I have observed, who is an overstrider. In fact, very few batters who overstride reach the major leagues. But I surely tried to cure it at Michigan."

Rickey took justifiable pride in this work and in his team's execution of baseball fundamentals, strategies and surprises. Early in a tight game with Syracuse at Michigan, he ordered a runner squeezed home from third base with a bunt. Catching or guessing the sign, Syracuse called for a pitchout and the Michigan runner was out by twenty feet. The special dispatch in the Sunday Detroit *Free Press* called it a very bad play in certain terms, and cast aspersion on the wisdom of a coach who would go through with such ill-advised strategy so early in the game, particularly when "everybody in the ball park knew the squeeze was on."

The criticism was especially biting because the writer was a close friend who sat next to Rickey in law class. He was Clarence Eldridge who had earned the nickname of "Dope" by constantly seeking the "latest dope" at the Athletic Office.

Rickey found him quickly and asked, "Clarence, how could you write a thing like that about a classmate and good friend?"

"Because it has nothing to do with friendship," Eldridge explained. "I'm a correspondent for a big newspaper. I'm paid to tell the truth. That comes first."

Rickey used most of the summer in 1910 to recapture his old health and endurance. Physicians in Cleveland advised him to work carefully and steadily at it. There was no guarantee against a recurrence when his resistance was lowered.

"It is like a busted boiler," he was told. "It's mended but you can't maintain the same steam pressure as before."

With Jane at his side, he went to Colorado Springs and then on to Trappers Lake in the high, mountainous northwest part of the state. There he resumed his rugged life, sleeping on outside porches in good weather and bad, and fishing the treacherous White River.

Michigan's 1911 season was fairly good, but baseball now was secondary to "the jealous mistress." The Law Department' Class Day came on Monday, June 26, when University Hall was filled with joyous, though somewhat restless, students. In the Law Department the number of degrees awarded was 199. Near the head of the marching line was the baseball coach, Branch Rickey.

The law firm of Rickey, Crow and Ebbert came out of the Karnea, or biennial convention of the Delta Tau Delta fraternity chapters, held at Chicago in early August, 1911. Branch had first proposed a partnership to Eldridge who already had plans to enter law in Chicago. The three selected Boise, Idaho, primarily because of its high, dry climate. That a majority of arguments in Boise were still settled out of court with unholstered .45's did not dampen their enthusiasm. Crow received his Idaho bar admission on September 16, 1911, and Rickey got his three days later. The firm rented Room 409 of the Idaho Building, best in town, for $17.50 a month.

Branch Rickey was engaged in a business lunch at the Union League Club in New York City some forty-five years later when a tall, elderly man paused at the table and asked gruffly, "Which one of you is Branch Rickey?"

Somewhat startled, Rickey admitted the responsibility. A large hand was thrust before him.

"I'm Judge Davis of Boise, Idaho," he exclaimed. "Just wanted to shake your hand. I heard your first case and you lost it. Haw-haw-haw!"

"I sure did lose it," Rickey sighed after the greeter had left. "I was appointed defense counsel by the court, and I never knew a man could be guilty of so many crimes. Nowhere in my client's make-up was there a shred of innocence."

Shortly after the first of the year, he wired Bartelme at Michigan: AM STARVING. WILL BE BACK WITHOUT DELAY.

It was considerably more than a slight exaggeration, but exactly what Bartelme wanted to hear. Within a few weeks Branch had turned the law office over to Crow and Ebbert with a promise to return in June, and was at Ann Arbor launching the new intramural baseball program. It was February.

"Candidates for several varsity baseball teams were reporting," Rickey said in describing one more pivotal moment in his life, "for registration, assignment and tryout. Here before me stood a handsome boy of eighteen, with dark brown hair, serious gray eyes and good posture. He was about five feet eight or nine, well built but not heavy, and he wore a somewhat battered finger glove on his right hand. He said he had pitched on a high school team in Akron, Ohio, and that he was George Sisler, engineering student in the freshman class.

" 'Oh, a freshman,' I said. 'Well, this part of the program

is only for the varsity. You can't play this year.' He showed extreme disappointment. I said, 'You can't play this year, but you can work out with the varsity today.'

"The workout was unforgettable. He pitched batting practice and, for the next twenty minutes, created no end of varsity embarrassment. His speed and control made him almost unhittable. All of his moves were guided by perfection of reflexes, which made him quick, graceful, accurate — the foundation of athletic greatness. It was all there."

Later in the spring, he heard a student assistant say, "That freshman engineer — I think I'll start him in a game tomorrow." He remembered saying, "Good, I'd like to see him." He remembered all this afterward.

But, the next day and, with no thought of the freshman, he was scouting for the varsity when Bartelme arrived, somewhat out of breath. The student manager of the freshman class had run to Bartelme with the news.

"There's a little kid on the far field striking out everybody." Bartelme relayed the news and Rickey was first on the scene. The Michigan *Daily* did full justice to the performance the next day:

UNEARTH "FIND" IN
INTERCLASS GAME

Sisler, Freshman Engineer, Twirls
for Seven Innings and Strikes
Out Twenty Men.

E. F. "Tommy" Hughitt, of Buffalo, a prominent football official, once volunteered additional data on the historic game:

"I played third base on the freshman engineering team in that game. Our catcher was Steve Wilson. Poor Steve just couldn't hold George Sisler's speed and had a number of passed balls. The last strikeout victim went to first when the pitch got past Wilson, and a few passed balls later, Sisler tagged him at the plate for the final out!"

Five days later Branch Rickey looked on soberly as Sisler pitched a full nine-inning game. The frosh not only won, 4-0, but young Sisler permitted the varsity only one hit and struck out eleven. Sisler himself made one base hit in two times at bat. Through late May and early June, Rickey arranged short practice games almost daily with the strongest freshmen he could assemble. Sisler played the outfield when he wasn't pitching.

After completing the schedule, he used Sisler to pitch for the varsity against the Michigan Alumni as part of the term-end festivities. The varsity had only a fair record with fifteen victories, nine losses and a pair of ties. The Alumni, with six former captains in the lineup, were justifiably confident. But they got only four hits and no runs off the freshman south-paw in losing by 3-0, and fifteen Alumni were strikeout victims.

Whenever possible, Rickey made quick visits to scout nearby teams of the South Michigan League — Flint, Adrian, Jackson and Lansing. When he liked what he saw, he made a note of why and the player's name. On one occasion he wrote a detailed report on three players in the league and sent it to the owner of the St. Louis Browns, Hedges.

"I had not forgotten Mr. Hedges' kindness and courtesy," Rickey explained. "He let me skip the post-season series, six years before, when I had to report for a college coaching job, and I'm sure he was responsible for the players voting me a full share of the playoff money."

Rickey boldly recommended that all three players be purchased immediately, since only one could be obtained in the

fall player-selection draft. All three might even be sold before then. Hedges failed to act soon enough. When he
decided to move, the rival St. Louis Cardinals had already
purchased the big eighteen-year-old catcher on the Flint
team whom Rickey had particularly liked. He was Frank
"Pancho" Snyder, of San Antonio, Texas.

Hedges appeared in Ann Arbor to express his appreciation
in a most flattering way. After two record-breaking seasons
financially in 1907 and 1908, he had rebuilt Sportsman's
Park with the first concrete grandstand in baseball. However,
failure on the field in succeeding seasons had diminished attendance and the previous year, 1911, it was only 207,000, a
third of the 1908 figure. This year was little better.

He wanted to launch a program of expansion with the purchase of the Kansas City Club in the American Association.
He would buy the Kansas City Baseball and Exhibition
Company outright if Branch Rickey would operate it as President and general manager.

This was an important moment for both Hedges and
Branch Rickey. In view of what happened in the next half
century, it was pivotal for baseball. Hedges was forty-three
in 1912 and a wealthy man. He had mature ideas about multiple ownership of teams. Branch Rickey, aged thirty, had a
most definite idea of what constituted skill and latent ability
in a baseball player. He had seen thousands of players as a
big-leaguer and college coach.

Multiple ownership of baseball teams was not original
with Hedges. Even ownership of one major-league club by
several clubs, known as syndicate baseball, was not new. Corporate stock interest in the New York Giants of the 1890's
was held by owners Brush of Cincinnati, Soden of Boston
and A. G. Spalding of Chicago. The Baltimore and Brooklyn
clubs of the twelve-club National League in 1899 had the

same owners and board of directors. By financing both the Cleveland and Boston clubs in the early 1900's, Charles Somers, Cleveland shipping magnate, had made the American League possible. He owned several minor league franchises, as did Charles Ebbets in Brooklyn.

This activity resulted from a desire to have more and better players than another owner. A long-standing rule against the "farming" of young or excess players had frustrated acquisitive owners, but not entirely. Most of them circumvented the rule by simply loaning promising players to minor-league clubs under a "gentleman's agreement." Unfortunately, the trusting owners lost too many players when the custodian ceased being a gentleman and sold the player to another owner.

Well, would Rickey take the Kansas City proposition?

Branch couldn't say. He was flattered. He was grateful. But he had talked two fraternity brothers into setting up law practice in far-off Boise, Idaho. He was paying his part of the office expenses from his coaching salary, and taking nothing from the firm. But he owed them his time and — well, he just didn't know for sure.

Hedges had another idea. He needed players. Why couldn't Branch check up on the office in Idaho, and go on to California and study the players in the Pacific Coast League? Then when the fall draft meeting was held, the Browns would know which players to select. He could take Mrs. Rickey and do the thing leisurely. There would be expenses for two and a generous allowance for time away from the Boise office. That, Branch replied quickly, might work out.

By October, 1912, the days of Rickey, Crow and Ebbert were numbered as a law firm. The boys had eaten regularly, but the partnership had not prospered. Moreover, while Rickey and Ebbert were espousing the Bull Moose Republican movement of Theodore Roosevelt for the presidency, Howard Crow was talking people into voting for Woodrow Wilson, a Democrat.

Branch and Jane Rickey had visited the Los Angeles area in behalf of Mr. Hedges. They enjoyed the country and climate, watched baseball games and scouted the Pacific Coast League. At least three players, Rickey declared with his customary assurance, were of big-league caliber, Agnew, a catcher; Leverenz, a pitcher; and Patterson, an outfielder. It was his first scouting assignment, but he justified Hedges' stubborn faith.

Midway in the month came a surprise call from the Browns' owner. He and Mrs. Hedges were driving west and would reach Salt Lake City on a certain day. Could Branch be there?

Rickey went down and returned with the best possible news. He was to be second in command of the St. Louis American League Baseball Club, a presidential assistant, responsible for carrying out policy, seeking players, planning and arranging player transfers, and generally strengthening the Browns in every way possible. He was to get a high salary, $7500, and he could coach the Michigan baseball team once more, bringing his income to $9000. After the baby was born, they would return to Ann Arbor until June. By that time he would have living quarters in St. Louis. It was perfect, he assured Jane, as she boarded the train alone for Lucasville, Ohio.

6

After reporting to the St. Louis Browns in January, 1913, Branch Rickey was quietly named second vice-president and secretary, but there was no official announcement of his exact status and duties. The press didn't know what he was up to, but knew something was up and conjured a variety of explanations that included the probable ousting of one or two old retainers.

A baseball organization rarely has room for an extra man anywhere, for the reason that operators of the game, on the field and in the office, have always tried to "take care of their own." Few workers or players leave a baseball job voluntarily, because the one held is usually better than anything they might get elsewhere. When Rickey joined the Browns in 1913, the working staff consisted of President Hedges; his nephew, Hiram Mason, who later served as road secretary; one part-time scout, Charlie Barrett; Lloyd Rickart, a combination ticket man and traveling secretary; and, in May, Roscoe Hillenkoetter, fifteen, a baseball-minded youngster who began as office boy.

Rickey's very entrance into St. Louis brought a newspaper headline, "Rumor Rickey to Succeed Rickart." The new man couldn't dispel this and other rumors. He wasn't certain of his own plans. His title had no bearing on his job. Writers, meeting him in the club's downtown quarters, noted he had no private office. Loquacious and accessible, he sat in plain view at an old desk with nothing on it or in it. He talked eagerly and intelligently on baseball. He exuded enthusiasm for his undefined duties. The writers observed that he was just past thirty-one and still in "tiptop playing condition," not knowing he had recently spent anxious days in southern Ohio trying to regain weight lost in a near-fatal battle with blood-poisoning contracted in Idaho after Jane had left.

Most frustrating to a curious press during those early months were Rickey's unscheduled trips to scattered points that were not identified until after his departure. One terminal point in early February was Lucasville where he became the father of a baby daughter. They named her Mary Emily for the two grandmothers. His return to Ann Arbor for a final term of coaching was no mystery until he suddenly appeared in major-league cities without his college team. He was back in the downtown office on June 1.

President Hedges ignored the erroneous explanations of Rickey's duties and whereabouts until one writer stated that the nomadic vice-president would replace the provocative playing manager George Stovall, whose retention was in doubt after a one-month suspension in May for spitting tobacco juice on the white linen coat of an umpire. Rickey had heavy baseball and coaching experience and did not chew tobacco. But Hedges replied quickly:

"I regard Branch Rickey as one of the brightest men in baseball, but that doesn't necessarily mean he is to become manager of my club. Because Rickey picked up four of the greatest young players in the league today — I mean Leverenz, Agnew, Lavan and Patterson — I consider him capable of sizing up the situation on our club and, for that reason, he has followed the team in three cities. Stovall is my manager right now and I'm not thinking of making a change."

Finding ball players of potential promise was a factor in Rickey's early experience with the consequences of having things that others wanted or needed. Immersed in his immediate plans, spurred by irrepressible hope, he was oblivious to the price tag on working for survival within the competitive framework of big business. He was not immediately aware of the jealousies and outrage he had precipitated in a comparatively small business, and less aware of those he would cause in the future through his unbridled methods.

Actually there was no way of defining Branch Rickey's thinking and doing in 1913. His work, having no precedent, could have been misinterpreted and hampered by partial understanding. It centered around the production in quantity of young players with high promise as insurance against fading veterans at the top. Fans could be assured of a winning team for the future along with a pennant now and then.

The new approach was combined with Hedges' understanding and analysis of baseball finances. Transient attendance in New York, for instance, equaled both resident and transient attendance in St. Louis. That, added to the many millions of available patrons in the New York area, made it difficult for a town like St. Louis to compete favorably with the large metropolitan cities for the pennant year in and year out. The alternative was to have literally millions of dollars to spend for more-or-less finished playing skill, which had to be purchased from the AA, or top, minor leagues. The answer was to be found in the farm system of player development.

"But let's get right, once and for all, the really early beginning of the farm system," Rickey once said in reconstructing his start with the Browns in 1913. "Nobody had fabulous amounts of money to spend for finished ball players from the minor leagues or from one another. Our Browns club was so-so, though not the worst team in the league. I brought to Mr. Hedges a wide acquaintanceship in college circles throughout Ohio, Indiana and the Western Conference, and beyond those universities through Kentucky, Tennessee and even Georgia, because of the annual spring vacation trip of our Michigan team. I had coaching friends also throughout the East. I cultivated those contacts and kept in close touch with them when I went to St. Louis.

"They told me about players, more than I could take care of because of our low player limit. With no place to put these recommended players, I had to find minor-league clubs to take them and sign them on a title basis. They owned the contracts and, in return for recommending and signing the players, we tried to have a gentleman's agreement on later purchase. There was no rule against it at the time. There shouldn't be any rule against it. It was the only way for a major-league club to get players except by outright purchase.

"It was very easy to place players with a minor-league club on an arrangement that gave you the right to purchase them later at a fair price. If that kind of arrangement could have been maintained and kept realistic and honest as just that, there is no reason for the gentleman's agreement not being in use and entirely legal today. Unfortunately there was a disposition of the minor-league clubs owning these college contracts to find a market far in excess of anything we could pay. Indeed, they sometimes manufactured a market to realize the highest dollar.

"For that reason, some clubs where I first placed my players — Montgomery, Alabama, was the chief repository and later party to the first written working agreement — took the players and refused to be honest about it. Since the verbal agreement could not be proved, they simply sold the players to another major-league club at a higher figure. That didn't pay and it wasn't right. It occurred to me that I had to have something more than an oral understanding. Friendship was vital and friendship is the best thing you can have, but when a man who is your friend has controlling or determining interest in a minor-league club, and dies or sells out, then all your agreements amount to nothing. This complex problem arose and begged for solution all during my first year with the St. Louis Browns."

The pioneering job that Hedges and Rickey tried to do against the handicap of a world war and another with a rival third major league was staggering in size and scope. Promising players by the dozen had been located and assayed through Rickey's contacts. But their plan to buy one or more high-classification clubs for the seasoning of players was ended by a confidential bulletin in mid-season from the National Commission, baseball's governing body, stating that ownership of minor-league franchises by major-league teams would be barred after January 1, 1914. The deadline gave owners like Somers and Ebbets more than six months to dispose of their multiple franchises, but Hedges and Rickey were prevented from launching their program at all.

Outlawing ownership was a companion piece to the original "no farming" rule which, in 1903, decreed that no player could be "farmed" from a major-league club to one of lower classification. Seven years after this ruling, 1910, and by actual count after investigation, Brooklyn in the National League had 61 players under contract to Philadelphia's 31. Cleveland in the American League had 60 to Washington's 29. The hazardous practice of gentleman's agreement made the lopsided situation possible. Rule-makers tried to legalize it somewhat during the winter of 1912-13 by raising the big-league player roster to 35, with mandatory reduction to 25 a month after opening the season.

Hedges and Rickey solved their own problem by devising baseball's first open and aboveboard working agreement. They consented in July, 1913, to finance four Montgomery, Alabama, merchants with $12,500 to help purchase the ball club in their city. Hedges and Rickey agreed to supply the club with a full roster of players at no expense to the club for the privilege of buying any or all of the player contracts for a flat $1000 each at the end of the season. When one of the merchants tried to change the agreed financing in his favor, Hedges and Rickey pulled out and the unique agreement collapsed.

The importance of this pioneering maneuver can best be realized after a study of the so-called draft meeting, a procedure in baseball that provides the "unsold" minor-league player with an opportunity for advancement by selection at the end of each year. It was held shortly after Labor Day in 1913 in order to meet the activity of the Federal League organizers who needed players badly.

Baseball officials were astounded at the meeting in Cincinnati. Of the 108 minor-league players selected in turn by each of the sixteen clubs, 30 were called by the St. Louis Browns.

"Branch Rickey must have had two hundred names in a book," one stunned observer reported. "He kept crossing off names as they were called by other teams, but he always had another choice ready when his turn came. We never saw anything like it before."

Nor had any big-league club ever contracted to pay more than $100,000 for drafted players. Wise heads called it a poor gamble.

"Poor nothing," Rickey argued. "Two outstanding players

will be worth that. Meanwhile, we'll look at twenty-eight others besides our regular team of thirty-five."

More than a third of the Brown's thirty draftees were able to play in the major leagues, some for many years. Perhaps the top prize was "Big Bill" James, a right-handed pitcher. Another was Leon Cadore, who, eight years later, pitched the longest game on record, twenty-six innings. The Browns lost him in the traffic of players within a year of the draft. More important than quality was that Branch Rickey had evolved in 1913 an entirely new conception of baseball operation. It violated no existing rule. Hampered in its earliest stages by wars and other obstacles that made all but survival secondary, it was still the birth of the farm-system idea.

Most big-league managers serve as coaches or apprentices, but Branch Rickey took over the St. Louis Browns in early September, 1913, almost without warning. He didn't want the job. He preferred to continue ironing out the wrinkles in the new idea. But Stovall had dissipated his value as a field leader. During the final week in August the Browns played seven days without scoring a run. Team morale ebbed low, jeopardizing the future of green youngsters on the club, and of those to come. Hedges prevailed upon Rickey to take over and forestall catastrophe.

The appointment [wrote Bill O'Connor] will be one of the biggest experiments. He has been called a theorist who has a working knowledge of baseball, based on limited experience as a catcher . . . Hedges has made a more radical change than most major league magnates would have dreamed of. He has made the baseball world sit up and take notice.

In addition to managing, Rickey made trips to Ann Arbor

for players, to Cincinnati for the draft meeting, and to Florida for next years' spring training arrangements. He signed two catchers from the University of Michigan ranks to relieve the loss by injury of Agnew and McAlester. With each signing he volunteered opinions to the press with a frankness that was almost naïve, and invited the critical second guess.

"I wouldn't try to pick a hitter from the college ranks," he said. "You can arrive at a clear idea of how he can field, throw and run the bases. You can also learn if he is a 'bonehead.' But whether he can hit in the big leagues will keep you guessing. He seldom faces the same college pitcher more than once in a season, and his weaknesses are not revealed. In professional baseball a new player may make one swing around the circuit and hit above three hundred. But the pitchers soon inform each other of batting weaknesses, and they're all waiting for him, especially the college player, on the next trip."

Rickey's preference for positive statements made him a target of newspaper crossfire shortly after he joined the Browns, but it was intensified after he had succeeded Stovall. The former manager, a good first baseman, remained with the team, enlisted sympathy from a few writers and then broke with Rickey. He wanted his unconditional release. Rickey spoke sharply:

"I would consider it a huge mistake to unconditionally release Stovall. He's a good ballplayer, an asset to our club and he'll not get away until another asset comes in his place. You can make it as strong as you like that Stovall will not be released unconditionally."

After the Browns and Cardinals, managed by Miller Huggins, had tied each other in a long and dull post-season series, Rickey revealed the extent of the trouble caused by the deposed manager.

"I didn't wish to make it known at the time, but Stovall cast his lot with the Federal League while still under contract to the Browns and then began tampering with players on my club. I refused to permit him on the ball field during the fall series. Prior to that, having learned that he was not working for the best interests of the club, I asked him to stay away from the games. When he refused, I did the only thing possible: I removed his uniform from the locker."

Near the end of the year Rickey was thrown into "open warfare" with a man for whom he had only admiration, Miller Huggins. A writer had interviewed Rickey on his extensive and unusual plans for training the Browns at St. Petersburg, Florida, the next year. Without his knowledge or consent, the interview was run as a personal account "By Branch Rickey." A writer on another paper then visited Miller Huggins and prodded him into commenting. The barbs in his remarks were:

No ballplayer can learn to steal by sliding into sand pits.

How long do you think I would last if I was compelled to hit the dirt 15 or 20 times a day? I am no longer a kid and it would cripple me.

I would not ask an old ballplayer to slide in a pit just because the veterans have been in the pastime long enough to do such things properly, else they wouldn't be carried as regulars.

I released Larry Quinlan to Oakland for the reason that he runs flat-footed. I don't think he could be taught how to run.

Lee Magee is fast, but he never would learn to run bases in the sliding pit. I am a self-made ballplayer and I had to run bases the best way I could. I never slid in a pit.

Yes, this theory stuff is all right, in a way, but I don't think much of it.

Publication of the Rickey story, which he denied writing, though admitted he may have inspired, and the Huggins critique, brought forth a torrent of rebuttal from Branch Rickey on his thirty-second birthday. He may have left doubt in the minds of St. Louis fans on some points, but not on his sincerity. The substance of his harangue follows:

"It seems somewhat like sounding brass and a tinkling cymbal for managers of two eighth-place major-league teams to be engaged in an argument over the development of a ball club. Not because anybody in St. Louis or anywhere else cares a rap about my beliefs in this matter, but just for the sake of a little self-satisfaction, I shall have three batting cages, three handball courts, one sliding pit and a place for running dashes at the training camp in St. Petersburg. If this is theory, it is blamed good practical theory.

"That ballplayers could be and are being developed is a fact that can easily be supported as against the contention that players coming into the majors may assume to be finished players. In five weeks' practice at St. Petersburg, participating only in games, it might be that this or that player would have to slide only two or three times, and then come back north and enter the season no better than when he went south. I have had a good many men slide daily in sand pits and never have known anyone to be injured or bruised.

"It is also a matter of common knowledge that development of a foot-runner is comparatively easy to obtain by a competent instructor and is very noticeable to a looker-on. To say that you do not want a recruit just because he has not all the speed he is capable of giving is, to me, only silly twaddle.

"To exaggerate the importance of means anyone may use in the development of a ballplayer is very easy. The main thing is a big amount of inherent ability. After all, a man's development is up to himself, and the power within a man to develop himself establishes with me a standard of his brain power. It is just as much an achievement of a ballplayer, as anyone else who develops into his best in other lines of work.

"I confidently expect to know that Mr. Huggins will be employing sliding pits, and possibly a batting cage, before he is through with management of the St. Louis Cardinals baseball club."

In mid-February of 1914, Branch Rickey led the advance squad of St. Louis Browns into St. Petersburg, Florida, thanks to the persistence and civic-mindedness of Al Lang and opened baseball's first all-purpose training camp, the most novel to date and one of the most rugged of all time. The entire party consisted of forty-seven players, Manager Rickey, Charlie Barrett, scout; veteran Joe Sugden, the catcher who loaned Rickey the mitt in his first big-league game; George Palfrey, team photographer; and five St. Louis newspapermen. Five wives who made the trip did not include Jane Rickey. She remained in St. Louis with her second child, born on January 31, and named Branch.

After a prolonged struggle among real estate promoters, the baseball training grounds had been located on Snell and Hamlett's Coffee Pot Bayou district, today a select residential area. The sandy stretch, cleared of pines, cabbage palms and palmetto bush, now contained a large wooden grandstand, handball courts, three net-covered batting cages, sprinting lanes for speed tests, and sliding pits.

An innovation first seen in big-league baseball at St. Petersburg was the "pitching strings." A part of every Rickey training camp thereafter, they consisted of two upright poles at either side of a home plate, connected by two horizontal white cords across the front edge of the plate at average knee-height and shoulder-height. Cross strings were then connected by upright cords seventeen inches apart to indicate the plate-width. The white rectangle outlined the strike zone. The catcher squatted behind the strings and plate. The pitcher stood at the regulation distance and tried to "hit the strings" to develop plate-edge control.

Modern players training at St. Petersburg's Al Lang Field, a steel and concrete memorial to the civic pioneer, know little of the rigors endured by the 1914 Browns. Their biggest complaint came from the compulsory walk of a mile and a half from Fifth Avenue North and Second Street to what is now North Shore Drive and 30th Street, with a return trip after strenuous workouts. The road was sand and shells, hot and dusty and all of St. Petersburg's half dozen saloons were in the opposite direction. Rickey ordered everyone up and eating, whether asleep or awake, by eight-thirty each morning. He had no retiring curfew.

"After the running trials," he said, "and the pitching strings, the batting cages, the sliding pits with stress on the hook and fall-away slides, handball, and the three-mile round-trip walk, they had my permission to stay up as late as they wished, or could."

Opening of the exhibition schedule was a holiday occasion in Pinellas County. Special trains brought crowds down from Tarpon Springs. Decorated excursion boats steamed from Bayboro Harbor up the bay to Coffee Pot Bayou for 25 cents a head. The St. Petersburg *Independent* published an extra. Sports writers filed a "record" 15,000 words. The Chicago Cubs made the two-hour trip across the Bay from Tampa on the *Manatee*. Some three thousand jammed the new wooden grandstand and lined the field to see Branch Rickey use nineteen players to beat the Cubs 9 to 5.

During 1914 and 1915 Branch Rickey managed the Browns in about three hundred championship games. Modern writers are almost unanimous in claiming that he had little or no managing ability. No one bothers to look beyond the league standings or the last "authority" who wrote that he was a flop, talked over his players' heads, was too theoretical, or was merely "satisfying an unconquerable itch to manage."

Some startling contradictions of these appraisals were part of the *Post-Dispatch* game coverage in 1914.

Boston, May 15 — "It has been years," said Ban Johnson at Fenway Park today, "since I have seen the Browns play with the life, fire and ambition they showed against the Red Sox. Manager Rickey has succeeded in getting them right on their toes and keeping them there. They are playing the sort of game that must eventually be a winner."

Boston, May 16 — "If Rickey can keep his men up to any such clip on the bases," says Bill Carrigan, Red Sox manager, "the Browns will be the greatest base stealers in either league."

St. Louis, June 6 — Clarence "Tilly" Walker has vindicated Rickey's judgment. The $15,000 purchase is making Rickey the most talked of manager in the American League. For years cheap baseball material has been palmed off on the indulgent public hereabouts. But with the coming of Rickey, the analyst, came a new era.

A few days later:

Manager Branch Rickey's team is arousing the interest of the country with its remarkable spurt from last place in 1913 to a near-championship position. He is no longer referred to as a baseball theorist. He has put to flight penners of the sarcastic criticism and skeptics who predicted that practice, not theory, won ball games. His applied theories have made the Browns one of the country's best and most exciting teams. He has shown himself a master of the science of the game, a capable handler of men and a man who can practice what he preaches.

Rickey never discussed his years of managing — or the career of any manager — from the viewpoint of greatness.

Greatness, as such, does not exist among managers on the ball field, because it is, at best, a hindsight calculation on the basis of won-and-lost figures. Hundreds of decisions are made by a manager during a game, and the manner in which these crises are met determines degree of managing skill, or the lack of it, to baseball people. Rickey is quite positive about it.

"John McGraw was an outstanding field director," he always insisted. "Almost beyond compare. I regard Rogers Hornsby and Barney Shotton as the closest approach to McGraw. Managing a baseball team means molding individuals of varying temperaments and intelligence into a cohesive unit of coordinated action toward the achievement of a common purpose. McGraw's ability in this is amply demonstrated by the presence of two 'opposites' in the intellectual Christy Mathewson and the unfortunate 'Bugs' Raymond, both winning pitchers. Of course, a manager's players must be good to begin with. Poor material can make the best of managers mediocre, and has."

Overlooked by his critics in Branch Rickey's case was the fact that, while managing, he continued his duties as assistant to Hedges, working to build a better team through a new kind of baseball system. Rickey summed up that side of his work with the comment:

"We will have between fifteen and twenty new youngsters coming up next year. Most of them are green, but they are lightning fast. Whether the Browns can obtain immediate strength from any of them is a question. They all need experience, but we may pick up a player or two who can help us."

On August 25, 1914, Rickey appeared in his last major-league lineup, and right where he had broken in, Philadelphia, but this time in five-year-old Shibe Park. The Browns were losing the first game of a double-header, 7–0, to a nine-teen-year-old southpaw, Ray Bressler. Rickey had used one pinch hitter and needed another. Ira Thomas, now the A's coach and catcher, bellowed across the field to his former New York teammate, "Why don't you hit, Rick!"

The whole St. Louis bench took up the cry. Even Connie Mack caught the spirit of the moment. So Rickey agreed on condition that Bressler stop throwing curves.

"In spite of the 'condition,'" Rickey laughed in recollection, "I was sure they'd curve me to death, so I wasn't set for the first pitch, which was a fast ball and strike one. Well, I thought, they did that to build up my complacency. I just knew the next one would bend over. A second fast ball went by for a strike. Now I really got ready for the curve, and was utterly amazed to see a third fast ball go by for called strike three. My last turn at bat taught me that nothing is gained by distrusting your fellow man."

After winning the fall city series with the Cardinals, Rickey plunged into a heavy campaign of appearances at churches, Y.M.C.A.'s, clubs and banquets in an effort to combat the stiffest competition in Browns' history. The Cardinals led in attendance, but only by 11,000. The third bid for major-league patronage, the Federal League "Sloufeds," playing only a few blocks away, had dented the gate receipts of both rivals.

Much of the winter's work was devoted to hunting for ways to meet the ruinous competition while hoping that recurring rumors of peace were true. The St. Louis Feds were owned by wealthy Philip DeCatsby Ball, who showed no worry over his losses. He said all peace reports were due to fright within organized baseball.

The weeks of spring training in Texas were punctuated with rumors or threats of defection by players to the Federal

League. Injunctions, restraining orders and damage suits clogged the federal courts and even the decisions conflicted, what with reversals and delaying appeals. Rickey was extremely busy, fighting to hold his players in line, tutoring his green recruits while the foundations of organized baseball were shaking. But late June brought a refreshing sight, that of George Harold Sisler, who joined the Browns in Chicago, ending one of the most bitter disputes over a single player in baseball history.

Rickey had returned to Michigan for a successful season of baseball coaching in 1913. George Sisler pitched 57 innings in his sophomore year, allowing only twenty hits and eight runs. He struck out 84, an average of fourteen every nine innings. Because of his great batting, he alternated at all three outfield positions and first base. He went to bat 104 times and made 46 hits for an average of .442. He stole bases at will, five in a single game and, in that one, two in the same inning.

Rickey built and left a championship team. Sisler was captain as they went on to become champions of 1914 with twenty-two victories and six defeats. Yet, had it not been for Rickey's prompt and decisive action, Sisler's college career might never have happened.

The Sisler case, a simple one when he reported it to Coach Rickey in 1912, became complex only when a big-league club owner acquired an illegal contract that developed value.

"A part-time umpire named Gailor," Sisler volunteered, "said that he could get me a professional pitching job with Akron of the Ohio-Pennsylvania League, and I took it."

"Did you sign a contract?" Rickey asked.

"I guess so. It was called articles of agreement."

"That's a baseball contract. Did your mother or father sign it?"

"No."

"Did you take any money, any at all, from this man or the club?"

"No. The contract was for a hundred a month," Sisler explained. "Gailor wanted to give me an advance, but I never took any. Soon after I learned that my high school catcher, Russ Baer, was coming here to Michigan. I wanted to come, so I changed my mind and came."

Rickey assured him that the contract was not binding. When Sisler drew attention as a freshman star, Columbus, which had acquired the contract, "suspended" him, and assigned the contract to the Pittsburgh Pirates, owned by Barney Dreyfuss, who insisted that the suspension be enforced, even though the contract had never been promulgated through the National Commission offices. Sisler's eligibility was threatened by the cry of professionalism. Rickey took protective steps in the boy's behalf. Mayor George B. Cobb, of Detroit, wrote to the National Commission chairman, Garry Herrmann. Rickey visited Ohio, verified the absence of parental consent and had Sisler's father write the Commission to that extent. James O. Murfin, member of the Michigan Board of Regents, advised the Commission in Sisler's behalf, and was disappointed when the player failed to sign with the Detroit Tigers.

"You must not force recognition of this illegal contract," Rickey advised the National Commission, and at this time, 1912, he had no thought of returning to organized baseball. "If you do, you will forever alienate parents and colleges and even high schools. For who is going to trust you, if you cajole minors into signing contracts and then declare them suspended — as you have tried to suspend Sisler — when they change their minds?"

Chairman Herrmann cast the deciding vote against Dreyfuss, a member of his own league, and ended a long friendship when the Pittsburgh owner remained adamant for many years.

Sisler completed three years of varsity competition with a batting record of 120 hits in 297 tries for a grand average of .404. He pitched a total of 153 innings, allowed 20 runs and 58 hits and struck out 232 batters. He won thirteen games and lost only three. He could have signed with any one of several big-league teams and for a substantial cash inducement. He chose St. Louis to play for Branch Rickey.

Sisler's first pitching start came on July 3 in the first game of a double header at Sportsman's Park. It was something of a personal nightmare, and he could hardly see catcher Severeid's signs. He walked nine Cleveland batters, but he also struck out nine. Cleveland left fourteen runners on base, and failed to score until the ninth inning. At that time the Browns had three runs and Sisler had his first major-league pitching victory, 3–1.

In late September a St. Louis writer said:

> Branch Rickey may not have lifted the Brownies to the pennant level, but he has done one thing to prove the wisdom of R. L. Hedges: he has shown a decided ability to recognize young talent when he sees it. Rickey is thus far responsible for what Clark Griffith calls the best crop of young baseball prospects in the country.

Branch Rickey was rewarded with a new contract for 1916 at the same salary, $7500, and none too soon, either. December brought peace between organized baseball and the Federal League, and the purchase of the Browns by P. D. C. Ball. Hedges had given a purchase option on his 90 per cent of shares to John Bruce, secretary of the National Commission, and Walter Orthwein. They sold the option to Ball for $525,000 and cleared a profit of $90,000.

The new officers were named, and Rickey was not one of

them. In fact, Ball gave writers to understand that Rickey would not be part of the new operation, since he wasn't responsible for the contract. Rickey said nothing, but reported each day to the Browns office, confident that the contract was valid.

"My philosophy of life makes me grasp this situation rather easily," he said, doing a little verbal tightrope walking. "The new owners of the Browns are successful businessmen. Obviously they are going to maintain their successful system with men with whom they are acquainted.

"They don't know me and that's my only consolation. I might be a great baseball man without them knowing it. I might not be, too. But if the new owners don't see fit to 'place me,' I shall not take it as a personal affront. I'll just do the best I can."

Robert Hedges had done a tremendous favor by giving Branch the 1916 contract, but he had also favored Ball without the new owner realizing it. Combining the two St. Louis teams left Ball with a roster of sixty-two baseball players of great value. Rickey alone knew what to do about them, where to put them.

Ball was a gruff and growling Iowan of fifty-six who had been everywhere and done everything. He had been a cowpuncher, a construction-gang worker on a Tennessee railroad, and a killer of buffalo for hides in Texas. He played baseball in Louisiana and roamed many states, finally settling down in St. Louis to build a prosperous ice business. He was a sort of self-made man who worshiped his creator, and used excessive invective to make you realize he wasn't afraid.

Roscoe Hillenkoetter brought Ball in to see Rickey for the first time at Sportsman's Park. Branch looked up and saw the fleshy, pear-shaped face twist slightly. Ball rubbed a stubby hand through his iron-gray, brush-cut hair and bellowed: "So you're the God-damned prohibitionist!"

7

WHEN SALARY PAYMENTS continued, as Branch Rickey felt certain they would, the lack of a title was meaningless. He reported daily to the Browns offices, which had been moved to Sportsman's Park during the summer, and worked long hours, carefully placing the surplus players. Not only was he especially fitted for the task; the new team manager, Fielder Jones, was not. By joining the Federals, Jones had sacrificed many of his old and loyal baseball friends.

A disturbing note developed in the office when confidential news items on options, waivers and proposed player moves leaked through the switchboard attendant and appeared in newspapers. The offender was quickly dismissed. The switchboard, left without regular attention, was a problem until "Blind Bill" Nordeman, manager of the concessions department, produced a candidate.

"He's only a kid," Nordeman said to Rickey, "but he packs the correct number of peanuts and keeps track of other things for me. Comes in after school and I know he wants to work all summer."

Presently a bespectacled youngster of thirteen in short pants stood before Rickey. His large blue-gray eyes, hardly visible through the very thick lenses, stared straight ahead as he stood at attention, his hands tight against his sides as though ready to recite the day's lessons. After a few brief questions and answers, Rickey hired him. With that William Orville DeWitt began his front-office career in organized baseball at $3.50 a week, staring at the flip-switches of a small monitor board. The job lasted until school reopened, after which he took a post as night messenger for the American District Telegraph.

Roscoe Hillenkoetter enjoyed the status of a shorthand secretary, helping Rickey with the player problems and the glamour of big-league baseball. His joy ended abruptly the June morning he casually mentioned that his father "can get me an appointment at Annapolis — "

"What did you say?" Rickey barked. Then he described his own bitter disappointment in failing to win an academy career. He dramatized the tragedy of youth failing to grasp opportunities that are denied so many who would give anything for them. He made the same case again to the boy's father the next day. Forty years later Roscoe was Vice-Admiral Hillenkoetter, Naval Inspector General.

The Browns finished a most encouraging fifth and improved their wretched attendance of 1915 by more than doubling it with 335,000 paid admissions. This was 110,000 more than the last-place Cardinals whom they defeated again in the post-season series. Branch Rickey was rewarded with another contract for one year at the same salary. He toiled through the winter on his lengthy player lists and personal score books, his key to mass evaluation. He was kept from the February baseball meetings in New York and pressed into legal service to defend the Browns against a claim of $15,000 for false arrest. Defendant James C. Reach charged mental anguish and humiliation. Rickey argued that the evidence clearly indicated a new ball had been purloined and that it was scuffed by Reach himself. The case turned largely on that point, not as a legal question, but because Reach had made it a major issue and was shown to be in error on the point. When the fracas was over and the verdict returned for the Browns, Rickey made Reach a gift of the ball.

Coincident with this was the visit from James C. Jones,

attorney for the hard-pressed St. Louis Cardinals. Their financial plight was no secret. Mrs. Schuyler Britton had inherited the club six years before. She had used considerable wealth trying to keep it afloat. Now, Jones confided, out-of-city capital might come in and move the historic franchise from St. Louis, if a way couldn't be found to take it off her hands quickly.

"All this I knew," Rickey said in explaining the first steps of his controversial switch to the National League which wound up in the courts. "Many wanted the club, but no one had the fair price that Mrs. Britton asked — three hundred and fifty thousand.

"What I didn't know, and Jones told me, was that several businessmen had just met at his home to discuss his own plan for buying the club and keeping it in St. Louis. His partner was Mrs. Britton's personal attorney, and easily got a purchase option, which was good until March third. Jones then explained to me his Knothole Gang idea. It was based on the public sale of stock at a nominal price per share, with two shares entitling the holder to sponsor a full season of free admission for one boy. I thought the idea splendid and suggested the age limit.

"Then Jones said, 'If we go through with the plan, will you be president?' I said I couldn't reply, being under contract to the Browns. However, Mr. Ball and I had discussed the possibility of improvement when I last signed, which is usual, and he said he wouldn't stand in my way if anything came up. So, I told Jones I would speak to Ball as soon as possible."

Rickey reported the approach and offer to his employer.

"Why those sonsabitches want to buy that ball club?" he exclaimed.

"It's to be financed by a public sale of stock," Branch reminded.

"If you've got a chance to go with them," Ball said, "I wouldn't keep you down for the world."

Thanking him, Branch asked, "Then you want me to pursue it?"

"Let me know what they offer you," Ball replied. "I think I can get them to beat it, and I will help you on that contract."

Rickey met with Jones and repeated the conversation. After verifying it in Rickey's presence by telephone to Sol Swarts, Ball's secretary and attorney, Jones and Rickey discussed duties, authority, noninterference and salary. They agreed on $15,000 a year. Rickey reported back to Ball. The Browns' owner said, "Good. Have you got anything in writing?" When Rickey said he hadn't, Ball continued, "Get it. I'll help you with the contract. Have another meeting with those bastards and get enough to make it good."

In reconstructing the dialogue, Rickey deplored Ball's choice of words, but he felt obliged to include it on account of what followed.

"He had made rough language a part of his gruff nature," Rickey added. "The idea, I suppose, was to disarm you by shock, or something. But he was very kind and cooperative during the several meetings we had on the subject. Our final talk lasted a half hour and he promised to 'look up three or four of those so-and-sos' among the purchasers and tell me whether or not they could be trusted. That was from ten-thirty until eleven.

"At noon I was in Jones's office. We went over the contract, and I signed. Just as we were about to leave for lunch at the Noon-day Club, a call came for me from Sol Swarts. He said Mr. Ball was at the Missouri Athletic Club and wanted to see me immediately. It was very important. I was completely mystified and told Mr. Swarts it was too late, that

I had signed. Jones said to go over, since everything was all set now."

Rickey went and found a completely changed Phil Ball.

"I've just talked to Ban Johnson," Ball announced. "It's all off. He said under no circumstances must this fellow be lost," and he imitated Johnson's characteristic intonation, "to the gre-a-at American League."

"But I have no choice now," Rickey protested, and then, "I only signed after you said it was all right. You gave me your word. We shook hands."

"I don't care," Ball replied with a shrug. "Just tell those bastards you can't go through with it."

"You can't go back on your word. They're giving it to the press."

"If they do, I'll deny I ever said it."

Rickey rose, his face taut and pale, as though slapped.

"Mr. Ball," he said, "whether or not I ever go with the Cardinals, I'll never work another day for you!"

Branch Rickey looked back over forty years of trials and tribulations and happiness, success and failure, and emitted a deep sigh.

"I wish I had gone out of baseball at that moment," he murmured. "I was overwhelmed by mortification and shame at hearing a man of big business and responsibility feel obliged to say such a thing. I learned later that Ban Johnson had raised the devil on the telephone with Ball, who was very much under his thumb. I didn't speak to Mr. Ball for many years."

The mention of Branch Rickey's name as possible president had brought the matter into the open. Rickey promptly issued a formal statement saying:

I have accepted a position with the Cardinals organization. Mr. Ball told me prior to and at the time of acceptance of terms between us, and has confirmed it several times since our contract was signed, that I should feel privileged to accept any position at any time whereby I might better myself and told me, further, that he would release me in such event and voluntarily added that he would "help me to secure it."

I notice that he does not deny he told me this, but I am surprised and shocked to learn that he qualified his promise. I relied upon it, for he told me "My word is my bond." I believe the chief Cardinal idea is "a winning ball club." And my hearty support shall be given to this cause. I regret to leave all the boys on the Browns, most of whom I induced to join that club. There will be some more just like them on the Cardinals, and I hope both clubs will represent St. Louis well, not only in 1917 but always.

He then pledged to purchase two hundred shares of stock for $5000, which he didn't have. He used his last $1000 as a down payment on a three-story, tree-shaded brick dwelling at 5405 Bartmer Avenue. Furnishing the twelve rooms was another strain that left him dependent on the success of the Cardinals to satisfy a mortgage of $9500. But he had his own home at last for the three children, Jane, and her sister Mabel, who had volunteered to stay on, and a maid, Clara, coaxed down from Ann Arbor.

He headed his own stock-selling team and began a race with Jones to see who could bring in the most purchasers.

"I got a lot more buyers than Jones or the others," Rickey confided, "but mine were hundred-dollar boys. Of our seven hundred stockholders, I don't think Jones got more than thirty, but each of his ran to five and ten thousand apiece. Of the hundred and seventy-five thousand raised, Jones accounted for three-fourths of it."

Presently Ball had to back up his position by applying for an injunction to restrain Rickey from a breach of contract. Neither Jones nor Rickey worried. Their position rested with forcing Ball to deny under oath that he gave Rickey permission to negotiate with the Cardinals' syndicate.

Rickey repeated key portions of his verbal agreements with Ball, and made Ball stir uneasily by repeating the aspersions he had cast against the leaders in the purchasing movement. All this and more is a matter of public record.

Ball escaped the odium of denying or admitting anything through a face-saving "decree by consent," which his attorneys presented and Rickey's attorneys accepted. It enjoined Rickey for twenty-four hours. Rickey would have none of it. The matter was settled over his protest. Jones explained it to the press:

The injunction by consent for 24 hours is, in substance, no injunction, and I was perfectly willing to agree to the form where we got the substance. This form is, in my opinion, merely a "save my face" process, as they say in the Far East, and in Chinese laundries, and if anyone feels he has "saved his face," I am glad for him and his face.

On May 2, 1917, the incorporation papers were duly filed for the St. Louis National Baseball Club, and half of the purchase price, $175,000, was paid over to Mrs. Britton. Branch Rickey was first on the list of incorporators with a purchase of two hundred shares of common stock at $25 a share. Sam Breadon was not an incorporator; nor mentioned at all.

Down in Ohio, J. Frank Rickey and Emily Rickey mortgaged 287 acres of Duck Run farmland and buildings for $5000 and wired the money to Branch, because, as he said, this was a great opportunity, and he believed in his ability as president to make it valuable.

8

THE FACTS about the origin of the Knothole Gang idea have long been treated loosely. The policy of free admission to big-league games for children was first popularized during Branch Rickey's stewardship in St. Louis. Today it is a part of every major-league club's promotional plans and accounts for upwards of a million free admissions for boys and girls each season. The best ideas may not be, as wise heads say, common property, but they wind up as such. Branch Rickey explains the origin of the innovation by saying:

"The Knothole Gang was Jones's idea. It was new and constructive. Unfortunately the men who bought the shares knew boys with ample spending money, and hardly any who needed to be taken off the streets. Because the overprivileged boys, so to speak, declined the gratuitous admissions, we had no Knotholers at all at the first half dozen games of that first season.

"After three or four meetings with the stockholders, I got all of them to assign their free-attendance rights to the club for discretionary use, and wound up with three thousand season passes for boys between ten and sixteen. I didn't care whether it was three or thirty thousand. I started to assemble a Knothole Gang with meaning. I went to the heads of nine or ten organizations — Sunday School Association of St. Louis, Big Brother Movement, Jewish Council for Boys, Y.M.C.A., Y.M.H.A., Boy Scouts, Public Playground Association, and a few Catholic youth groups. They honored me by appointing heads of those organizations as Knothole committee members, the only time in my life till then that such a diversified group rallied in a single voice to a common cause.

"After several meetings the committee agreed on two rules for attendance: One, no boy could attend without his parent's consent and two, no boy could skip school. Two simple rules and they worked. At one time two hundred and seventy-five agencies in metropolitan St. Louis were issuing passes to boys for Sportsman's Park. We could have an attendance of three thousand for any given day on forty-eight hours' notice.

"We drew some bad publicity and deserved criticism when boys got out of hand, but the escort idea — one adult supervisor for every ten or fifteen boys — corrected that. We extended the Knothole Gang throughout the Cardinal organization as we grew. I've had it everywhere I worked since. It is one of the most rewarding experiences of my life."

Branch Rickey had scarcely become identified with the Cardinals when a well-wisher within the Knothole age limit telephoned to ask for a job. Since he had experience and a record of diligence, Rickey hired him, and William DeWitt left the Pierce Oil Company to resume his career as a baseball front-office "man."

Congress passed the Selective Conscription Act of 1917 in May. Because of the draft, all of Rickey's plans for the placement in quantity of promising players on minor-league teams had to be postponed for a second time. His only hope now was to keep leftovers from the draft and provide Miller Huggins with additional playing strength through trades with other clubs.

As both manager and man, Huggins thoroughly justified the high esteem in which Rickey always held him. He was cooperative and understanding in the shifting of players off the field, for which Rickey alone was responsible. A stipulation in every contract Rickey signed as a Cardinal, and elsewhere thereafter, gave him this responsibility. Reciprocally, his manager was always boss on the field, once the players had been placed there.

"A manager who is not in sole charge of his players," Rickey always said, "cannot run his team, serve his employers best and, indeed, cannot call himself a manager. A few players will soon find his weakness and start managing him."

Huggins led a fighting team from start to finish, paced by twenty-one-year-old Rogers Hornsby, a rising star of unmatched magnitude. St. Louis fans liked the team and 288,000 paid their way into Robison Field to see the Cardinals finish a heartening third. A week later there was much ado over the "coup" of American League president Ban Johnson. He had, they said, helped the New York Yankees "steal" Miller Huggins from Branch Rickey. Actually he left with full consent and good wishes. Said Rickey:

"Miller Huggins came to me and talked over the whole situation. I advised him to accept the New York offer and he was quite surprised at my attitude. I assured him that my willingness to have him go was not due to my dissatisfaction with him as manager. His salary was high for us, that was true, but I again assured him that I'd be glad to have him stay. His surprise was expressed in just one sentence, 'Do you really mean it?' I laughed and said that I did.

"There was no stealing or breach of ethics. My word was good, and there was no pressure on me to change my mind. I wouldn't have changed it anyway. Miller Huggins had a great opportunity to capitalize on his skill as a fine manager. And he succeeded with six pennants and three World Series victories for the Yankees."

The Cardinals, barely solvent, began 1918 with very little cash, and less hope for improvement in the second year of American participation in the World War. They still owed half the purchase price to Mrs. Britton. To buy uniforms was a major consideration.

The pall of war and penury shrouded spring training in the South. A squad of overage and otherwise nondraftable players went through the motions. Overseas the Germans began shelling Paris at long range. Their Somme offensive was disheartening. Slowly Rickey's thinking began to dwell more and more on how much people were doing and how little he did by comparison.

Friends high in the councils of the Y.M.C.A. had approached Rickey the year before about "doing something." They operated an important program of augmenting the military, socially and spiritually, in training camps and overseas. He could help put down some of the unsavory rumors that similar auxiliary organizations had to fight — that they sold doughnuts, hawked cigarettes at a premium price in the front-line trenches or extended favoritism. He had declined with thanks.

"Standing at the corner of Sixth and Olive one day," Rickey said, "I saw a sign on a store that really floored me. It read 'Closing up after six months in business. I am going to war.' No other single thing had a greater impact on me at the time.

"Perhaps it was foolish," he went on, "but I developed a deep desire to fight, in combat if possible. I imagine many men my age plagued themselves the same way. If so, we were all frustrated by a growing sense of uselessness. We kept telling ourselves we not too old to die."

In New York he met Percy D. Haughton, former Harvard football coach. Haughton, an intense, forceful and serious man of forty-two, was president of the Boston Braves. The topic of baseball was dropped quickly when Haughton learned of Rickey's feeling about helping in the war.

Haughton explained that Canada had taken coaches and others from non-industrial fields and put them to work devising new ways and means of launching surprise attacks in gas warfare, and the U.S. was going to do the same. The powers that be were reluctant to take skilled and well-trained specialists from military work. They wanted men from fields that wouldn't feel the loss.

"Branch," he confided, "I've just come from an important meeting in Washington on this very matter. They have asked me to recommend intelligent leaders to take charge. You're my first nominee."

"I hadn't thought of fighting that way."

"You're nearly thirty-seven, Branch, with four little children. Let husky kids do the fighting. This calls for brains and leadership. You'll have to help the Commission by naming others with good qualifications."

"When is this supposed to begin?"

"Right now. You and I are going to Washington."

When the United States entered the World War in April, 1917, there was no chemical-warfare organization. The effects of the deadly medium were no secret, but action on the subject was hampered by the dispersal of responsibility for it among five separate government agencies. In 1918 the various activities were combined into the Chemical Warfare Service, National Army.

Less than twenty-four hours after lunching with Haughton, Branch Rickey was signing army papers. A colonel surmised aloud, as the meeting ended, that Branch might have made a mistake.

"Joining?" Rickey asked.

"No, I think you should have asked for a colonelcy."

"I'm perfectly willing to be anything."

"Yes, but as a major you'll have to instruct officers who out-rank you." He shrugged. "Of course, it *may* work out."

Ten crowded days followed. Jones called an emergency meeting of the Cardinal Board. Resigning over their pro-test, Branch Rickey was now "unemployed" for the first time in many years. He drove the family to Lucasville, leaving the Bartmer Avenue house to be rented for the duration, and reported to Washington at the very end of his terminal leave. He was in Hoboken, New Jersey, the next morning, and sailed soon under sealed orders on the *President Grant*.

Three days later he was one of hundreds aboard who were ill. Most of them had influenza and one hundred and thirty were buried at sea on that single trip. Rickey was moved to an upper deck and virtually abandoned. He lost track of time. Finally, a doctor appeared at his bedside. He listened and tapped and felt. Then he laughed.

"No influenza," he said. "You've got pneumonia. And you're going to get well."

But Rickey was still weak when the "floating hospital" reached Brest. Two orderlies tumbled him onto a stretcher and down the gangplank to an ambulance which sped him to an infirmary.

As soon as his strength began to return, he began to worry about being sent back to the United States because he might have developed tuberculosis again. Luckily, he had not.

The war of chemicals was on in earnest. The First Gas Regiment supported assaults made by infantry and tanks dur-ing the Marne-Vesle operation and again in the St. Mihel and Meuse-Argonne offensives. Using Livens projectors and Stokes mortars, the regiment had conducted 152 gas opera-tions.

A high spot of Rickey's brief war experience came with the arrival of twenty young noncommissioned officers who had distinguished themselves in recent battle, some at a terrible price. They reached the camp with orders from President Wilson to grant them every opportunity to gain an officer's rating in the Chemical Warfare Service. Rickey moved from his quarters into the barracks with these men, for here was a job that needed special attention. One boy was shell-shocked, wouldn't answer reveille, eat or drill. Branch got him to play chess. Another had a face black with powder burns. Rickey felt that they simply had to be made whole men again and leave as officers. He prepared himself ahead of time and helped them bone up at night for the next day's classes.

All of them qualified for commissions and Rickey's reward was a private dinner given in his honor after the Armistice by the twenty grateful heroes. They cooked and served the food in the barracks and gave him their most prized combat souvenirs.

Major Rickey arrived in New York on December 23, 1918, and reached Lucasville the day after Christmas.

9

IN MID-JANUARY Branch Rickey returned to St. Louis and to another emergency meeting of the Cardinal directorate. The problem was an empty treasury. Few of the twenty-one board members attended, because all that any of them could have contributed to relief was cash. Yet, had all been able to appear with checkbooks and poised pens, the problem would not have been solved.

Here is a graphic example of the financier caught in a downward spiral of baseball investment, helpless to save his holdings. More money simply was not the answer and, at best, would have provided only temporary relief. Money can buy playing strength from within the big leagues, but at the added cost of weakening another club, and subordinating the basic and major cause of the fan's attraction to baseball: healthy, league-wide competition.

The efforts of Rickey and Hedges to solve this problem six years before had produced the pioneering steps of the farm-system idea. When Connie Mack sold his stars after 1914, he made the Athletics a doormat of the league by failing to replenish the lost skill. The A's supremacy passed on to the two American League clubs that bought his stars, Boston and Chicago. After winning several championships, Boston fell upon evil days through front-office financial mismanagement. To obtain needed cash, its playing strength and greatness had to be shifted to the New York Yankees.

This began with the sale of Babe Ruth's contract for $125,000, and a cash loan of $400,000, secured by a mortgage on Fenway Park. The loan was repaid over the next several years as part of player "trades." The stars Boston shipped out helped make the Yankees invincible through the 1920's. Meanwhile, the Boston Red Sox, by failing to replenish lost skill, replaced the Athletics as perennial doormats of the league.

The Cardinals failed to rehire Jack Hendricks as manager after his return from the war for the very good reason that they awaited the return of their business partner and director, Branch Rickey. The directors knew little about the office operation of a baseball club, and absolutely nothing about field management. They were attorneys, insurance men, real estate operators, automobile distributors, merchants.

All agreed that Rickey should manage on the field, and Jones, when offered the presidency, declined it with a move to have Rickey take that office, as well.

"It's too much for one man," Branch protested. "I probably wouldn't do either job right."

But Jones recalled Rickey's words of the time they took over the Cardinals, "Already minor-league clubs want our surplus players, and in return will promise an option on their entire teams in the fall." By handling both jobs, Branch would have complete freedom to locate and develop young players. Jones swung the others over and Branch Rickey became president-manager, with a three-year contract at $15,000 a year and a share in the profits.

"Within a week I made one of the best of all my deals," he recalled. "I traded Douglas Baird, Gene Packard and Stuffy Stewart to the Philadelphia Phillies for Milton Stock, Dixie Davis and Billy Dillhoefer. Though Billy died suddenly three years later, the values at the time were tremendously one-sided in our favor."

Rickey drove the Cardinals through a rugged spring training, made more so by necessary economies, at nearby Washington University. Equipment was scarce. Baseballs were guarded like precious jewels. Wearing apparel consisted of odds and ends because last year's uniforms were patched and laundered and put away for the regular season. There were no luxuries.

In early April he turned the team over to Joe Sugden for a few days and drove to Lucasville. He returned with Jane, the four children, Mabel and Mrs. Chandler Moulton, now a widow, who had observed her seventieth birthday on March 23. The old home on Valley Pike was closed and shuttered, its story just about told.

In operating the Cardinals, Branch Rickey became experienced, if not an expert, at running a baseball club with no treasury.

"We met current expenses by borrowing from the bank," he explained. "Our Board of Directors were substantial businessmen, and all of us — whoever was within reach — endorsed notes. That satisfied the bank — plus the fact that the notes were a first lien on the forthcoming gate receipts at Robison Field."

The Cardinals' poverty made them fair game for the clubs with postwar affluence. Chief of these, the New York Giants, had just been sold to Charles A. Stoneham, a Wall Street broker, and John J. McGraw.

"McGraw wanted Rogers Hornsby," Rickey revealed, "and I couldn't blame him, because I wanted to keep him just as badly. On the Giants' first trip west that year, McGraw came into my office at Robison Field and placed on my desk a paper listing the names of five important New York players.

" 'Look, Rickey,' he said, 'you play this fellow here, that fellow there, bat him second and this one fourth.' He made out a batting order for me and said, 'They're yours for Hornsby.'

"It was most flattering, because I had highest regard for McGraw as a field manager, and for his integrity. His fierce competitive spirit and hatred of defeat caused him some enemies, but I was not among them. His feelings on these matters were no deeper than mine, and I understood him. Off the field he was quiet-spoken, almost disarmingly so.

"He had surprised me in a National League meeting early in my first year as a Cardinals president. A committee was to be appointed for some purpose, and McGraw named me as a member. I protested that I was new and strange to the others, but he said, 'You can do it; take it.' And so I took it, though I didn't think he knew of my existence.

"McGraw was a master at handling assorted personalities, though sometimes not his own. As a baseball man he was quick, incisive, astute and thorough, with an unusual sense of justice. He had great personal affection for Christy Mathewson, yet Matty told me in France that McGraw once fined him five hundred dollars for gambling with his teammates, and said he made the fine more for Matty than for the others because Christy knew better. His deal of the five players for Hornsby was a good one, and sincerely proposed, but I turned it down with thanks."

McGraw tried again during the Cardinals second visit to New York. Present were Rickey, McGraw and Charlie Stoneham. McGraw explained that the Giants were anxious to bring a big star to the Polo Grounds to capitalize on the postwar interest in the game and the new Sunday baseball law. The St. Louis club needed capital, and Mr. Stoneham had it.

The Giants' owner nodded his naturally florid and fleshy face, and said, "We'll pay a hundred and fifty thousand dollars!"

"That's a lot of money," Rickey sighed.

When he failed to respond, the price was raised to $175,000. Here both parties began a discussion of probabilities and might-nots as a screen for their thoughts about the money. Stoneham wasn't accustomed to having his offers ignored this way, and his patience began to wear thin. Suddenly he jumped the offer to $200,000, a figure that represented 20 per cent of his investment in the Giants.

"I don't think I can take it," Rickey murmured, thereby increasing Stoneham's exasperation.

"Will you take two hundred and fifty thousand?"

"No."

"What do you mean, no?" Stoneham demanded. "What will your stockholders think when they hear you've turned down a quarter of a million dollars for *one* player?"

"I don't know, Mr. Stoneham," Rickey replied. "I don't see how they can be pleased. That amount would get us into the clear financially with a little over. But I'll tell you what I'll do."

All were hushed and expectant as Rickey paused. "You have a player I like," he said.

"I think that can be arranged," said McGraw.

"Not so fast, Mr. McGraw," Rickey cautioned. "This is a young college fellow. He's green and only played a few games."

"Who is he and what about him?" Stoneham barked impatiently.

"His name is Frisch," Rickey said, "and I'll give you fifty thousand dollars for him right now — "

"What's going on here!" Stoneham roared. "You haven't got fifty thousand dollars. You haven't got a quarter, Rickey. What are you trying to do, insult us?"

Stoneham had lost most of his patience. He didn't know that Rickey would "pay for" Frisch with money obtained for Hornsby.

"Look, this is the last," Stoneham said, leaning over the table which they surrounded. "I'll give you three hundred thousand cash for Hornsby and you can keep him till the end of the season. If the Giants are lucky enough to win the pennant, we'll add another fifty thousand to the price."

"You can't do that, Charlie," McGraw said almost instinctively.

"Don't tell *me* what I can't do!" the harassed Stoneham roared.

"Charlie, you've got me wrong," McGraw soothed. "I mean about Hornsby playing against us and our making additional payment if we win. You couldn't do that."

They talked around the point a while. McGraw wouldn't part with Frisch. The meeting broke up without a deal, and Rickey left with a feeling that he might be drawn and quartered in St. Louis for refusing the amazing offer of $350,000 for a single ball player.

The figure remained a record high until June, 1950, when Rickey offered a National League club owner more than $500,000 for a veteran left-handed pitcher. His proposal was $400,000 in cash and a young pitcher easily worth $100,000.

Branch Rickey's prophecy that he might not do either of his jobs right was near fulfillment before Labor Day. He confided as much to Jones. The Cardinals were in seventh place and they would not total 170,000 paid admissions for the year.

Jones wanted to know if Rickey thought the failure of the team on the field and at the gate meant he should give up managing and concentrate on building a team from his president's desk.

"It meant just the opposite, and I told him so," Rickey said in recounting the important steps of the period. "Being president of anything is a signal honor, a privilege and an

Grover Cleveland Alexander, pitching great claimed for the waiver price, $4,000, to help make St. Louis Cardinal history. *United Press Photo*

Roy Campanella, one of the first five Negroes signed by Branch Rickey. He became the National League's Most Valuable Player three times and caught in seven consecutive All Star Games. *Look Magazine Photo*

Another National League batting champion produced by the Cardinals' farm system, Joe Medwick batted .300 or better for his first thirteen seasons in organized baseball.

Martin Marion, known as "Mr. Shortstop" on the pennant-winning Cardinals, shown here as a Rochester rookie, 1939.

Michigan Daily

ANN ARBOR, MICHIGAN, THURSDAY, MAY 2, 1912.

PRICE FIVE CENTS

SWING-OUT COMES WEEK FROM TODAY

Tuesday May 14 Selected in Case the Weather Does Not Permit Swing on Thursd

CAPS AND GOWNS

Unless the weath
and puts a stop t
annual senior sw
on Thursday, N
May 14, as the
of the weather i
possible to "swi
The date was
idents of the v
at a meeting he
at the Union,
holding the aff
tival was reje
thought that it
Besides the N
spring contest
with Syracuse
would would
much.
Arrangement
monies have r
it was announ
ry B. Hutchir
address, and
would deliver
Prof. Albert
side at the or
The caps a
and may be
customary fee
at which the o

ALL SEI
IS BE

Idea is to Aid
Small
(

TO HAVE C

In harmony
movement loo
cation of Mich
es, the Stude
steps to hold a
seniors of all d
and June. The
way intended to _ _rtere _ _ul-
vidual class sings, which have become
a custom at Michigan, but rather to
promote acquaintanceship among all

TO HOLD INITIAL SING MAY 9.

Senior Lits Will Warble Evening of Swing-Out Day.

At a meeting of the senior lit sing
committee last evening, it was decided to hold the initial senior sing on
T'
ing, May 9, the date
ig-out. The lits will
ery Thursday even-
f the school year.
it 7:30, and the
on a rousing

RTS
AINTY

is Place
Hold

GANIZED

e deprived
s is an as-
near the
walks, di-
e, among a
n selected

new loca-
ion against
desire to
Prof. C. S.
nittee that
erected ci-
r the early
f Grounds
reviewed.
started to
ices, and
it the same
completed.
bers with
Manager
to be able
ext week."

N MEN
W CLASS

of Faculty
. Basis
0.

or law honorary
elected ten men
first year laws to its
hose selected were:
. . Allen, San Diego, Cal.
R. M. Gillette, Bay City, Mich.
E. P. Grierson, Manchester, Ohio.
G. C. Grismore, Pandora, Ohio.

UNEARTH "FIND" IN INTERCLASS GAME

Sisler, Freshman Engineer, Twirls for Seven Innings and Strikes Out Twenty Men.

ERROR MARS PERFECT RECORD.

To hold a team hitless for seven innings is considered more or less of a
stunt among those who are prone to
watch ball games, but when a pitcher strikes out twenty would-be sluggers in addition, it is a fact that is
seldom equalled on any ball field.
But such was the performance of Sisler, the fresh engineer box artist in
the game against the junior engineers
yesterday afternoon. One man was
passed and succeeded in getting home
with the aid of an error, thus depriving the star hurler of a perfect record. Sisler never allowed the junior
sluggers a chance and out of twenty
one put outs, all but one were by the
three whiffs route. And if ever a varsity future was open before a man,
it is easy to this freshman who sets
the interclass league on fire. Incidentally, in fact quite so, the freshmen won nine to one.
The fresh and junior laws also engaged in an encounter which was a
real ball game. the juniors winning
one to nothing. Quaintance and Black-
ie, of Amherst and Princeton respect-
ively, were the batteries for the freshmen, while Lanigan and Butler worked for the juniors. Quaintance allowed two hits and Lanigan one. Myers
was easily the defensive star of the
game, making some wonderful stops
and cutting off scores. The game was
a pitching duel throughout and Lanigan had a shade the better.
The senior lits took the sophs into
camp in the only game played that
was not spectacular, although this
contest was better than the average
class game. Pennell and Lewis worked for the seniors and Blake and Mil-
lard for the sophs. No games will be
played today.
were:
Fresh engineers 9, juniors 1.
Junior laws 1, Fresh laws 0.
Senior lits 5, soph lits 2.

S. C. A. TO HOLD EXCURSION TO JACKSON PENITENTIARY.

An excursion to the state peniten-

Elwin "Preacher" Roe, as a
Cardinal farm-club pitcher in
1940. After several years out
of the organization, Rickey
brought him to Brooklyn
where he became a pitching
mainstay.

Rickey called Ralph Kiner "one of the
nicest boys I ever met," but added that
his home-run greatness was not enough
to help in rebuilding the Pirates. *International News Photo*

Johnny Mize, "The Cat," during his
farm-club development at Rochester,
New York. National League batting
champion, 1939.

Albert "Red" Schoendienst, left, entered Cardinals' system through tryout camp. He starred at Rochester under Manager John "Pepper" Martin, right, who reached Cardinal tryout camp on the rods of a freight, 1925.

"Me an' Paul" Dean, reunited briefly during Cardinal game in Chicago, 1939. "Dizzy," left, had been sold to Chicago the year before, for $185,000 cash and three players. *Wide World Photo*

Rivals of the dramatic 1926 World Series—Babe Ruth of the Yankees, and Rogers Hornsby, Cardinal playing-manager. The Cardinals won in seven games despite Ruth's four home runs, three in one game. *International News Photo*

After eight years as baseball's first Commissioner, Kenesaw Mountain Landis "looked into" Branch Rickey's flourishing system of developing St. Louis Cardinal players through corporately owned minor league clubs. Before he could "do anything" about it, all remaining major league clubs had adopted the idea, which was permissible under the rules of organized baseball, approved at the time of Landis' election, January 1921. Through the last eighteen years of Landis' tenure and life his efforts to end or even curb the "farm system evil" were met with further development and rules permitting its growth. The minor leagues, decimated by war at the time of the Commissioner's death, late 1944, reached even greater growth

and success through the farm system, with Branch Rickey still leading the way in Brooklyn. *United Press Photo*

Branch Rickey interrupts study of famous "Little Black Book" (in hand) to weigh merits of Burt Shotton's casting rod. Looking on are presidents Al Banister of Columbus Red Birds and Oliver French of Rochester Red Wings. Shotton was then (spring training, 1939) manager of Columbus.

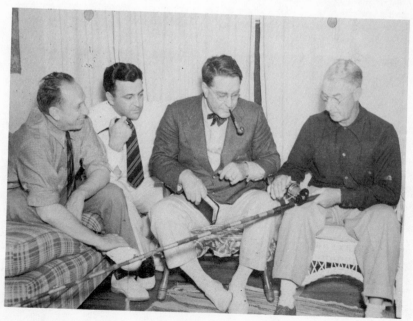

Rickey as a sophomore at Ohio Wesleyan University, 1902.

Vice-president and business manager of St. Louis Cardinals, 1925.

1957. As vice-chairman of President Eisenhower's Committee on Government Employment Policy, Rickey faces even more and bigger crises in all parts of the nation in connection with the Civil Rights program. *Courtesy of Pan American World Airways*

"Our position is not good," was a recurring reflection of Rickey's during frequent crises, such as depicted here. *Photo by Barney Stein*

Rickey in 1895. "It was the day of the flying tackle . . . flying wedge . . . flying teeth."

In the early 1920's, with only hope and faith in an idea.

The Rickey family on the fiftieth wedding anniversary of Mr. and Mrs. Branch Rickey, Sr., June 1, 1956, at Fox Chapel, Pennsylvania. Left to right, seated: Sue Rickey Adams, Miss Mabel Moulton, Jane Moulton Rickey, Branch Rickey, Jane Rickey Jones. Standing: Stephen Adams, Jr., Mary Rickey Eckler, John Eckler, Alice Rickey Jackle, Edward Jackle, Branch Rickey, Jr., Mary Imes Rickey, Robert T. Jones, Betty Rickey Wolfe, Lindsay Wolfe. *Lou Farris, Photographer*

With the volatile Dizzy Dean, left, and the voluble Manager Frank Frisch. "Between the headaches," says Rickey, "there was laughter." *International News Photo*

". . . if I owned a ball club 100 per cent, I would not hesitate having Durocher [above] as my manager. My estimate of Leo as a manager never changed." *United Press Photo*

Integration of the Negro, Jackie Robinson, into organized baseball, has been called one of the most important and significant steps ever taken in sports, or elsewhere. *Acme Photo*

indefatigable German. Bottomley, properly shod, had the grace and reflexes of a great performer. Had he been unable to walk, I'd have taken him on.

"Others with more or less appeal came. I had an increasing number of letters from many friends in baseball and in college coaching. I was confident of getting promising young players in quantity. And I could handle them best as manager. It was not a question of wanting to manage. It was simply an inescapable fact that I could do the club most good on the bench."

Rickey did not care who became president, so long as he could retain sole responsibility in the matter of players. Jones agreed and promised that his contract would be changed only to the extent of erasing the word president.

At intervals throughout the season Branch Rickey had gone without salary when money was needed by the club. It was during this period that he telephoned Jane and sent her hunting for a nonexistent bargain sale at a department store. While she was away from home, he borrowed a rug and some chairs from home to use in his office to impress an important caller. He was not proud of the things that had to be done at the time, even though they appeared in print later as whimsical recollections by others.

He collected enough back salary at the end of November to send his father and mother the $5000 he had borrowed. Rickey now owned his stock in the Cardinals free and clear. From time to time in the future, he bought more in small amounts.

During these difficult days Rickey saw Jess Haines pitch part of a game at Kansas City in 1919, and it was enough to explain to Rickey his fine minor-league record. Kansas City wanted $10,000 cash for his contract. The Cardinals had to borrow it.

"The list of endorsers made those twelve notes look like

the Declaration of Independence," Rickey laughed in recollection. "Maybe it was that kind of document. At any rate, it provided the money, and the money brought Haines to St. Louis for 1920. He remained with us eighteen years and won more than two hundred games."

Haines was the last player-purchase by the Cardinals for more than a quarter of a century.

After Haines, who dates the beginning of the farm-club Cardinals' operation, all of Rickey's players reached St. Louis through scouting and development on the smaller clubs, or were obtained by trade of contracts outside the organization.

Overshadowing player moves was the winter-long refinancing of the ball club. Without realizing it, Rickey had armed Jones with strong investor bait. The publicizing of the Giants' offer had put a tremendous value on Hornsby's contract as a corporate asset. Then, Rickey's attitude toward the presidency provided a premium for the biggest pledge of cash against a promise to increase the common stock by four thousand shares, and the capitalization by $100,000.

The presidency went to Samuel Breadon, already a small stockholder, and president of the Western Automobile Company. Adolph Diez, a wealthy dealer in leather findings, advanced $15,000 for spring training and a steady stream of thousands until the stock increase could be formalized.

"The man was truly an angel," Rickey declared at this writing. "And that goes both ways. His money made everything possible and he has been my great friend over the years. Still is."

Results of the formal election named Sam Breadon, president; Branch Rickey, vice-president and manager; and a board of twenty-one directors. Control of the club rested with a more wieldy seven-man Executive Committee, with Jones, Rickey and his attorney-friend, George Williams, holding fast on policy matters. Rickey's duties were announced as being the same until such time as Breadon could take full charge of office and park administration.

During this period of high finance Charlie Barrett came to Rickey with information he had long awaited. Blake Harper, a friend of Barrett's, had the franchise for Fort Smith, Arkansas, in the Western Association, which was re-opening after a three-year shutdown. He was willing to entertain Rickey's idea of part ownership.

"I had told Charlie to quietly look out for just such a situation," Rickey said. "He brought Harper to St. Louis and I pledged the Cardinals to finance half of the Fort Smith Club."

Understand that Branch Rickey's philosophy of player development from the lowest point of recognizable skill was based upon — depended upon — two pivotal factors in organized baseball.

One related to a pair of clauses in the uniform player contract that made possible assignment, sale or trade, and reassignment. In signing a contract, the player accepts, as part of the consideration, an obligation to observe the terms of the contract when or if assigned to another club; and to reserve his unique services to the club pending salary negotiations for the next season. This latter is the reserve clause. While claims of inequity or morality might be argued, there never was valid question of the legality of these clauses and, at this writing, none has yet been proved.

The second factor rested upon baseball's existing system of classifying minor-league cities. At the time, winter of 1919–20, the classes consisted of AA, A, B, C and D, rated according to the total population of a league's member cities. The greater the population, the larger the attendance, which in turn permitted a higher team payroll, hence stronger or more mature players.

Fort Smith was Class C and could take beginners like

Mueller. But where would Mueller go after succeeding there? He still wouldn't be ready for the big-league team. There would have to be participation in higher classification ownership to accommodate improved players. More clubs in the low C and D class would then be taken on to accommodate the fruits of heavier scouting.

The Cardinals trained at Brownsville, Texas, thanks to Adolph Diez. As the next step in his plan, Rickey turned his attention to negotiating for part ownership of the Houston club, then undergoing corporate reorganization. He knew the owners from his Dallas playing days. He had met the young business manager, Fred Ankenman, at the recent minor-league meetings in Hartford. The field manager was Al Bridwell, one of the old 1902 Portsmouth Navies.

Friendship was an integral part of Branch Rickey's early baseball associations, and he counted heavily upon it throughout his career. Without integrity, however, there could be no friendship, and so the two factors, to him, were synonymous. Loyalty also owed its existence to integrity. That he had loyal friends meant only that he had recognized integrity and was happy to have the possessor as a friend. He wasn't interested in those who lacked integrity or who abandoned it now and then as an economic expedient, beyond being sorry for them. He was always willing to extend a helping hand, if they needed it.

He was able to purchase 18 per cent, or 18 of the 100 shares that comprised the corporate ownership of the Houston Baseball Association. That he didn't happen to have the $15,000 price with him failed to jeopardize the deal. He shook hands, gave his word and said that the Cardinals would stand behind him. Young Ankenman was named secretary and business manager of the corporate operation.

The Philadelphia Athletics also trained in Brownsville in

1920, and Rickey got to know Manager Connie Mack well through exhibition games and long talks in a Pullman drawing room during the barnstorming trip that followed training.

"I had known Mr. Mack since my American League playing days," Rickey said, "but I saw him in a new light about ten years later when we were playing spring games in Texas. Fred Hunter was umpiring, hoping to get such a job in the American Association. A high wind one day caused Fred to make some very bad calls. Mr. Mack was furious and motioned across the field for me to get the umpire out of there. I motioned back that he would be all right. Later I went over and explained that yanking Fred might hurt his morale and his chances, and Mr. Mack thanked me for telling him. Fred, by the way, got the Association job.

"But I learned to know this fine manager best during our long train rides. I understood why he was so different from John McGraw, yet equally masterful in handling men. He was a pedagogue, a kindly instructor. It was his desire that his players should learn from him and then think for themselves on the field of play.

"An ideal example of his technique in handling men is found in the treatment of Rube Waddell and his catcher, Ossee Schreckengost. Both were inclined to eccentricity, and Mack once fined his catcher ten dollars for an escapade.

" 'But Mr. Mack,' Ossee protested, 'Rube was just as guilty as I was and you didn't fine him at all.'

" 'Now lookit,' said Mack. He often used that quiet expression. 'If you want to be treated the same as George Edward, we shall do it.' And Ossee retreated from his stand because he didn't want to be classified with the Rube.

"In his kindly way, Mack could handle all types of ball players, from eccentrics like Waddell and Schreck, to an intellectual such as Eddie Collins. Like McGraw, he was a master of the private interview. Unlike McGraw, he rarely employed the open clubhouse harangue. Quiet understanding and the heart-to-heart talk behind a closed door went deeper into the hide and heart of the recalcitrant. Burt Shotton and Walter Alston favor this method, too.

"I adapted Mr. Mack's daily pre-game meeting to my own use on the Browns, as did many others. I found it the best way to bring separated forces together. Some players don't like it, but there is no substitute. We all owe so much to many, but to some, like Mr. Mack, we owe more than others."

Rickey worked assiduously on the job of lining up farm-club affiliations. It called for personal diplomacy, and mutual understanding. The clubs were not easily satisfied. The plan was new and strange and therefore suspect in many quarters, calling for quiet caution. Rickey spent much of the year building toward a farm-club relationship with Memphis, of the Class A Southern Association. He sent Ray Blades there for tryouts. He had optioned Oscar Tuero, a Cuban pitcher. Before he could consummate the desirable arrangement after the season was over, he received unexpected "competition" from within his own organization.

Sam Breadon had met one Ernie Landgraf, president of the Syracuse Club in the Class AA International League. Breadon made a firm commitment to purchase half the Syracuse stock for $25,000. The Cardinals were in no position to buy into two high classification clubs and, as yet, they didn't have the players to satisfy even one commitment. And so Rickey wrote off the summer-long work on the Memphis project, took back Blades and Tuero, and began to incorporate the Syracuse purchase into his plans with considerable apprehension.

Once again the question of Branch Rickey's ability as a

manager will come up as he continues to try out and select
players, trade contracts, call plays on the field, hold daily
meetings, and compete with seven other managers for a common goal. It is safe to say that Rickey not only succeeded
in 1920, 1921 and 1922, but his record compares favorably
with the best, as the following figures indicate:

Team	Manager	Won	Lost	Pct.	Club Profit
New York	McGraw	273	188	.592	$546,213.
Pittsburgh	Gibson	254	207	.551	578,892.
St. Louis	Rickey	247	214	.536	374,309.
Cincinnati	Moran	238	222	.517	272,784.

Those three years ended for all time the appellation "poverty-stricken Cardinals." The figures include the sale of Robison Field, but also the liquidation of indebtedness and a
cash investment in several minor-league ball clubs.

But it was only the beginning of the fabulous millions
piled up and siphoned off as a direct result of his unique
operations.

10

THE WINTER of 1920–21 brought official termination of the old National Commission and the beginning of one-man rule for organized baseball. Plagued by administrative chaos and the shocking dishonesty of eight members of the Chicago White Sox who conspired to lose the 1919 World Series to Cincinnati, baseball sought refuge and a restoration of public faith in Federal Judge Kenesaw Mountain Landis. He was elected Commissioner for seven years at an annual salary of $50,000.

The old Major League Rules, virtually abandoned because of the Federal League war and then by the manpower emergencies of World War I, were completely rewritten. Heading the revisers was George Wharton Pepper, United States Senator from Pennsylvania, who had successfully handled considerable litigation in behalf of organized baseball.

The new rules went into effect on the same day that Landis was formally elected Commissioner of Baseball, January 12, 1921. Nowhere was farming prohibited, or even mentioned. Nowhere did the rules prohibit, or even mention, ownership of part or all of a minor-league franchise by a major-league team.

Under "Rules of Procedure" which were "Formulated by the Commissioner and announced pursuant to the Major League Agreement, and the Major-Minor Agreement," Article 15 read:

Section 1. The optional release of a player under a regularly filed agreement is valid under the following conditions:

Clubs of higher-classification may place with Clubs of the same or lower classification for repurchase at a later date, such players as they may desire, not in excess of

Six players by each Class AA club.
Five players by each Class A club.
Four players by each Class B club.
Three players by each Class C club.

This was the legal machinery that permitted Branch Rickey limited transfer of player contracts among his minor league affiliates. As part of the Major-Minor Agreement, it was approved by acceptance on the part of Commissioner Landis in January, 1921.

Landis also accepted a glaring inconsistency in the Major League Rules. Section 1 of Article II stated that no club "shall have title to or under its control at any one time more than forty (40) players" and stipulated a reduction to twenty-five between June 15 and August 31 of each year. With a surplus of fifteen players, club owners then were instructed by Section 13 (a) of the same Article, "Assignments of players' contracts by Major League to Minor League clubs must in general be absolute assignments; but in a limited number of cases — not exceeding eight (8) in one year — a Major League club may reserve a right of recall, exercisable on or before September 15th next ensuing . . . "

What owners were to do, or did, with the seven leftover contract players was ignored by Landis for many years. It was secondary, however, to the limitless possibilities of player-supply through ownership of minor-league corporate subsidiaries, such as Syracuse, Houston and Fort Smith, even though they, like the parent club, were restricted numerically from mid-June through August. Unlimited supply was a matter of forging links in an expanding chain by which the raw playing material could be hoisted to the top.

Branch Rickey was not only first in this baseball philosophy as far back as 1913; he was already "in business" when the machinery was built officially eight years later. His pioneer producers of raw material in the early 1920's were scouts Charles "Pop" Kelchner, of Lebanon, Pennsylvania, a specialist in college players; Dr. Charles Chapman, of the University of California; Charlie Barrett, who, Rickey said, "could assay the gold content in a handful of ore"; Jack Ryan, Joe Mathes, Carl Lundgren, who succeeded him as baseball coach at University of Michigan; Fred Hunter, who always looked out for "Rick" regardless of where he was working; and just friends who knew him when.

The salaried scouts were not even well-paid specialists. Rickey couldn't saddle a poor corporation with big pay on top of the guarantee of expenses, which had to be assured in order that scouts might move freely anywhere. Here again loyalty was the golden thread that held them to the St. Louis Cardinals. A gleam of this precious tie can be seen in a Jack Ryan story many years later when economy forced a curtailment of the scouting department. Breadon informed Rickey that they had to let Ryan go. Rickey hated the idea, but accepted Breadon's offer to relay the bad news.

And so Breadon informed Ryan that he was no longer a Cardinal scout. Ryan took it with good grace, but he was sitting on the bench in the small reception area the next morning. They nodded. When he was there a second morning, Breadon paused and said, "Jack, you understood what I said the other day, didn't you?"

"Yes, I did, Mr. Breadon."

"And that — well, you're off the payroll?"

"I understood you, Mr. Breadon," Ryan said, and without rancor in any degree, "but when I came here, I was hired by Branch Rickey and I worked for Branch Rickey. And until he fires me, I'm still working for Branch Rickey whether you pay me or not."

Twenty years later the question of dismissing Ryan arose once more in the Brooklyn Dodger office. Again Rickey approved cutting him loose, but expressed doubt privately that the letter would be mailed. However, the minor-league department acted and Ryan went off the payroll. Some weeks later Rickey was in a Chicago hotel enjoying a needed afternoon rest when Ryan appeared at the door, happy and smiling. Told that Rickey was asleep in the next room, he said, "I just talked to him on the phone. He told me to come on up."

Ryan, then well along in years, disappeared into the bedroom and emerged a few minutes later with handshakes and goodbyes. After he had gone a telegram was sent to Brooklyn, restoring Ryan to the scouting payroll for a "special assignment," which he discharged with satisfaction.

There were rare moments, of course, when Rickey was forced to doubt the sanity or sobriety of a scout. He got an awful shock in 1921 when he saw a rookie leave the clubhouse lockerroom and feel his way along the passageway to the shower. He turned to Joe Sugden.

"Who sent him here?" he gasped.

"Kelchner," Sugden replied. "Picked him up in New York. He's signed to a Syracuse contract."

"Why, he can't even see where he's going."

"He will, Branch, when he puts on his glasses."

It was George Toporcer, first big-league infielder to wear glasses, and a great natural athlete. Toporcer set the training camp afire with his hitting and fielding. To make room for him in the infield, Rickey played Rogers Hornsby in the outfield at the opening of the 1921 season. When the Cardinals got off to a bad start, Hornsby was restored to second base and Toporcer was sent to Syracuse for playing experience. He reappeared, however, to become an integral part of Cardinal success and glory, and an everlasting symbol of courage in battling a physical handicap. He also remained a symbol of scouting intrepidity, for all scouts had watched Toporcer play for five years around New York, but only Rickey's bush-beaters could see more than the thick-lens spectacles.

The Cardinals finished with a threatening rush in 1921, and looked for all the world like champions for 1922. Rogers Hornsby had become one of the all-time hitting greats. As a St. Louis hero, he had only one rival, but a real one. George Sisler had broken records in 1920 with his league-leading batting mark of .407 and his 257 safe hits. Hornsby, too, had led his league, and for the second time, missing .400 in 1921 by three percentage points. The Sisler *vs.* Hornsby fights among the younger set threatened peaceful assembly of the faithful Knotholers.

Sam Breadon had added to his original stock purchase enough additional shares to have the directorate reduced to seven. Now he was the largest individual holder of common, or voting shares, though he lacked control. January, 1922, brought his re-election as president. Manager Branch Rickey was renamed vice-president.

Four months later Breadon and Jones, still a large stockholder, reached a point of final disagreement on policies. Sitting in the grandstand at Sportsman's Park, where the Cardinals played after the sale of Robison Field two years before, Jones expressed doubt that they could ever resolve all matters to their mutual satisfaction. He suggested that either sell out to the other, and he didn't care which. Breadon accepted the offer, bought out Jones and came into control of the Cardinals by owning 67 per cent.

Early that season Rickey made several daring moves, all resting on the success of his farm system.

"Now, lookit," Connie Mack had told him one night in the compartment of a Pullman car, "don't let go of your older player until you have something just as good or better to take his place."

Bottomley, already called "Sunny Jim," and Heinie Mueller and Toporcer were ready at Syracuse. Ray Blades was ready at Houston. On Decoration Day he traded a young outfielder for an older outfielder. He needed the experience to offset the greenness of Blades and Mueller.

Big-league baseball felt the full impact of Branch Rickey's challenge in July, 1922. He had the hardest hitters in the National League and, through the recall of optioned players, he had one of the fastest and youngest teams. More important, he was right at John J. McGraw's heels, threatening to end the Giants' domination by winning the pennant.

McGraw met the threat with the money Rickey had spurned. He gave the Boston Braves $100,000 and a thirty-three-year-old pitcher, Fred Toney, for a twenty-four-year-old pitcher, Hugh McQuillan. Branch Rickey shouted his protest to the St. Louis Rotary Club, and invited civic protests. Citizens responded quickly, because the New York Yankees had also moved to stop the league-leading Browns by getting a great shortstop, Joe Dugan, as further reduction of the Boston Red Sox debt a few weeks earlier. Rickey's outburst against midseason purchases from competing clubs resulted in a subsequent ruling by Judge Landis that prevented such deals between June 15 and August 31 without offers to other clubs by the waiver list.

A month later, mid-August, with his second-place Cardinals only three and a half games behind the Giants, Rickey answered a knock on the door of his hotel room. The caller was one of his outfielders, Leslie Mann, scarcely able to speak. In his trembling hand he held a letter.

"I think you ought to see this," he said in a half whisper.

Rickey read the now infamous letter from Phil Douglas of the Giants, which said in part:

I want to leave here. I don't want to see this guy [John McGraw] win the pennant. You know I can pitch. And I'm afraid if I stay I will win the pennant for him.

Talk this over with the boys, and if it is all right, send the goods to my house at night and I will go to a fishing camp. Let me know if you all want to do this and I will go home on the next train.

"Judas Priest, boy!" Rickey exclaimed. "When did you get this?"

"Yesterday morning," the player murmured.

"Well, what are you waiting for? Go to your room and write a letter to Commissioner Landis at once!" Rickey suddenly hauled Mann across the threshold. "No! Sit down here and write it now. We may be too late!"

The story broke as "the New York Club's exposure of this sensational incident," and, "Before exploding the bombshell today, New York officials had notified Judge K. M. Landis, Commissioner of Baseball and John A. Heydler, President of the National League."

Branch Rickey refused to comment for publication at all. The mere thought of the letter was sickening. The tragic predicament of poor and ignorant Phil Douglas, a good spitball pitcher who had won eleven games for the Giants, thinking and scribbling such thoughts, was too awful to contemplate. Landis barred Douglas from baseball for life.

The Cardinals met the first-place Giants a week later, still only three and a half games behind. Public embarrassment from the Douglas letter prodded McGraw's team into playing beyond their very best. The Cardinals lost three straight and finished the season in a tie with Pittsburgh for third place.

Before the winter's end Rickey signed his third Cardinals contract for five years at $25,000 and 10 per cent of the profits before taxes. Breadon asked if he wanted to make it ten years. Rickey said no. An early example of Rickey's bold discernment of latent baseball talent was displayed that spring during the Cardinals' visit to Bradenton, Florida. The camp bustled with newcomers, thirty of whom claimed to be pitchers.

One of these, a thrower, proved to be less than mediocre, but in batting practice the next day hit the clubhouse at the leftfield foul line with a drive on the fly. Two more wallops dented the tin fence nearer center. Running to first base on the last drive was mandatory.

"Now, give it all you've got, boy!" Rickey called. "Run . . . run!"

After a night of study, Rickey handed Joe Sugden the lineups for a practice game. Presently Sugden waddled across the field to where Rickey sat.

"Branch, you've got a boy wrong here," he whispered. "Don't you remember working him out yesterday? Hafey . . . he's a pitcher."

"He *was* a pitcher, Joe," Rickey whispered in mock confidence. "He's an outfielder now."

That Hafey struck out in the game at Bradenton is unimportant. Rickey told him so the next morning while combatting the boy's tearful protests that he was still a pitcher.

"We'll send you to Fort Smith, son," Rickey consoled. "You'll strike out there, many times, and you'll be ashamed. But you have a God-given grace and quality in your swing that causes hitting power. You can run like a deer and throw as well as anybody in camp. A pitcher works once every four days. As an outfielder you'll play every day and you'll play well, I'm sure."

Hafey went to Fort Smith and set new strikeout records

for the team, for the league, and was about to put all such marks beyond reach when his bat started meeting the ball with all the hoped-for power. A hitting terror for the second half of the 1923 season at Fort Smith, Hafey, too, became a pillar of Cardinal success and glory, and National League batting champion of 1931.

One new idea at Bradenton in 1923 failed to materialize. On March 5, Rickey announced to the press:

"The Cardinals this year will number their players at home, as some colleges have been doing in football for more than ten years. The numerals will be on both sleeves, about six inches high. I think it will help the game, and I think we owe it to our patrons.

"Before another two years every team in the majors will be using the numbering system, in my opinion. The fans do not know all the players. Even I, a manager in the same league, must often call an usher aside and ask who is this or that player. And if I do not know the player, how is an ordinary baseball fan expected to figure it out? That's why I think we owe it to the public."

But the plan ran into opposition back in St. Louis. Concessions operators of Sportsman's Park feared that the numbers might hurt scorecard sales. At any rate, by the time Rickey returned, it was too late to force the issue. Five years passed before numbers appeared on baseball uniforms.

The Cardinals presented a disappointing year for 1923 on several counts, especially of turnstiles. With 338,500 paid, the home attendance was 200,000 less than in 1922. More important to Branch Rickey was failure on the field. The pitchers he depended upon most didn't deliver. Rogers Hornsby was superb, and batting champion again, when he played, which was only two thirds of the season.

Hornsby's year was highlighted, however, by a clash with

Branch in late August at the Polo Grounds in New York. Hornsby was on third base, impatient to score. The count on the batter went to three balls and one strike. Something on Rickey's face, or his hands, moved horizontally, meaning negative. It was the "take" sign. Hornsby reflected disgust immediately in a manner that even the opposing team could understand.

Rickey barked an order for Hornsby to "stay in the ball game" and answer to authority on the bench.

In the dressing room Rickey, still smarting from criticism of his sign, tried to remind the star that winning baseball depends upon respect for centralized authority, regardless of personal opinion. Hornsby interrupted with an ill-chosen invective.

Rickey's temper flamed. He charged at Hornsby. Surprised, Hornsby pushed him away, only to face another bullish charge. Before Rickey destroyed himself, helping hands dragged him away.

The story appeared in all the newspapers. The fracas made subsequent events all the more unfortunate. Hornsby developed a skin infection and couldn't play after Labor Day. Following a reasonable wait, Rickey asked the star to play and he begged off. The team doctor advised Rickey that Hornsby could play. When he still refused, Rickey asked Sam Breadon to suspend him. Hornsby went to the press with his story, forcing Rickey to speak for the first time about existing differences.

His formal statement said:

I have just read the report of Hornsby's statement in Friday morning's paper. It is incorrect in many particulars. I have at no time entered into any controversy in newspapers or anywhere else regarding the incident in New York and I shall not do this now, because the present discipline of Hornsby has nothing whatever to do with the New York affair.

Neither this nor the previous statements in the press are really Hornsby's statements, after all, but rather are those of his adviser here in St. Louis.

In one particular, the articles were particularly incorrect. He knows and everyone knows that I should not have shown resentment without very unusual cause. I have been in charge of baseball teams in one capacity or another for twenty years. And for the last ten years in major-league baseball. In that time only one player has ever spoken disrespectfully to me. I am not a "fighting manager." However, I am not sorry I resented the vile and unspeakable language used by Hornsby in New York.

The present suspension of the player is absolutely unavoidable. He not only refused to play in the game — he refused to work out in practice. Finally, I suggested that he might win the game, or enter the game as a pinch hitter.

He simply persisted in forcing discipline. It was a part of the plan. Most people will understand that it is not really possible to fail to discipline the star and expect good services from other players. In some respects, all players must be understanding as well as obedient.

In response to questions, Rickey amplified his written statement as follows:

The only reason I am entering this controversy is because of the fear that the public may accept Hornsby's statement as the truth.

Hornsby was fined $500 and suspended for the balance of the season.

11

THE PRECISE RELATIONSHIP of field management to a baseball team's victories or defeats has never been evaluated, and perhaps never will be. That the manager alone makes or breaks a team is a tenuous presentment of baseball writing that dates back to the late 1880's.

"More than twelve hundred games are charged against the records of teams in a full season of major-league play," Branch Rickey has always said. "A manager who has lost the pennant by one or two games can go back over his fifty or sixty defeats — and he does, you may be sure — and find situations which, if handled differently, would have turned upwards of forty defeats into victories. If those scale-balancing situations were not in baseball, the game would be uninteresting to manage, and worse to watch.

"I have told many times, as an illustration, how the great Ty Cobb and his intense, almost ferocious, desire to win once deprived me of victory in the last inning at Detroit when I was managing the Browns. He created his own opportunity and took advantage of it. He got a base on balls, stole second and drew a wild throw, ran to third, spilled the fielder there and continued on to score the winning run. And I had told my pitcher *not* to walk Cobb at all costs."

A baseball writer is charged by his editor, or his own competitive urge, with describing games readably, dramatically and, sometimes, sensationally. He cannot wax enthusiastic or dramatic over a losing or inept team. Just as such a team will not draw paid admissions, so the stories about it will not sell newspapers. The absence of an obvious explanation of victory or defeat makes it easier to rationalize the necessity of creating and embellishing it.

Baseball has fed upon this type of dramatized delineation for generations. It has grown fat and prosperous with the help of space-filling and eye-arresting fodder for the fans. The increase in space in the sports pages after World War I created a need for stories above and beyond the ball game. Here Branch Rickey became an inexhaustible source of material, though much of it went unused, because it did not fit the new needs, which were for "inside" goings on, feature material, rumors of feuds, trades, the lowdown on alleged controversies, and the story behind the story, especially if it was "offbeat" or spicy.

As a team manager and office executive, Rickey was unable to contribute such material. He knew almost everybody in baseball as a friend, and was genuinely sorry for anybody foolish enough to feud. Now past forty, he was far too busy to waste time on anything less important than the ball game, the players who played it, or the players who would play tomorrow.

He preferred limiting interviews to the game on the field and the skills involved, if any, the strategies or an interpretation of the results. He recognized the value of newspaper sports pages to help and also to hurt. He cultivated the good will and company of the sports writers as best he could, talked willingly and hoped "they got a story." He never knew. He simply talked to answer questions, the pointed ones too cagily for some, and talked on . . . and on.

Once a New York magazine writer, John Chamberlain, assigned to do an article on Rickey, had the good fortune to spend four uninterrupted days close to his subject on a midwestern flight of the Brooklyn Dodger private plane, in hotel suites, in dining rooms and baseball parks. Chamberlain never had as many laughs or as much fun. He returned to New York early on the fifth morning, and was missed at breakfast. Rickey inquired if "John was all right." Informed of the unexpected departure, he exclaimed, "What about his story? Oh, I should've spent more time with him. John came all this distance and got no story."

Chamberlain flew back with a foot-high stack of priceless notes.

Often it was otherwise, especially in the early days of his team-building. Rickey stands accused in print, and, of course, reprint, of breaking up the St. Louis Sports Writers Association on the "strength" of one writer's claim that he lied to the claimant. One rewritten version of "history" appeared in a 1947 magazine as follows:

A St. Louis writer who had passed up nothing containing alcohol during the course of the evening, and consequently feeling no pain, hopped up to challenge Branch. "What about that time you lied to me?" he wanted to know, digging up an old beef about a statement Branch had given him once denying that waivers had been asked on a certain Cardinal. The writer later learned that Rickey had asked for the waivers, and was not telling the truth when he denied the same.

A big rhubarb ensued when the emboldened scribe pressed his challenge. The subsequent minor riot was bitter enough to end meetings of the St. Louis Sports Writers Association for keeps. There never has been once since — with or without strong drink.

When questioned about this, Rickey vaguely recalled the meeting and row, but couldn't remember the heckler's name. "More important, the writer was drunk," he added. "That gave him courage enough to hurl the challenge, create confusion and deprive me of a chance to explain why he had to be mistaken. I have never discussed the contents of the confidential waiver list, given or received, with a newspaper man.

Rules forbid it and it defeats the very purpose of the instrument."

Branch Rickey's regard for truth, and his childlike dependence upon it in others, is the brightest facet of his nature. His spontaneous and unrehearsed method of thinking, living, saying and doing is such as to make simple truth the one thing that keeps occasional chaos in his life from being constant. He may be oblivious to his own whereabouts, the presence of his wife, the non-presence of money in his pockets, or any other matter that has no relationship to baseball and ball players. There simply is no time in his life or room to fit in lies or double-dealing. And he never suspects others.

His sublime faith in people received a severe test at luncheon one day when he, his secretary, Mrs. Rickey and two others from the office finished, and he called for the check, which was usual. He lacked enough to pay the bill, which was not unusual. He turned to Mrs. Rickey and negotiated a loan of ten dollars.

Seaching his pockets for a match at the cashier's desk, he came upon a folded paper, a check for a little more than $100, also not unusual. Since he was well known at the restaurant, the attendant cashed it. Before Rickey pocketed the money, one of his luncheon guests reminded him that he owed the guest $30. Another asked for $20 also due. His secretary said that he had better give her $50, since he owed it to his personal account for a loan she had made at his direction.

"Well, if everybody's getting paid," Jane Rickey said, "you might as well give me my ten dollars back."

He looked at the few remaining bills in his hand, somewhat bewildered by the speedy disappearance of his temporary affluence. He recalled none of the old transactions, but he trusted completely and paid happily.

He will countenance all manner of errors and blunders on

the baseball field. He will overlook an employee's mistake and blame himself for "not being close enough to the situation," but he will not countenance an untruth.

Once he faced a group of Brooklyn Dodger workers about to leave with him for the minor-league meetings in Minneapolis. They had finished discussing expendable player contracts. They had practically memorized the dossiers and each had a specific assignment to contact executives on other clubs for the purpose of iniating or measuring interest. One had a question.

"Mr. Rickey, just how much shall we tell about each player?" he asked, "and how will the others know what we've told?"

"Just tell the truth, boy, and we'll all know what you've said," Rickey replied.

Earlier that same year, 1948, he had reached something of a climax in his refusal to ignore aspersion cast at his regard for the truth. His big winning pitcher of the previous year, Ralph Branca, had come to terms after a long meeting. The signing was announced and Rickey left town briefly on other matters. Upon his return, a press conference was called. The large Brooklyn office was jammed with more than fifty sports writers, radio-television broadcasters and photographers. He picked up a newspaper clipping.

"I have before me a carefully prepared agenda," he began solemnly. "It is of greater news and feature value, I'm sure, than what I'm about to say. But I ask your indulgence while I take up a matter that concerns me deeply. I hold in my hand a newspaper story that contains about seven gross misstatements of fact, and perhaps a libel or two. I am not interested in those.

"I have been called many things in my time, and I expect to be called worse things in whatever time is allotted me on earth, but, gentlemen, no person has ever called me a liar without proving it or apologizing, and you, Mr. Young, are not going to be an exception. *Because,"* he thundered, and whacked the desk, *"I never lie!"*

"You say here," and he read from the clipping, " 'The auditory torture in Rickey's gas chamber lasted four solid hours, by which time, Branca, after wiping the blood off his ears, was more than willing to take two thousand less and escape with his life.' " Rickey looked up and added, "That's supposed to be clever writing, I guess." He continued from the clipping. " 'That session, incidentally, took place last Friday afternoon. Rickey, who has been known to employ circumvention but prides himself on his truthfulness, lied when queried later that day whether he and Branca had come to terms.' "

The room was hushed as Rickey summoned Branca through an office intercom. The big pitcher appeared and stood at the closed door.

"Ralph," Rickey began, "do you know why you're here?"

"No, sir, I don't," he replied, shifting self-consciously.

"When did you last see me, or talk to me?"

"Last Friday. You remember, when I signed."

"Do you recall my taking a telephone call from a Dick Young while we were talking?"

"Yes, sir."

"Do you remember my telling him you hadn't signed?"

"Yes, sir."

"Had you signed?"

"No, sir. We were still talking. At least, you were."

Welcome laughter broke the rising tension.

"Yes, I do talk a lot," Rickey went on. "And by the way, Ralph, what were we talking about?"

"Oh, everything. A lot about why I didn't get married."

"Did we talk about your contract?"

"No, sir, not until about two hours later."

"And approximately how long did it take us to come to terms?"

"Not long, Mr. Rickey. Five minutes. Wasn't that about it?"

Rickey nodded and thanked the pitcher, who left, still ignorant of why he had been brought down from Mount Vernon, New York.

"Gentlemen," Rickey said, "that is the fact. I talked at length with Ralph, as I do with many players at signing time. That's my only opportunity to get close to them and find out what's on their minds and in their minds and get to know them better. The rest of the year they belong to the manager, and must heed only one voice.

"And now, Mr. Young, if you please. Two things: tell these people who is the liar, Ralph Branca, Branch Rickey or yourself. Secondly, I want an apology now, and I want one with a retraction tomorrow in your newspaper. *Speak up, sir!*"

Young, red-faced and thoroughly trapped, stood and murmured his apologies. He resumed his seat. Rickey apologized for the "boring" delay and took up the agenda. The next day's editions of the New York *Daily News* contained the apology and retraction as part of Young's signed coverage of the press conference:

(5) Rickey's vehement contention that he didn't lie about his negotiations with Ralph Branca — and his shouting insistence that "I never lie!"

TOLD TRUTH: RICKEY

Rickey was deeply concerned over the charge that he had been untruthful in stating last Friday that Branca had not yet signed his '48 contract. The Brook boss explained that at the time he informed a reporter that Branca had not come to terms, it was the truth — that the righthander did not actually sign his contract till two hours later.

Rickey has received a sincere, unqualified apology. The reporter's big mistake was in failing to technically analyze Rickey's evasive phraseology — an innocent error which could happen to anyone, and usually does.

The "evasive phraseology" dodge was old back in the early days of Rickey's tenure with the St. Louis Cardinals, when he was less misunderstood than not understood. His life was too circumspect to be a source of gossip. He also could not give the hail-fellow-well-met type of spontaneous interview so often ignited at a speakeasy bar or from a bottle of bootleg liquor secreted in a desk drawer. He did not have a bad press but he was not exciting "copy."

Sports writers, in St. Louis and elsewhere, simply were not aware of what he was doing with or to the Cardinals. He received sincere praise now and then for his many advantageous trades, but the gauge of his contribution was the result of the day's game and the standing of the clubs. When he failed to win, or a young player failed to deliver as promised, Rickey received the blame, which he regarded as fair. Whether or not he could have conveyed it, he never explained the depth, extent and significance of his player-production plans, beyond "they are young and green, and it will take time." In fact, he never went much beyond that, even with the impatient members of the Cardinal directorate.

Rickey's over-all plan and purpose went unrecognized until long after it was an unqualified success. Sports writers could hardly be expected to know what was happening within the Cardinals, if official baseball itself didn't understand. Rival owners tried to match Rickey's quantity production by boldly ignoring rules clearly outlined under the Commissioner's sponsorship. Landis was openly challenged on flagrant option violations during the minor-league convention of 1924, and again seven years later by Yankee owner Colonel Ruppert. Landis ignored both challenges.

The Cardinals were a losing ball club in 1924. However, Rogers Hornsby turned in the most dramatic season at the plate in modern history. His fielding, always unfairly criticized, was topnotch, and he was among the leading second basemen in double plays. If he was trying to prove that the outburst at the Polo Grounds had nothing to do with his ability or willingness to play for Branch Rickey, he succeeded.

"It is not surprising," Rickey said. "It is typical of athletic greatness. Winning transcends all else."

The 1925 Cardinals foundered. When they reached Pittsburgh for a four-game series over Decoration Day, Sam Breadon appeared at Rickey's room in the Hotel Schenley early on the morning of May 29 and told him he was no longer manager. Rogers Hornsby would succeed him.

"There were no hard feelings," Rickey explained in calling the occasion to memory. "I was shocked and hurt, not over the loss of the post — my contract was not affected — but by the unnecessarily dramatic and clumsy way it was done. Sam could have made the same move more than a year before. I had asked to be relieved of management while he was visiting our first training camp in Stockton, California. But you couldn't get angry with Sam Breadon for his lack of tact. It was part of his nature. He honestly couldn't think of any other way to take me off the field, and he was frightened by falling attendance.

"His choice was an abvious one. Hornsby had led the National League batters for the past five years, and looked as though he would make it six. He was an outstanding hero. George Sisler managed the Browns and they doubled our home attendance while we were away. Our gate receipts, which had fallen off for cause, might be improved by a dramatic change to a popular manager, and they were."

During a taxicab ride immediately following the meeting, Rickey told Breadon that his Cardinal stock was for sale. Hornsby, sitting at his side, said he would take some part of it, if he could get financial help. Breadon said he would finance Hornsby's purchase and buy the rest himself. The deal took two minutes. The price was $250,000.

The Cardinals were in the visitors' clubhouse at Forbes Field when Rickey arrived.

"This is my last pre-game meeting with you," Rickey said. "I am turning the club over to Hornsby. Give him all you've got. Until now, I have been your manager and I could not associate with you as one player with another. Now it is different. I want you all to know that my latchstring is always on the outside for you."

Later Rickey revealed that "Sam came out to the training camp the year before as a fan, which was his custom. He had no special mission. I brought up the subject of a new manager because the organization work was growing. Details of the player transfers were staggering. Young players were not getting my attention on the field, either in St. Louis or the minor leagues, because of time necessarily spent in the office.

"The recent Hornsby difference had nothing to do with it. He was a great star, but still a ballplayer and therefore would conform. But the pressures were shortening my temper. I started after some friend of young Ray Blades in the St. Louis clubhouse after one disheartening loss to the Phillies. I ordered this fellow out of the clubhouse, where he didn't belong and, when he failed to obey, I charged him in earnest, not knowing, of course, that he was some kind of welterweight boxing champion. I think Burt Shotton saved me that time. I was always ashamed of those outbursts afterwards."

It is doubtful that Breadon, in his eagerness to halt declining attendance, and placate at least one segment of an impatient press, realized the emotional damage to the manager he had summarily fired. It was most embarrassing to Rickey's friends in St. Louis, for he was more than a manager to them. He was a corporate officer and a big stockholder. Sports writers, of course, rallied to Breadon's cause. They pinpointed specific maneuvers to show that Rickey simply "couldn't manage," and they stressed the evidence that he had "managed the ball club into last place." Eventually Rickey was able to discuss the trying period of criticism somewhat objectively by saying:

"From a standpoint of technical knowledge and experience, I was always able to manage. That I never really wanted to [be a manager] was subordinated on both occasions to the necessity of becoming one. There was no alternative in September of nineteen-thirteen, because of our plans for the Browns. And none in January six years later because of the Cardinals' empty treasury.

"To correct an impression that got out over the years, I don't think I ever overmanaged. I had had enough coaching to know that you couldn't teach a fellow ten things at the same time, and it might be true, as Hornsby has honestly stated, that I talked over the heads of the fellows at times. My fault as a manager, as I diagnose it, was due to my apparent zeal. I discussed the game every day, dealing with the game of the previous day in my discussion, as if the game coming up was the game of the year.

"I think I was a corking football coach, because there you talked all week for the game on the following Saturday, and that was all right. But you couldn't keep men at high gear for a hundred and fifty-four games, playing practically every day. My tendency was, I think, to have men press — do more in effort than was really natural for them to do."

12

RELIEVED OF HIS field duties, Branch Rickey began to lead a somewhat different life, though one just as busy. He spent more time in his home and with the circle of intimate friends that he and Jane had gained through early attendance and activities at the Grace Methodist Church. He increased his work as a board member of the Y.M.C.A. and a country day school. He heard and heeded a growing number of personal pleas for help, and he was physically closer to a household that now comprised six active children. The two youngest, Susan Moulton, born in 1922, and Elizabeth Ann in 1924, appeared in March while he was in training camp.

Rickey never learned to categorize the handling of his multiple activities and interests. More than ever now he considered them in heterogeneous bunches to a point where the Bartmer Avenue house became a sort of annex to his Sportsman's Park office. Coordinated into family affairs were telegrams, telephone calls and personal appearances at all hours, unexpected and always involving a baseball emergency. They vied with, and usually triumphed over, Jane Rickey's dogged efforts to maintain a planned domestic program. Not even the combined assistance of the cook-maid, Aldine, or Miss Mabel and Mrs. Moulton, now an active seventy-five, could overcome the disadvantage. Aldine's recurring threat to quit was met with a reiteration of Rickey's promise of a thousand-dollar bonus for staying ten years.

She stayed and collected. But as a result of his varying and unpredictable activities, the menage thrived in happy confusion, benign but constant.

One of his first moves, after the firing in Pittsburgh, was to seek protection for the future of this family. Admitting he was headstrong, and perhaps foolish, to sell his Cardinal stock, Rickey also knew that a minority holding is none at all when subject to the whim and caprice of a larger one. If Sam Breadon could have ideas that quickly on managing, he might have similar notions, honestly conceived, on Rickey's front-office job when Rickey's contract expired two years hence. And so he invested heavily in life insurance, buying as much as possible through the next several years. For a considerable period, the first $14,000 of his annual income went for premiums. Eventually he carried $400,000 of coverage.

"To force change or conformation to our routine meant hurting Branch," Jane Rickey once explained, "because he had to saddle himself and his time with his many affairs and obligations without regard to people or circumstances elsewhere. It wasn't a matter of bringing his baseball work home; the work never left him. It was his life. To get his attention at times was like calling him back from a journey. Then he would put his thoughts aside, give every consideration to what you were saying, express his opinion, and then resume his journey.

"We had a constant fear that he would 'help' around the house, for I don't know of any person who could create catastrophe sooner than Branch Rickey in a helping mood. Once he almost bled himself to death merely trying to polish some old shoes in the bathroom. Somehow he smashed the bottle and then used up a few days' supply of linen trying to hide the accident from me. Another time, merely taking an empty trunk from the second to the third floors at Bartmer, he scraped the side of a beautiful bed getting the trunk on his back, and knocked off the newel post ascending the stairs. In whirling around at the top, he broke the gas fixture and yelled for everybody to leave the house before we got asphyxiated.

"Over the years and wherever we lived, we postponed countless dinners and finally dined without him. He was always sincerely sorry when he came home late, sometimes without having had his own dinner, and the reason would come out in a day or so. He had negotiated some enormous baseball maneuver that had occupied his thinking around the clock for weeks.

"But no father could have been more devoted to his family, especially his children from the first moment he saw them. Each was like a little island that he visited and enjoyed as a tourist. And when he made the excursion, it was a special holiday for the Island, too. He enjoyed the neighbors' children as well."

There were important personnel changes in the Cardinal organization in 1925. Hornsby named new coaches. Rickey concentrated on administration. William DeWitt, the Browns' switchboard boy of 1916, had obtained his education through night school and after-work classes, and was elected treasurer of the club. Warren Giles had joined the St. Joseph, Missouri, Club, of the Western League, after quitting in protest of his employers' renege on a handshake deal with Rickey in early 1920. Subsequently, Giles had taken players on option from the St. Louis club and its subsidiaries, and also worked with Minneapolis, an AA club. After the baseball season he officiated football games to augment his income. He was so engaged when Rickey sent Charlie Barrett to find him in the fall of 1925.

"Branch introduced me to Mr. Breadon," Giles says in recounting his visit to Sportsman's Park, "and left us alone. Breadon talked, but I couldn't understand what he was driving at. The idea of the visit, I suppose, was to expose me to him, and it barely served its purpose. After fifteen minutes, he excused himself.

"Branch came in and ended the suspense by saying, 'Warren, how would you like to take over as president of the Syracuse club? Phil Bartelme has resigned to enter business in Florida. It's booming down there. What about it?' I was just as abrupt and said yes. Barney Shotton would be my field manager, which delighted me."

In spite of a growing business schedule, church activities, and civic, fraternal and charitable responsibilities, Branch Rickey found time for play, simply by stepping up his pace, and squeezing in more activities. Yet, he so coupled his relaxation with his work that they often became interchangeable.

Rickey's penchant for coordinating work into his play often taxed both patience and friendship. Once he came close to exhausting both when he took Fullerton Place and Forrest Donnell on what he promised would be a hunt for quail in the Ozark Mountains.

"Two things puzzled both of us," Place reported many years later. "How on earth he found such wilderness spots, and how he survived them. This time he led us into the home of what is pictured in the cartoons as a typical Ozark family. It was right out of fiction. Branch's explanation was that one of the boys was a pitcher and he wanted to get acquainted with his family background.

"Well, we waded through snow and we shot guns and I suppose somebody bagged quail. I was so cold and so near complete exhaustion from the walking that I didn't know, and most certainly didn't care. We returned to the house, which consisted of one room with a dirt floor, and a small dining-kitchen lean-to off one end. It had a single pot stove in the center with the stovepipe extending through the roof. Newspapers and catalogue pages had been stuffed into cracks and chinks along the wall and seams to keep out the cold. This was the home of the father, mother, three sons and a daughter.

"Dinner came, and the table groaned with food that was most satisfying and warming. It was Saturday night and we gathered around the stove to talk. Forrest Donnell and I huddled close, but it seemed too warm for the father and the boys. They kept moving away until their backs were against the chinked wall, where they tilted their chairs in comfort, *barefooted.*

"Bedtime came. The father and mother gave up their bed to Branch. Donnell and I climbed a ladder to a loft containing corn-husk mattresses and restless mice. We covered ourselves with horse blankets, which were identifiable even in the dark. Forrest and I couldn't sleep much, because we knew that you always freeze to death quicker by sleeping.

"In the morning we broke the ice in the washpails and dampened our faces. Then Branch produced our jackets and guns and insisted we get some early shots. After I got warm again, a few weeks later, I wondered whether or not he had signed the pitcher, but he wasn't in his office when I called. One of the French boys had telephoned to report flocks of geese visiting Charleston, Missouri."

From 1920 through 1925, Rickey had bought up sufficient blocks of stock in the Houston club to give the Cardinals control. H. L. Robertson, the president, simply couldn't accept the philosophy of selling a contract to the Cardinals for $2500 if it had a greater value to rival major-league clubs.

That it had been sold to Houston for perhaps $250, with no charge for scouting and other contributions, meant nothing. It wasn't "good business." Even as a minority shareholder, Robertson insisted on the maximum price.

His associate, Crooker, disagreed with Robertson's attitude and sold out. Fortified by nearly 75 per cent ownership, Rickey held a stockholders' meeting and voted in Fred Ankenman, the secretary, as president. As an incentive and also to continue the fact of local ownership, Ankenman was sold five per cent of the corporation. He was protected with a guarantee of his purchase price at any time in exchange for a promise to sell at cost to the Cardinals on demand, plus six per cent cumulative increase, which would double his investment in sixteen years.

This seemingly arbitrary handling of the Houston stock situation was not as iron-fisted as it sounds. The club had chosen immediate profit over almost certain appreciation of corporate holdings through continued operation as a Cardinal subsidiary. Given the opportunity, Rickey bought it. In later years a number of minor-league club owners retained 100 per cent of their holdings and still saw the properties turn into bonanzas through working agreement contracts with the Cardinal system.

That mushrooming system was reflected on the east wall of Branch Rickey's office by a large blackboard on which were chalked the subsidiary teams. Under each club the playing roster was listed in groups — manager and catchers, then pitchers, first basemen, infielders, outfielders, in that order. Rickey knew every player on every team down through Class D.

Beside each name chalked on the blackboard was an asterisk or other sign to indicate the option status of the player. In his pocket was a loose-leaf book with a scuffed and coffee-stained leather cover which contained the names and status of the players in the organization for quick reference, and separate pages for reports on players he had seen elsewhere and liked.

It wasn't a thick book at that time. Eventually it became heavy and achieved a degree of fame and reputation during deals and at meetings in smoke-filled rooms with his growing staff of managers and scouts. Once when he couldn't get a desired player in a trade he threw the book upon the desk of a major-league general manager and shouted, "Well, what *do* you want? There they are! Make your own deal!"

But the official pushed the book aside as though it were a time bomb and insisted that he didn't want to deal at all now.

A year-long crescendo of shining hours was heaped upon St. Louis baseball fans, players and executives through 1926. It began with a report of nearly $80,000 operating profit for the previous year, thanks to an increase of 125,000 in attendance. Then the Browns enlarged Sportsman's Park. Phil Ball spent more than a half-million dollars almost doubling the seating capacity.

Finally, Breadon and Rickey grabbed Billy Southworth from John McGraw for Heinie Mueller even-up on June 14, and claimed Grover Cleveland Alexander, Chicago Cubs pitcher, on waivers a week later. It was one of the biggest $4000 bargains on record.

Within one more week a new milestone was reached when 37,196 filled Sportsman's Park to overflowing for the well-advertised Sunday game in which Alexander defeated his former mates 3–2 in ten innings, thanks to a home run and later the winning run by Southworth. Alexander, known affectionately as "Old Pete," allowed only four hits.

Unfortunately, throughout the season, Manager Hornsby

suffered from an old Cardinal malady: failure of key players to maintain their best form. He was among them. His batting average tumbled from its astronomical heights to a figure that many players have tried in vain to achieve, .317. Ray Blades caught his spike in a protective wire screen on the outfield fence at Ebbets Field. He was carried off the field and his speed went with the shattered knee.

During this period of tension and hope and doubt, Sam Breadon opened the door to Rickey's office. His good-looking features were pale and drawn. His blue eyes glared as he said:

"He's got to go, Branch!"

Rickey looked up from his desk, knowing he meant Hornsby.

"He's got to go. Nobody can talk to me that way."

"What did he say?" Rickey asked.

Breadon's head moved from side to side. "I'm ashamed to repeat it," he murmured. "But he also told me to get to hell out of his clubhouse. *His* clubhouse. Practically threw me out. He's got to go."

"If you really feel that way, Sam, he'll go."

"Can a trade be developed?"

"For Hornsby? Oh, yes."

"When? How? What can we get? You name the deal and he goes."

Rickey wasn't anxious to discuss the matter at the time. The pennant race had to be settled and the Cardinals, with Hornsby as manager, still had a good chance. Breadon was angry and upset. His pride had been hurt deeply. He could calm down enough to discuss the situation rationally if the team stayed in the race.

It would be difficult at any time, however, to tell a club owner and businessman that he had committed an unpardonable breach of baseball etiquette by arguing with his manager in the clubhouse. An owner is at a distinct disadvantage there, even though he pays the rent.

A baseball clubhouse is like a foreign embassy in that it is beyond ordinary regulations. It is a sanctuary for flaring tempers, flying shoes, vocal outbursts, or anything that relieves pent-up emotions. Manager and players have no other place for such explosions, and their ground is protected by right of eminent domain, or its baseball equivalent. Chances were Hornsby never would have said whatever he said had the conference taken place in Breadon's office, for there he would be an employee. In his own clubhouse Hornsby was supreme boss, and knew it.

Rickey purposely speculated with Breadon about possible trades for Hornsby and finally Breadon cooled down enough to accept Rickey's assurance that something would be done. Branch had won precious time.

Hornsby led his team to the pennant. The Cardinals had the lowest winning percentage in league history, .578, but they made it.

City and County went wild. News of the long celebration dwarfed that of the celebrated Veiled Prophet Ball, highlight of the St. Louis social season.

The World Series against the Yankees was very close. Rickey did not go to New York for the deciding games. His neighbors, the Mudds, were listening to the seventh and deciding game broadcast on Sunday, October 10. The series was tied at three apiece and the Cardinals were rallying when the bell at the back door rang.

"Right at this time!" Gene Mudd muttered, rising to answer. "Wouldn't you know!"

He was startled to see Branch Rickey at the back door.

"My radio set broke down right in the fourth inning!" Rickey gasped. "What did Thevenow do?"

They caught up on the progress of the Cardinals three-run rally in the fourth. Now Jess Haines was leading by a score of 3–1. Then came another Yankee run, and, in the memorable seventh, a blister on Haines' pitching hand. Old Alexander relieved him dramatically to strike out Tony Lazzeri with the bases full. The game went on to the finish with the score still at 3–2.

"Gene, you can't possibly realize what this means to me . . . to the club," Branch Rickey sighed. "Not only vindication of all I've dreamed of and fought for, but it means capital to reinvest and spend for expansion and scouting and large training camps and more teams for developing the finest players . . . "

A rising cacophony drowned his words. Automobiles were already careening down Bartmer Avenue with roaring klaxons and screaming occupants. Then the whole city in full cry that swelled throughout the night proclaimed the St. Louis Cardinals baseball champions of the world!

13

Two WEEKS later Branch Rickey was on the stage at the Portsmouth, Ohio, High School, starting a series of lectures. The auditorium was sold out. Rickey stood before his audience resplendent in white tie and tails.

Though bent on getting and holding their attention, he heard a tittering, and then laughter. He had said nothing funny. He continued, only to hear scattered guffaws. Now he paused to make a mental checkup of dressing. Yes, he had buttoned everything. Still they laughed, and then he felt something brush his jaw and cheek. He grabbed and caught a loose end of his wing collar. It had broken free from a tight mooring to an undersized collar button. He held it down with one hand and continued talking, only to have the other end break loose and fly up. He caught it quickly with his free hand. A fresh kid in the front row cheered. Red-faced and silent, the speaker held the recalcitrant ends of the collar as the auditorium echoed with laughter. Suddenly a booming voice in the rear pierced the outburst with:

"Branch! Take that thing off!"

Rickey lowered his hands slowly to his sides and let the free wings hug his jowls. He felt a warm sensation of comfort and ease as he waited for the laughter to subside.

"I know that voice very well," he called firmly. "But thirty years ago the owner of that voice would not have told me to take that thing off and acknowledge defeat. Thirty years ago Jim Finney would have said, 'Branch, you button that thing down and make it stay down!' and, ladies and gentlemen, that's exactly what I'm going to do!"

He wiped his hands with his kerchief, pulled the white tie loose, buttoned the collar firmly, and retied the bow. Once again the auditorium echoed, but this time with cheers and applause. After the speech, a gentleman gripped his hand, leaned close to his ear and said: "I'm Dr. Bright of the Bigelow Methodist Church. I do considerable public speaking outside of my pulpit work. I'd like to ask you a very personal question."

"Go ahead," Rickey whispered. "What is it?"

"In your opening remarks, did you have that collar come off on purpose?"

"Oh, no!" Rickey gasped. "Certainly not."

"No?" The good doctor seemed somewhat disappointed. "I thought that was the very best part of your speech."

Rickey's continuing hope that Breadon would change his mind about Hornsby ended in their last discussion prior to leaving for the annual major-league meetings at New York in early December.

"Are you sure you still want to go through with it?" Rickey persisted. When Breadon said he did, Rickey added, "because I can handle him, Sam. If you two can work something out, I can handle Hornsby."

Breadon was adamant. Rickey would see McGraw in New York.

"Had I been in sole charge," Rickey declared many years later, "Hornsby never would have left St. Louis. Depriving the Cardinals of a known quantity of greatness in batting and competitive spirit wasn't right. Whether Frisch was as good or better, personal affront is never enough to justify a move of such magnitude.

"McGraw was delighted at the chance to get Hornsby for Frisch and the extra pitching help I felt we needed. His elation was apart from the personal coolness that had developed between him and Frisch since June. He would not have parted with Frisch for less than Hornsby. Personal relationships never affected McGraw's evaluation and use of playing skill. His great record proves it.

"McGraw said, 'Let's bring Stoneham in on this.' I said that I was turning our end over to Sam Breadon, provided the pitching help was satisfactory. He assured me that a good man would be included. Then I asked him if he was aware of Hornsby's natural desire to take charge and manage. He said he could understand that, and liked it in a player. He could handle it in Hornsby.

"As a matter of fact, I had the same conversation two years later with Joe McCarthy, manager of the Chicago Cubs, when they were about to get Hornsby's contract from the Boston Braves. It was less warning than discussion. I felt that McCarthy should understand the player."

Breadon and Stoneham concluded the deal on December 20, 1926, Rickey's forty-fifth birthday. With Frisch came Jimmy Ring, a right-handed pitcher, who was not the help Rickey had hoped for. Had Ring won even two of his four losing games, the Cardinals would have won the 1927 pennant.

Storm clouds broke and public indignation reached a new high in St. Louis when the trade was announced. Mark C. Steinberg, a broker and Cardinal stockholder, called the trade "an insult to the fans and to the directors of the Cardinal club" with whom Breadon had not discussed the move.

Within a week, the new manager was announced as Bob O'Farrell, veteran Cardinal catcher. He was a hard-working receiver and a strong hitter. Whether or not he was a good manager depends upon the gauge used. O'Farrell lost the pennant by a game and a half but he lost. He had a good club and great pitching. Pittsburgh won on the last day of the season and McGraw's third-place Giants were closer to

St. Louis than the Cardinals were to the Pirates, thanks to Hornsby's great season. A record 750,000 paid to see the Cardinals.

In August of 1927, Breadon reduced his capitalization to $320,000 by retiring $30,000 worth of common stock. At that time he reported assets of $847,705.62 against liabilities of only $110,860.88. He signed Branch Rickey to another five-year contract, this time at $40,000 annual salary plus ten per cent of the profits before taxes. At the year-end the Cardinals reported an operating profit of $235,000.

O'Farrell began a period in which Branch Rickey demonstrated his belief that fine players will make a winning manager, and the same manager will not win without them. From the time Hornsby left until Rickey himself departed sixteen years later, the Cardinals did not have a single high-priced "master mind" in the dugout. Of the nine listed below, all were either players on the Cardinals, coaches on the Cardinals or managers in the Cardinals' minor-league system. With the successor always ready when the change was made, the parent team was never without a manager:

Manager	Until
Bob O'Farrell	November 7, 1927
Bill McKechnie	November 21, 1928
Billy Southworth	July 23, 1929
Bill McKechnie	October 31, 1929
Gabby Street	July 24, 1933
Frank Frisch	September 10, 1938
Mike Gonzalez	November 6, 1938
Ray Blades	June 8, 1940
Billy Southworth	November 7, 1945

These men could tell a thousand stories of heartbreak and triumph, of hope and despair, of victories and defeats, and of greatness and lapses in individuals and in their teams.

14

A BUSINESSMAN could readily see the merit of the new baseball philosophy, but not because of the profit alone. Rickey had created an ideal instrument for absorbing earned surplus. Baseball parks could be built and the value added to corporate worth. This is especially appealing if you happen to own 75 per cent of the stock in the profit-making corporation about to be raised in value.

Branch Rickey got a free hand to proceed at an unbridled pace. With Ankenman on the scene to supervise, he bought acreage in Houston, and then sold off enough to pay for the whole parcel. A new Buffalo Stadium was erected and stands, even today, as one of the best. He bought land and erected another, though smaller, in Danville, Illinois, and then rushed into Rochester where he bought that franchise, sold Syracuse to help pay for it, and then transferred Warren Giles and the team to the new location. Feeling that he might be straining the Cardinal treasury, he held off spending $72,000 for eighteen choice acres.

"Why didn't you buy the property?" Breadon exclaimed. When Rickey explained that he didn't want to go too deep on his own, Sam said impatiently, "We agreed on a land purchase. I thought you'd swing the whole thing. The property may not be for sale tomorrow, Branch. You should have bought it. Why not go back and get it?"

Looking back, Rickey regarded this incident as the only

time Breadon "criticized" him in twenty-five years of business association.

"Perhaps it wasn't even criticism," he reflected. "Sam was anxious to create a repository for an anticipated profit and surplus in the coming year. I wasn't sure of income, because I thought in terms of ballplayers, victories and defeats, and we had been lucky two years in a row. Sam thought in terms of the upward business spiral of the late 'Twenties that was carrying everybody along and pouring money into the corporate reserves as never before."

Breadon was right and Rickey was "lucky" again. The Cardinals won their second National League pennant in three years with new attendance records and a half-million profit. Rickey's income for 1928 totaled $95,000. The once poor Cardinals showed a three-year profit bonanza of more than a million dollars.

Through its two top subsidiaries the assets of the St. Louis Cardinals National Baseball Club were now conservatively one million dollars in minor-league ball parks and real estate. It also owned many contracts of baseball stars, major and minor, with a current value of nearly a million more. Both evaluations, of course, depended upon the continued prosperity of organized baseball.

Now, in late 1928, Commissioner Kenesaw Mountain Landis "discovered" the St. Louis farm-club operation officially. It had existed for nine years, and eight while he was in office as guardian of a public trust. The door of his Michigan Avenue office bore one dramatic word: BASEBALL. Through that door had passed a formal record of every transaction made by the St. Louis Cardinals and their subsidiaries during the past eight years.

But not until Branch Rickey had developed and refined his farm system to the degree that the Cardinals dominated the baseball world did the Commissioner decide that the "thing needed looking into." His new interest was first reflected in the record of a joint meeting of the two major leagues, held at noon in the Congress Hotel, Chicago, December 13, 1928, and reprinted here verbatim:

LANDIS: Now, Gentlemen, for the information of the commissioner's office, and for the information of all of you, I would like to have a statement from each club here today of its ownership or control of minor-league clubs. That is necessary for the intelligent administration of the code of rules; and it is fair to all members of this organization that they should know of the ownership by members of the two leagues of minor-league clubs, or control over minor-league clubs, or contract relationships for the operation of minor-league clubs. Will you call the roll, Mr. O'Connor, and we will get this memorandum as the clubs are called.

O'CONNOR: National League. Boston.

BOSTON: Boston Club owns and controls the Providence Club; has no other interest in any other club outside of its own.

BROOKLYN: The Macon Club.

CHICAGO: The Chicago Club owns a controlling interest in the Reading Club. The Chicago Club has no interest whatsoever in the Los Angeles Club, which is owned by Mr. William Wrigley, Jr. And the Chicago Club and the Los Angeles Club have worked independently and have no working connection whatsoever.

CINCINNATI: Columbus, Ohio, and Peoria, Illinois.

NEW YORK: Not any.

PHILADELPHIA: Not any.

PITTSBURGH: Columbia, South Carolina, and Salisbury, North Carolina.

ST. LOUIS:	Rochester, Houston, Danville, Dayton, Topeka. Have not settled on Waynesboro and Laurel yet. [The Laurel association was in the process of abandonment.]
O'CONNOR:	American League. Boston.
BOSTON:	Not any.
CHICAGO:	None.
CLEVELAND:	The Cleveland Club owns the Frederick Club of the Blue Ridge League; and has an arrangement with the Terre Haute Club of this nature: It has no interest whatever in the Terre Haute Club other than the Terre Haute Club agrees to handle its players, and in return the Cleveland Club agrees to stand any deficit of the club. If it makes any profit, the Terre Haute owners get it. Last year it cost us $14,000.
DETROIT:	Evansville; Fort Smith; have a working agreement similar to Mr. Evans [Cleveland] with Hanover Club.
NEW YORK:	No interest in any club at present but expects to have.
PHILADELPHIA:	We have an interest in Portland [Ore.] Club, but I do not think we have a controlling interest.
ST. LOUIS:	St. Louis American League Baseball Company has no interest in any other club.
LANDIS:	Has the owner of the American St. Louis Baseball Club an interest in any other club?
MR. BALL:	Tulsa, Muskogee. Last year, speaking of losses, Tulsa lost $27,000. Muskogee, $17,000.
WASHINGTON:	None.
LANDIS:	I suppose in view of what you gentlemen have said about losses, common ordinary frankness requires I should say to you my regret is that the losses were not about fourteen times that much.
MR. BALL:	Thanks.

A year later Commissioner Landis launched a Pearl Harbor type of attack, to declare open warfare on the farm system. In Chattanooga, Tennessee, he openly denounced the farm system and major-league ownership of minor-league clubs — "the octopus of common ownership and the people responsible for it" — in the strongest possible language before a large mixed baseball gathering.

Within a week, Landis met with the major-league club owners in New York, to discuss the question. He called no names now. He never did in executive sessions. He was there to listen. Branch Rickey was absent, unable to trust himself in the same room with his detractor. Speaking for the Cardinals, Sam Breadon read into the record five telegrams to Rickey from presidents of minor-league teams involved in the farm system, extolling the very situation that Landis had excoriated at Chattanooga. They loved the system because they were assured of financial support and good teams made up of players which major-league teams found for them and placed with them without scouting expense to them. Landis tried to explain his antipathy to common ownership on the grounds that the practice among part of the membership of a league forced the rest to follow.

"As to whether I *was* right about that or not," he said, "it is enough to say that at Chattanooga probably nine out of ten of the minor-league clubs represented there were begging some major-league clubs to take them over. That is the condition that exists today."

He admitted there was no rule to enforce when he said:

"We have a bulletin that goes out, the purpose of which is to acquaint each club owner and everybody else connected with the situation with the actual facts as to the status of every ball player but *we have got no rule that goes to the question of another club owning the entire personnel of a minor-league club through its ownership of a franchise. I* have no remedy. I still think the ideal situation is for the territory where the baseball club operates to support the ball club that operates in that territory. I cannot get away from that. None of them want that now. They want to be supported from the outside."

No solution to the problem was reached at this joint meeting. Instead, it was decided to appoint a committee of six to work out some kind of peace with the five high minor leagues which refused to participate in the draft, quite another problem but of vital importance, as will be seen, to all those major league clubs without a system for player development such as Branch Rickey's. These five leagues, by refusing to participate and therefore not permitting their players to be drafted by the majors for the comparatively low draft price, became a serious problem when they asked staggering prices for choice talent in the depression. Landis and Rickey, as the meeting adjourned, still were in opposite corners on the farm system.

Two months later Commissioner Landis dealt Branch Rickey another blow that widened the breach. He nullified an outright transfer of catcher Gus Mancuso's contract from St. Louis to Rochester. After citing that Mancuso had first been optioned to Minneapolis and to Rochester the next year, the third transfer, he said, constituted a violation of Article II, section 13 (b) 1. "Such assignments shall be known as optional agreements, and shall be permitted for not more than two successive seasons in the case of any one player."

The Commissioner's letter inferred that "control" of Mancuso, and hence any other Cardinal player, could or might lead to perpetual bondage. Landis or someone in his office launched the derisive term "chain gang," by usage in official comment and correspondence.

"This is neither ruling nor decision," said Rickey. "It has

no basis of fact in baseball law. It is simply an edict! The Mancuso transfer is not an option *per se,* but an outright disposition of the contract which is tantamount to a sale. Outrighting placed the contract beyond so-called control, since the player must be exposed to selection by fifteen major-league clubs before he can be reacquired, and then only through purchase, by the St. Louis Club. If he is not drafted by any of the fifteen clubs, St. Louis has a right to repurchase the contract at *any* price, the same as it has the right to purchase the contract of any other player not selected, regardless of so-called common ownership. That is baseball law. Landis stated two months ago that common ownership has no status in the rules. He is empowered to interpret all rules, but he is not empowered to interpret a rule that does not exist. I repeat, this is an edict."

15

THE ATTACK on his revolutionary and successful baseball program was only one of Branch Rickey's major difficulties. Landis struck two months after the market crash of October, 1929, had wiped out his financial backlog of $300,000. He was left with a heavily mortgaged home in a new development called Country Life Acres to which he had moved his family during the summer.

He was in debt again. He was ashamed of the predicament, mainly the result of trying to protect his wholly owned Air Reduction stock, which he had started buying fifteen years before, with a single purchase of more on "margin." After escaping with a few hundred shares at a fraction of their original value, he worked at keeping his indebtedness a secret from business associates and his teen-age children, happy in their new home.

Baseball at this point, early spring of 1930, became a blessed sanctuary to Rickey. He plunged into his favorite recreation — watching young and green "free agents" run, hit and throw in tryout camp. A free agent is a player who has no ties of any kind to a team in organized baseball. He is found on sandlots, among semi-professional teams and anywhere except in high schools and the American Legion program. The high school student or his class must graduate, and the American Legion program must be completed. Free agents are the backbone of the farm system for they "feed" the C and D clubs.

The tryout camp, another Rickey innovation, was a departure from baseball's antiquated gesture of offering opportunity to those who cared enough to come out and get it at the ball park. The St. Louis Cardinals packed up crews of scouts and coaches and brought the opportunity to the boy. A tryout camp was planned and placed wherever a fertile baseball spot loomed, and as long as weather permitted. In the spring the camp was also a laboratory for analysis of the hopefuls signed during the previous summer and fall by the scouts.

The camp in the ball park at Shawnee, Oklahoma, was exhibiting a swarm of would-be Cardinals from the Oklahoma and Texas area. Branch Rickey wanted most to see the pitchers. They were parading now to the mound, pitching an inning, if they could, against equally hopeful batters. It was just another day at camp until Pop Kelchner whispered: "This is the one!"

A tall, hunch-shouldered figure hustled to the pitcher's box, scraped at the rubber and took a few mature-looking warmup throws. Rickey leaned forward, watched a strike and another strike and then leaned back to watch seven more strikes. No batter got even a foul.

"Let him stay in and pitch to the next three," Rickey said.

The pitcher was happy to oblige. Well aware of what it meant, he made only nine more throws, eighteen pitches to six batters, all strikes, without allowing a foul tip.

That evening in the lobby of the Aldridge Hotel, Rickey heard himself greeted: "Hello, Branch!"

He looked up at the grinning face of the strikeout pitcher and said, "I'm sorry, but I don't know you."

"Yes, you do. I'm the pitcher that struck out all them batters an' you asked me to stay in and strike out more. I'm Dean."

"How do you do, Mr. Dean," Rickey said stiffly.

"When's you an' me goin' to St. Louis?"

"To where?"

"To St. Louis. When're you takin' me to join the Cardinals? I can win the pennant up there for you, Branch."

That did it. Rickey rose from his chair with the most serious frown he could command. He stretched up as close as possible to this gangling young man's face.

"*Mister* Dean," he said sternly, "I don't know when or where you're going. The men in charge will decide and let you know. Meanwhile, *Mister* Dean, I'd like to continue reading my paper."

"Okay, Mr. Rickey," the pitcher said, and backed away, never to use "Branch" in conversation with Rickey again.

"Dizzy" Dean came to the Cardinals through the zeal of a Missouri, Kansas & Texas Railroad brakeman on the Waco to San Antonio run, Don Curtis, part-time scout for Houston. He had heard of Dean and his pitching for the Power and Light Company, a semi-pro team in San Antonio, and knew the manager, Riley Harris. His off-duty hours didn't coincide with Dean's pitching schedule until late in the 1929 season when he finally was able to see him pitch.

Curtis made up his mind before Dean had pitched a full inning. He arranged to have Harris bring the pitcher to the Hamilton Hotel that night. Curtis danced out of the lobby a few hours later with Dean's name scrawled on a Houston contract for 1930 at $300 a month. His success blinded him to a rather important factor when he mailed in the contract with a glowing report. Dean still had to be pried loose from the Army.

At this time, Dean and his younger brother, Paul, lived with their father. A back injury prevented the father from working. Paul, seventeen, supported them with his job in a San Antonio filling station. Pitcher Dean's Army pay was $21 a month.

The only doubt about Dean's future greatness lay in the possibility that his ego and misbehavior would hinder his career. He had reached the Shawnee camp without money or clothes, which is not unusual. John Leonard "Pepper" Martin reached the Greenville, Texas, camp in 1925 on the rods of a freight.

But Dean acted as though he owned at least half of Shawnee. He was nearly six feet four inches tall, 190 pounds, and moved with the ease and confidence of a camp boss bully. He was optioned to St. Joseph, of the Western League.

Dean started trouble in his very first game. He pitched shutout ball and nearly died laughing at his opponents' inability to get hits. However, when one of them singled sharply past him and called, "How do you like that, you S.O.B.?" Dean saw red and rushed over to get him. The first baseman stepped in between them and Dean felled him with a solid right to the chin.

By mid-August, however, Dizzy Dean had won 17 games. He had struck out 134 and walked 77 in 217 innings. He was "the ball club." It was so easy for him and he was so thoroughly irresponsible that elevating him to the Houston club and greater responsibilities was now a necessity to protect him from himself as much as to strengthen that team.

Dean was neither bad nor incorrigible. Rather he lacked a sense of values. He had scrambled so long for the bare necessities, that with success his appetites were suddenly ravenous. Unexpectedly, he was a big shot, but he was unprepared for it.

When the news of his impending departure for Houston got out, he owed a large clothing bill and a large hotel bill and had little or nothing to show for it, having charged items and either lost or sold them for the cash he always seemed to need. Then the manager of a U-Drive-It appeared with a whopping bill for car rentals.

"Yes, and our car was abandoned somewhere out in the country," the renting official said. "We had to go get it. He ran up nearly three hundred dollars of rental time that way. I've got to account for it."

It was small wonder Dean pleaded to Oliver French, St. Joe business manager. "Just get me there [Houston], Oliver, an' I'll pitch for nothing!"

In six weeks at Houston Dean compiled an amazing record. He allowed only 62 hits in 85 innings, struck out 95 and walked 49. He had a record of eight victories and two defeats which, added to his record at St. Joseph, gave him twenty-five wins and ten losses on the season. His dream of reaching St. Louis had to come true.

Jess Haines put the finishing touch on the Cardinals' thrilling stretch drive by beating Pittsburgh, 10–5, on September 26, 1930, to give St. Louis fans their third pennant in five seasons. Two days later Dizzy Dean arrived to close the season with a simple request to Manager Charles "Gabby" Street, "Just tell the boys to get me a couple of runs, Charlie." He defeated Pittsburgh, allowing only four hits. Young Dean told the reporters he just fogged it "thoo" and that the Pirates were lucky to score at all in losing to him, 3–1.

Late that night newspapers were hawked outside Dizzy's hotel with his smiling features on the front page. He bought dozens of copies, crossed the street to the refreshment stand, pawed over the apples, selected a large one and bit into it. The proprietor asked for his money. Dean laughed, pointed to the front page picture and said, "Don't you know who I am?"

Rickey's problem was what to do with Dean now the season

was over. Should he advance him money against next season's salary and turn him loose? If so, what would he do? Where would he go? He had no home, no mother, no girl and no money. He had no job except baseball.

Branch Rickey found the solution by prevailing on Oliver French to take Dean into his home for the winter. The Frenches then had two small boys and lived with Mrs. French's parents in Charleston, Missouri.

"He was a good boy," declared Grandmother Brown a quarter century later, but, under prodding, she couldn't recall a bad one.

"He had us worried," said Mrs. French, "for his sake."

"As long as we heard the clink of the coal," Oliver French said, "we knew he was happy and all right. It was hard on our fuel supply, but it helped. Dizzy used to open the furnace door and stand at the other end of our long cellar to throw. A piece of chestnut coal into the furnace was a strike. Missing the opening was a single. Missing the furnace was a double. When the house got unbearably hot, we knew Dizzy had set another strikeout record."

The Frenches taught the boy to play bridge. In the competition he found another opportunity to express himself. He became aggressively sound at auction bridge. He learned to handle a gun, and, of course, wanted to bag more quail than anyone else. The day's hunting was never over until Dizzy had the biggest kill.

But he was young. He grew restless and developed a teenager's desire for a car. The local Chevrolet dealer loaned him one. When he drove, he used only half the street, but it was the center half. He went aloft in a Piper Cub, not once but several times. He quit when the engine threw a piston and the plane crashed through a fence and plummeted into a field.

Dizzy wanted money. Oliver obeyed orders not to give

him more than small sums, and had warned people in town not to make loans to the boy. Dizzy pleaded, and was so unhappy that Oliver finally drove him into St. Louis for a discussion with Branch Rickey. When they reached Country Life Acres, Dizzy's eyes popped at the beauty of his surroundings. His hopes for a higher allowance rose as he entered the long, well-furnished living room and said, "Wow! That'd be a pretty fur piece to hit a ball!"

Three hours later, Rickey emerged beaming, but Dean was scowling. Dizzy voiced his disgust to French as they headed home.

"A fine friend you are!"

"What did he give you?"

"All I wanted was a hundred an' fifty dollars, an' all I got was a lecture on sex. Golly, Oliver, when he first begin talkin' about the facts of life, I thought for sure he meant money!"

Finally, the inevitable happened. Dean found a girl. She was pretty, awed by his reputation and his ceaseless flow of words and teen-age boasts. He made a slight tactical error at Christmas time by presenting her with the most costly set of silk pajamas he could find. She returned them with thanks, because her parents did not think it appropriate.

Dean was smitten and wanted to marry her, even though she was scarcely halfway through high school. He wrote Rickey about it.

"Ballplayers should marry," Rickey telephoned in reply, "I'm always for it. But this isn't for you, boy." Rickey ignored the protest. "Look, I'll give you five hundred dollars to marry —"

"You *will?* You mean that?"

"Certainly I mean it," Rickey said, "but I mean the right marriage. I don't want to put a premium on any old marriage."

As time failed to heal Dizzy's wound, Oliver thought it best to get him out of town and into training camp ahead of schedule. Perhaps throwing a baseball would take his mind off his romance.

It was a terribly desperate and lonesome Dizzy Dean who, after missing one train by running away at the station, finally was headed for Texas and the great season the Cardinal organization knew he would have one day. He had twenty-six victories in 1931, 303 strikeouts in 304 innings, and an earned-run average of 1.53. He was the fulcrum of the outstanding team in Houston history.

16

RICKEY'S FIRST PARRY to the Commissioner's attack on the farm system at Chattanooga in 1929 took place a year later at the Mount Royal Hotel, in Montreal. The Minor League Convention of 1930 deplored a situation that had become desperate for everybody but the St. Louis Cardinals. Their organization was at the top of the baseball heap.

Because its scouts fed good talent to the minor-league teams which it owned or with which it had working agreements, these teams were strong and prospering, and gave the parent Cardinals an enormous pool of experienced players to draw on as needed and at reasonable prices. Surplus skill, never as good as that retained, was sold to competitors, increasing corporate prosperity. The success of the Rickey plan was complete. Other major-league clubs, lacking the player-development system, simply could not match his teams at any level.

But the minor leagues were in a state of revolt, especially the higher classification leagues. Because of the depression, the five of them that refused to participate in the draft plan could not sell ball players at prices they needed to survive. The small clubs that did not have working agreements were being pinched out.

With Landis sitting only a few feet away, Branch Rickey "poured it on" in such a way that no one in organized baseball could misinterpret his feelings or his fiery speech.

"Three Class D leagues, two in B, and one in A, may not open this coming year," he reminded them. "Thirteen leagues have closed down since 1926. Not one of the thirteen that failed has had major-league affiliation. And what are we doing about it?

"The farm system is not an ideal system, and nobody is talking about whether it is ideal or not. When people are hungry, they eat food which may or may not be ideally cooked and served. No questions asked because it is not an issuable point. The point is, do we have food and can we live on it? Is there sustenance in it? Yes. Then eat it and don't complain too much about where it came from, who cooked it, how it is served.

"It is all right to have a physician," he challenged and looked at Commissioner Landis, "who will feel your pulse and look at you and say you are a sick man, I think you are going to die. He offers you no medicine, none at all. He gives you no change of climate. He just says you are sick, he's awfully sorry. Then along comes somebody else who says you've got epizootic and he can cure epizootic and he doesn't have to cut off the epi. He doesn't have to take out an eye. He can make you live. Here's pill number one and here's pill number two and when you get through with one you can take number two.

"I claim that such a doctor in a hopeless case should be acceptable both to the patient and to the helpless doctor who has had the case. In no way should it be said, in my judgment, that anyone should say to the new physician who is offering assurance of a cure, if, in a rational hope a thousand held interest, 'You can't give him those pills! You can't give him anything!'

"Ladies and gentlemen, the Cardinals are interested in eight minor-league clubs, Rochester, Houston, St. Joseph,

Danville, Fort Wayne, Laurel, Fort Smith and Scottdale. We are minor league conscious. Our minor-league interests are two to one over our major-league interests and we are the National League champions as of now. Golf, motoring, economic conditions and bad management have played havoc with minor-league operations. Our farm clubs have been hurt, of course, but we have not suffered at all in comparison with those who are unable to continue, and those champions of local interest who may fail in midseason. I deplore the philosophy of indifference to what is going on.

"For without the minor leagues, baseball can get nowhere. When the majors get to the point where they think they do not have to consider the status of the minors, then a great danger exists to the structure of baseball."

Again he looked pointedly at Commissioner Landis.

"Baseball is bigger than any one club. I owe much to this game. It is bigger than I am. It is bigger than any one man!"

A thundering ovation followed Rickey's closing declaration. Commissioner Landis spoke an instant later and, of course, made no reference to the challenge. His brief talk was largely a tribute to the value of baseball in making good young citizens.

Having limited news value, the speech was soon forgotten. Rickey preferred it that way. He could not indulge in name-calling, or defy the Commissioner openly. He could not cajole the press into presenting his side. He was not a club owner; just a contract employee. But he was a formidable foe. He had proved it many times in the past when his back was to the wall. Landis, perhaps, had an edge on Rickey in law, for he had been a good jurist, with well-publicized integrity.

"Saying a person has integrity is like saying he breathes," Rickey would snap. "What's so unusual about having integrity? It's common. It's so usual that you don't have to keep repeating it."

"No doubt about his sincerity."

"Absolutely no doubt. A person can be so sincere about rules and law as to blind himself to justice."

"He's a self-made man!"

"That relieves God of a tremendous responsibility!"

As if to emphasize his attitude on his difference with Landis, a month later he consummated a significant deal with Larry MacPhail of Columbus, Ohio.

MacPhail, a stranger when he entered Rickey's office and life, had red hair, blue eyes and a purchase option on the Columbus Senators. His proposition appealed to both Rickey and Breadon. The Cardinals could well afford nearly $100,-000 for another top classification franchise from an operating profit of $230,000.

It would be a bigger project than Houston, and justify doubling the number of lower-classification clubs. It would mean jobs for scouts, managers, business managers, a larger staff and other expansion, in spite of the depression.

Rickey took the alternative to paying MacPhail a straight $10,000 commission. He paid $90,000 for the club and gave MacPhail a two-year contract as president at $10,000 a year.

17

FEW YEARS in Branch Rickey's life were as memorable as 1931. June brought graduation from school for Mary and Branch, Jr., and both would enter Ohio Wesleyan University in the fall. June also found Rickey in Columbus on a successful real estate hunt with Larry MacPhail for property that would hold another modern stadium.

Business was declining everywhere, it seemed, except in the Cardinal organization. Rochester attendance was good, but crowds at Columbus were 20 per cent better than in 1930. Houston was heading toward an all-time high, and the parent Cardinals would go over 600,000 paid admissions for the fourth time in club history. In August Breadon declared a dividend of $100,600, equal to 20 per cent of the profits.

And things were so good in September that the Cardinals clinched the pennant nearly two weeks before the season's end. They went into the World Series, however, against a Philadelphia Athletics team that had won 107 games, second highest total in American League history. Grove, Walberg, Earnshaw, Cochrane, Simmons and Foxx were on that team.

But the story of the World Series was all St. Louis. The base hits and base running of Pepper Martin stole the show. The reason for his great series, Martin insists, was a speech from Rickey before the first game.

"The National League hadn't beat the Americans in the

last four tries," he said. "The National League officials' pride was hurt. Mr. Heydler, the league president, talked to us first; then Mr. John McGraw spoke; but then came Mr. Branch Rickey. His theme was THE GREATEST ATTRIBUTE OF A WINNING BALL PLAYER IS A DESIRE TO WIN THAT DOMINATES! I have never forgotten those words. He brought every single Cardinal off his seat with an address that beat anything I ever heard. He reminded us that we had dreamed of this moment from boyhood. We had schemed and scratched and fought and gone hungry to get here, and here we were, and what in heaven's name were we going to do about it?

"Well, we rushed out of there cheering, and I personally got down on my knees in front of our dugout and I kissed the ground, and I actually prayed to God to help me have the desire to win that dominates. And I meant every word I prayed. I really did."

Martin's "desire to win" dominated the games. He totaled twelve hits in the first five games, which equaled the record. He lost a thirteenth in the final game when the official scorers decided Foxx had committed an error. Martin then stole his fifth base of the Series. In the fifth game, which the Cardinals won at Philadelphia, 5–1, Martin had a home run and two singles and drove in four of his team's five runs. During the seven games he scored five runs and drove in five. He handled ten fly balls in centerfield without an error. By taking the final game, 4–2, St. Louis again became champions of the baseball world. Pennant victories by both Rochester and Houston emphasized the organization's dominance more than ever.

Branch Rickey's voice dominated the Minor League Convention at West Baden, Indiana, two months later, especially behind the scenes. That gathering was made memorable by a rush of the few surviving leagues to overthrow a self-perpetuating group that directed the National Association of minor leagues but who had long refused to budge in the direction of forestalling disaster. Mike Sexton, president for twenty-two years, and John H. Farrell, secretary for twenty-eight years, were unseated and replaced by an executive committee to supervise the minors for a year.

"Bob Connery was my leg man in persuading club owners on the fringe to go for the change," Rickey said, recalling the administrative upheaval. "We picked William Bramham, president of the Piedmont, for front running, because he was a good lawyer and could carry water on both shoulders. He was elected chairman the next day. Then Bob Bookwalter, president of our Danville club, was my man on revising the antiquated rules, a thankless job well done. Warren Giles stayed close to Bramham."

This was only one of Rickey's answers to the do-nothing admission of Commissioner Landis.

The convention was made more memorable by the acquisition of the top-classification Newark, New Jersey, minor-league club by the New York Yankees. Three years before, when the roll was called before Judge Landis, the Yankees had expressed their intention of acquiring interests in other clubs. They had moved slowly, but now, from the Newark purchase sprang a baseball dynasty that was to dominate the American League from then on. The Yankees hired George Weiss at West Baden to do the job and he started the only equal to his own powerful farm system that Branch Rickey ever knew. Six years later, 1938, Yankee-owned Newark and Kansas City met in the Little World Series.

"This was one of the best things that happened to baseball," Rickey said. "We welcomed another strong operator in the other league, and wished there were more. The farm system had finally ended the undercover work of gentlemen's agreements, which were bad because they were covert. The farm system caused the aboveboard optional agreement. The wording of the optional agreement was the outcome of trial and error. Down through the years I sat with many business managers of major-league clubs in a discussion of the details of working agreements. I have given many printed copies of my working agreement form to other clubs in both leagues.

"Why, the next year — that would be 1932 — Eddie Collins went to the Boston Red Sox as part owner with Tom Yawkey. Collins came to St. Louis and spent two full days with me. I told him everything I could about the farm system, how to eliminate the errors we had made and the many 'don'ts.' He carried away with him a copy of every kind of agreement and correspondence in the handling of players, minor league clubs and farm system. Many others had a like experience. We helped wherever and whenever we could."

As a fitting climax to a great year, the major-league meetings at Chicago in December, 1931, saw Branch Rickey effect his most spectacular deal. He obtained the contract of a player he did not need or want and, within twenty-four hours, realized $45,000 on the effort.

"Hack Wilson is available," he told a number of the club owners after one Drake Hotel session. "Chicago doesn't want him and neither do I, but I'm going to get him and sell him to you."

Rickey appeared next day with Wilson's contract. He approached Brooklyn, whose operators had gone heavily into debt enlarging Ebbets Field. Rickey knew they needed a drawing card to fill it. He sold Wilson's contract to Brooklyn for $45,000 and an outfielder.

It has been written often and erroneously that Branch

Rickey "got 10 per cent of the sales price on every deal." The truth is his 10 per cent clause depended entirely on corporate operating profit. Actually he did realize $4500, or 10 per cent, on the Wilson deal, but only because 1931 was a profit year. Had he made the deal in January, a month later, it would have meant nothing to him personally, because the Cardinals reported a loss of $73,895 for 1932, and $80,198 for 1933. He made substantial contract sales in both years and collected nothing above his salary.

18

THE LOSS of 1932 was caused principally by the construction of the Red Bird Stadium in Columbus. The job went far over the budget, owing to incorrect figuring on the light towers. With his job as president at stake, Larry MacPhail was in deep turmoil. The union workmen didn't like him because of his interference and around-the-clock prodding. One of them, in a fit of temper, threw an eight-pound wrench and missed MacPhail's red head by inches. Branch Rickey interceded and sat far into the night with union representatives to placate workers on the job. Building the beautiful and modern Columbus Park reduced the Cardinals' reserve to nothing.

Sam Breadon was unhappy about the runaway project. It couldn't be ready by opening day. Old Neil Park would have to be used until the paint was dry and the sod ready. The situation was especially serious to Branch Rickey, whose five-year contract was about to expire. The economic depression was in full swing. Recalling Breadon's impetuous move in relieving him of management seven years before, Rickey now wondered if he was expendable as an employee. To prepare for the unforseeable, he got in contact with Sidney Weil, of Cincinnati, when both the Cardinals and the Reds were playing in the east.

"I'm leaving for South Carolina," he said to Weil. "Ride to Washington with me."

Weil would have gone anywhere with this man, and asked no questions, for Rickey was a true friend to him. No one else in baseball would have let Weil, in his precarious financial state, go "on the cuff" for $50,000. At Bradenton that spring, Weil had bought Chick Hafey from the Cardinals on an I O U. He was delighted to ride as far south as time would permit. His outlook was brighter when he left Rickey's drawing room in Washington.

"We had an agreement that was most flattering to me," Weil said in fond recollection. "If Branch got his release from St. Louis, he would come with me as general manager and vice-president of the Cincinnati Club. He would have complete charge of doing in Cincinnati what he had done in St. Louis. I felt that my troubles might be over.

"Several weeks later he called me and said, 'Sid, we've just got to call the whole thing off, as much as I'd like to come to Cincinnati. When I talked to Sam Breadon about leaving, Sam took off his glasses and put them on the desk and said, 'Branch, if you leave me I've got to get out of baseball.' "

Rickey was sincere when he made his conditional pact with Weil. Breadon had given no hint of his intentions on the new contract, and the Columbus project had become a hazard. To his surprise, they came to terms quickly on a new five-year contract, and at a raise, $50,000 yearly, with the usual 10 per cent of operating profit.

The new Red Bird Stadium at Columbus opened in mid-June with 18,000 on hand, including standees, twice as many as the old park held. Two weeks later its giant steel towers illuminated a night game for a sellout crowd. In August the quiet young brother of Dizzy Dean, Paul, pitched the Association's first no-hit game under lights against Kansas City. Columbus, which had never totaled 200,000 paid admissions for a season, was heading for 300,000.

The player who openly questioned Branch Rickey's managing methods nine years before, whose unspeakable language had provoked Rickey into physical violence, and who took over his job two years later, was released as manager of the Chicago Cubs in midsummer 1932. Financially embarrassed from horse-race betting, which was no secret, Hornsby needed help. Rickey, with typical coincidence, needed infield help and a pinch hitter. Even though Hornsby was a "hot potato," Rickey planned a contract and an advance against next year's salary. When Commissioner Landis roared no, because Hornsby was a "bad influence," Rickey demanded reasons, with equal dramatic emphasis, why this "demoralizer" had remained in baseball so long.

"I will write a contract," Rickey said, "and I will describe the gambling that Hornsby will not do, and he will sign it. Will you then deny this man the right to earn a living as a baseball player?"

Hornsby signed such a contract in October and remained a most helpful Cardinal until, through Rickey's efforts, he was hired as manager of the Browns in midsummer.

By that time Rickey was hit hard from another direction. The Cardinals, with Toporcer, Thevenow and then Charlie Gelbert, had given St. Louis fans a decade of great shortstops. Gelbert shot his leg while hunting in late 1932 and quite possibly would never play again. The organization did not have a star replacement ready. To fill the gap, Rickey had to trade in the open market. In May, 1933, he met with Sid Weil, and confided that he was going to Philadelphia to buy shortstop Dick Bartell.

"You can't," Weil said. "I tried. We needed his hitting in our infield. Nugent won't trade or sell just yet."

"Well, I can try, too," Rickey said. "Will you phone Nugent and tell him I'm on my way over? I'll call you when I get back."

Rickey returned without Bartell. He called Weil as promised. Weil and his manager, Donie Bush, appeared to satisfy his need of a shortstop, but on their terms. Rickey lacked his usual good bargaining position, but to improve Weil's situation, now at the desperation stage, would be no crime. Paul Derringer was only twenty-six, with his best years of pitching ahead, but he needed new surroundings. Rickey offered the contracts of big Derringer, Allyn Stout, another pitcher; and the veteran utility infielder, "Sparky" Adams, for those of shortstop Leo Durocher and pitcher John Ogden.

All taking part in the discussion were old friends, yet they bantered and badgered, cited strong points and weaknesses in these players, suggested others, and haggled in general, but Rickey got his shortstop, and Weil some badly needed cash. Said Donie Bush, as he mopped his brow in the elevator, "We sure had to swim the river to make it."

Durocher burst into Weil's room the next morning with chips on both shoulders.

"Donie just told me!" he exclaimed. "I won't go, Sid. I won't play for any chain gang, and especially for Rickey. I know all about him."

"Take it easy, Leo," Weil soothed. "So you don't want to play for Mr. Rickey. All right, but I made a deal. At least we owe him the courtesy of telling him why we can't go through with it."

At Rickey's hotel, a tight-lipped Durocher shook hands with the bushy-browed "monster" he had heard so much about. Rickey didn't exactly resemble a monster. Suffering from a cold, he sat in bed, wearing an old-fashioned flannel nightgown. A Gideon Bible rested in his lap.

"I'll tell you what I told Mr. Weil," Durocher began. "I won't play for your chain gang. In Mr. Weil I found a friend, the only one I've had in this world since Miller Huggins died. He's treated me like a son, and I'm not going to leave him. I just won't play for you."

Rickey made no effort to halt the rather heated and personal abuse. Durocher finally ran out of ways to say that he wouldn't leave Sid Weil to play for the Cardinals.

Rickey then told him quietly that the deal was final and added, "We've got a double header in Brooklyn this afternoon. You may not play for us today. But how are you going to feel if our shortstop bobbles, and we lose both games? And how are you going to feel at the end of the season, if we lose the pennant by the two games that you could have won by being in there at shortstop? Answer that, son."

The possibility was real enough to dissipate Durocher's final resistance. It was a fact that he was a Cardinal and, since he liked to win, he agreed to play.

The shortstop problem was barely settled when Rickey was called to Columbus to tackle a charge of salary limit violations by MacPhail. Newcomers to the intricacies of farm-system baseball, hopeful of accomplishing in a few months what it took Branch Rickey twenty years to evolve, often stubbed their toes. Larry MacPhail stubbed all ten of them and fell flat on his face.

He had broken the rules by adding incentive conditions to the contracts of players obtained from St. Louis. He neglected to incorporate them properly into the reports which carried sworn affidavits of limitations in salary and increments. Adjustment of the wrong called for immediate transfer of about ten players, disrupting at least three ball clubs already "set" for the summer.

Valuable time and — even more valuable — the options would be lost. To reassign contracts, adjust salaries and move players around was a night-and-day ordeal. Rickey did his sleeping in short takes on the office couch. He demanded MacPhail's resignation. When MacPhail refused to resign, he was dismissed.

President Bramham, of the National Association, levied fines against the players, and ruled:

> In the case against the Columbus Club the penalties for such violation are a fine of $500 upon the club and the suspension of the offending Club President from further participation in National Association affairs for a period of two years from the date he is found guilty.

By removing MacPhail from the presidency first, Rickey had placed him beyond reach of suspension and fine. Presently Rickey was sitting at the Columbus ball park with the young secretary of the Columbus Chamber of Commerce, George M. Trautman. He had helped run one of the most successful and pivotal minor-league conventions at Columbus six months before.

"Would you take the presidency of the Columbus Club?" Rickey asked bluntly.

Trautman nodded a head of red hair and said, "Only if MacPhail is out of the picture."

"He is, quite definitely."

They talked terms briefly and shook hands on $8000. On the way home Trautman realized that quick acceptance left him with $500 a year less than his Chamber of Commerce income. He telephoned his new boss to explain that he shouldn't work for less than —

"Yes, it's all right," Rickey barked, "but make up your mind!"

MacPhail's defection was costly to the organization, and a dent in Rickey's pride. Branch blamed himself for "not staying closer to the situation," his usual excuse when inexperienced personnel was floored by complicated farm-club challenges. He showed no outward anger toward MacPhail, and, indeed, eagerly sought to help him when opportunity arose, as it did twice later. The first time was when Cincinnati, under new ownership, offered him the top post. He declined and recommended MacPhail. A few years after that he turned town a similar plea to be Brooklyn's general manager, and "sold" MacPhail as a substitute.

Rickey returned to St. Louis to see his Cardinal manager, Gabby Street, surrendering to the pressures of a maverick team out of hand. This was one of baseball's tragedies that is never publicized, because it reveals a rather ugly side of a ball player's competitive nature. It was tragic to Rickey, because Street was a helping hand in the earliest days of farm-system success. Rickey had seen twenty-year-old Tommy Thevenow play one game for Street in Joplin, Missouri, liked him and asked about him. Street helped obtain the boy's contract for the Cardinals.

Gabby had been signed as coach of the parent team to teach and bolster young players under Billy Southworth and then McKechnie in 1929. When McKechnie left to better himself at the end of the season, Street took over and led the Cardinals to championships in 1930 and 1931. But now he had "lost" some of his players. They had somehow detected a weakness in Street. Rickey had watched it grow in silence, refusing to invade the clubhouse or ball field. It was the manager's domain and duty. Street's failure in handling the irrepressible Dizzy Dean was a contributing factor. Rampant disobedience in 1932 became open revolution in 1933. Silent but hopeful that Street would act, Rickey heard the ringleaders and their satellites ridicule "Old Sarge" and even suggest "get rid of him . . . I can manage better than he can."

Yet in undeserved justice to them, their carnivorous treatment of Street may have been to preserve health in their flock, for they knew they could not win without leadership.

Street made regular visits to Rickey's office in the last days of his harrowing ordeal, during which period the Cardinals lost ten of fifteen games.

"Gabby, can't you sense what this means?" Rickey pleaded.

"What else can I sense?" Street muttered. "They won't obey my signs, Branch. One said only yesterday, 'We're runnin' this team!'"

"But you're running out, Gabby. On them . . . on *me!*" Rickey said impatiently, and walked the floor with his arm over the manager's shoulder. "You fine them. I'll make it stick. Just name the players, Gabby. You know I won't. Name the players and I'll trade them. If you don't discipline them now, they'll run you right out of your job!"

Street sighed and slumped into a chair. If he named the players, Rickey would surely stand by his word. But what good would it do to trade five or six great players who could win any given game if they put their minds to it?

"I'm through, Branch," he sighed. "I'm pushed."

It was July 24. Frank Frisch, captain and second baseman, was appointed manager. The entire team settled down under his authority and rattled off six straight victories at home and sixteen of their next seventeen at home.

19

THE BROTHERS DEAN, of the St. Louis Cardinals, transformed their great story into baseball legend in 1934. At the Florida training camp, Dizzy launched the "Me an' Paul" saga with a promise they would win "forty or forty-five games." Good "copy" till now, Dizzy suddenly materialized as the wildest dream come true for sports writers. He was quoted at length, in and out of context, in and out of order, and in six different versions.

The Cardinals and Branch Rickey encouraged Dizzy's talent for getting publicity from the start by failing to discourage it. The pitcher's uninhibited antics and expressions were amusing. The colorful stories, often exaggerated or distorted, meant newspaper space which sold tickets. Not until too late did they realize it was also a form of Frankenstein monster.

For two years Eugene Karst, first publicity man hired by a big-league club, had serviced the press with information about the expanding St. Louis farm system. Now he was ready for the advent of the Deans. He augmented Dizzy's expostulations with effective background data. He had clarifying statements on the pitcher's conflicting declarations. To help the pitcher, Rickey assigned Bill DeWitt to handle the many commercial off-field exploitations of Dizzy's time and tongue. As agent, DeWitt eventually processed $35,000 in extra income and received 10 per cent for his work.

From the start, Dizzy Dean was infatuated with his fabulous press. He volunteered opinions on everything imaginable, and early in the season, he had the effrontery to stage a "strike" in behalf of his brother, claiming he was underpaid. Dizzy's senseless effort to have Paul's contract adjusted before he would "throw another ball" was well publicized before Manager Frisch could get him into a room with Paul and explain the facts of legal documents. Even when Paul said he was satisfied, Dizzy claimed the boy didn't mean it.

The Cardinals played consistent baseball, winning three of every five games at home and away. Dizzy's pitching was truly spectacular, the kind seen but once in a generation. He threw with a full overhand motion that imparted great speed without loss of good control. Paul threw with a side-arm delivery, bringing his right arm around at or slightly above waist-level. Dizzy had won twenty games the year before, but had lost almost as many. Now he lost hardly at all. He was by far the most important cog in the machine. But in August the team was in third place behind the Giants and the Cubs.

In that month, an exhibition game was scheduled. Neither Dizzy nor Paul appeared for it. Dizzy had deliberately skipped previous exhibition games and had been fined. This time Branch Rickey fined them both and suspended them indefinitely. The move was big news, but the story behind it was never divulged. Manager Frank Frisch considered it tantamount to throwing away his pennant chances. It was so reflected in Breadon's report of a conversation he had with Frisch.

"Frisch wants the suspension lifted," Breadon announced.

"It can't be lifted, Sam," Rickey exclaimed. "If you lift the suspension, you'll never be able to hold Dean again."

"Frisch wants it," Breadon sighed. "What'll we do?"

"Do whatever you please, Sam," Rickey replied quietly. "But you'll have to make a choice between Frisch and me. If you lift the suspension, I'll have to resign."

Breadon thought an instant and said, "Will you go to Detroit and talk it over with Frisch?"

Rickey caught a plane and met Frisch. The manager was dispirited, as would be any manager who has lost the two best pitchers in baseball. Rickey assured him that far more was at stake than a National League pennant. Dean had defied a big-league manager trying to run his team. He had flouted authority and was laughing at the very instrument responsible for team success: leadership. Rickey pointed out that this same type of defiance had run a fine man and manager off the Cardinals just a year before. The situation had to be handled with firmness to hold the respect of your team, even if doing so cost a few victories.

"You may do what you think best, Frank," Rickey concluded. "It is your team. But it is also my team and my organization. They stand suspended with me. That makes it either you or me, Frank. If you lift the suspensions, I must resign."

After returning to St. Louis, Frisch called the press to confirm the relatively small fines and the indefinite suspensions. Dizzy put on a great show of temper. He tore up one Cardinal uniform and, when some photographers pleaded for another shot, he tore up a second. He declaimed and he threatened. Paul was silent, having been trapped in the situation by his brother. But neither pitcher was allowed on the field at Sportsman's Park in uniform or out. Neither would receive salary during the period of suspension, and the cost of the uniforms would be deducted from Dizzy's salary check, when or if he received one.

Dizzy carried the case to the acknowledged defender of the little fellow, Commissioner Landis. Granted a hearing in Chicago, Dizzy and the hapless Paul received a severe castigation for violating their contracts and hurting the good name of baseball by challenging authority when they were wholly in error. The boys trudged back to St. Louis and waited meekly for the suspension to be lifted.

But Frisch was in no hurry now. The show of authority had convinced the team that Frisch, and not Dizzy Dean, was running the show. They reacted as if a great weight had been lifted from their shoulders. Given the opportunity to prove their independence of the Deans, they started a winning streak that soon mounted to five straight. They scored twenty-seven runs in the last two games. They lost to Boston and then defeated them twice. Seven victories in eight games without the Deans!

With its new self-confidence, the hard-running team was now an explosive yet cohesive unit in spite of Dizzy. Thus the "Gas House Gang" emerged.

The Gas House Gang was, in its fashion, the most fabulous team in the history of the game. On the field, it was aggressive to the point of daring and it held the spectators at its games and baseball fans across the country breathless with excitement because it introduced this element of danger and developed it as the trademark of a baseball era.

The uniforms that Pepper Martin dirtied and tore sliding into bases head-first symbolized the team's style of play. Rowdy, noisy, arrogant, the "gang" fought to stay on top against the opposition, and fought each other to stay in the lineup. Joe Medwick once threatened to use a bat on somebody's head if he couldn't swing it in his rightful turn in batting practice. Dizzy Dean and Tex Carleton swung at each other with their fists. Some even traded punches with sports writers. The team's youthful exuberance, its competitive spirit thrilled Branch Rickey as they did everyone else. The whole gang's desire to play in every game and to win every game was the direct outcome of his farm-system operation. The struggle among low-classification players for promotion not only eliminated complacency at the top;

it forced the big-leaguers to maximum effort, and mirrored Rickey's lifelong attitude toward play on the field.

Off the field, the Gas House Gang's antics were more of a headache than a thrill for Rickey. Pepper Martin rode fire engines to fires day or night. He used so much energy pushing his midget auto into a start at the night races he couldn't play his best the following days. After listening to Frisch's complaint, Rickey asked Pepper for an explanation.

"I only own half the car and my partner drives, Mr. Rickey. I'm saving the winnings to buy a midget racer with a self-starter for myself."

When the team's leading hitter, "Ripper" Collins, was fined $25 for missing a train, he appealed to Rickey, who refused to override his team manager. On his way out of the "front office," Collins appropriated a dozen new baseballs. The sympathetic team trainer gave him another dozen and he sold the twenty-four for a dollar apiece. In fairness to all, it must be added that Collins missed the train while helping the trainer take care of a player who had been taken suddenly ill in the station.

On the road, the team pranks usually resembled those of all hearty but fresh youngsters. In Philadelphia on one occasion, however, a quartet of the "gang" bought work clothes and tools, pretended to be workmen, and made a shambles of a luncheon meeting, the kitchen and the barbershop of their hotel. Rickey was hard put to convince the management that his team should not be barred from the hotel forever.

When their suspension was lifted, the Dean brothers rejoined a team that couldn't be stopped and added their own great support to its winning ways. In the first game of a double-header with Brooklyn in late September, Dizzy won 13–0 and had a no-hitter going for eight innings. Paul pitched a no-hitter in winning the second game. The Cardinals passed the Giants in the final week and won the pennant. Dizzy won thirty games and, almost as remarkable, lost only seven. Paul won nineteen and lost eleven. "Me an' Paul" had accounted for forty-nine of the team's ninety-five victories.

The Gas House Gang then stormed into Detroit for a most colorful World Series. Dizzy Dean, in street clothes, interrupted one Tiger batting practice to give Detroit practical instruction. Borrowing a bat, he whacked a half dozen line drives into the outfield; then retreated to the sidelines amid applause and laughter. He won the first game, lost the fifth and won the deciding seventh. Paul won the third and sixth games. During the fourth game, Frisch was looking up and down his bench for a pinch runner when he heard someone say, "You got one, Skip, Diz just went out." Dizzy was already telling the umpire he was the runner. Trying to prevent a double play a moment later, Dizzy got in the way of the relay throw. The ball struck his forehead, knocked him flat and he was carried from the field unconscious. Playing the entire series with an injured arm, Pepper Martin starred in the seventh game with two hits, two stolen bases and three runs scored. Leo Durocher was superb at shortstop. Joe Medwick retaliated from a "kneeing" inflicted as he slid into third base and had to be pulled from the flying fists of the third baseman. When he subsequently returned to his leftfield position, Medwick was met with a Niagara of vegetables, bottles and other debris thrown from the bleachers by Detroit fans. As both a protective measure and so that the game could be finished, Commissioner Landis had to remove Medwick from the lineup. Dizzy allowed only six hits. The Cardinals scored eleven runs.

Once again, the St. Louis organization was champion of the baseball world, for Columbus added a Little World Series triumph to the Cardinal victory.

20

THE SELF-PERPETUATING "old guard" directing the minor-league administration had been ousted in 1931. The cobwebby Board of Arbitration was replaced a year later by a new Rickey-picked president, William G. Bramham; and a three-man Executive Committee to hear appeals from the president's decisions. Warren Giles, a key Cardinal administrator, headed this Committee. Farm-system legislation subsequently passed made this change historic.

In a desperate move to salvage the tottering structure, Branch Rickey had come into leadership of minor-league baseball. The strength and wealth of his organization made it possible and Rickey assumed the control to preserve his baseball life. Commissioner Landis, empowered only to enforce rules, stood by, but not in silence. He warned owners of the pitfalls he thought might arise from too much control of players and of low-classification clubs.

Although Landis had no alternative plan for alleviating baseball's economic desperation, he was far from idle, for he watchdogged the option maneuvers. He uncovered a number of player transfers that violated the rules and declared many of them free agents. In fining the offending clubs, however, he seldom failed to imply deceit, dishonesty, or willful unmorality by the club owner. Critics of Landis pointed out that his value to major-league club owners, many of whom were often uncertain about procedure, diminished when he failed to advise beyond the rules to the same extent and vigor that he criticized. Even Landis partisans grew weary of his stock reply to seekers of counsel on procedure, "Do it and I'll rule on it."

Under the energetic direction of Bramham and the Executive Committee, new minor leagues were encouraged and dormant ones brought to life. The administrative house was cleaned from trashy cellar to musty attic. They shored the central treasury by raising the transfer-handling fee; protected player salaries by instituting the territorial guarantee; protected local mechanics, workers, merchants and others against financial loss by recognizing liens; and they clarified rules of option and working agreement as problems arose through the early 1930's.

Many legislation changes were influenced, if not initiated, by the staff of administrative eager beavers that Rickey assembled and augmented at every opportunity. Giles was his key man. Bartelme, Rickey's assistant and "buffer" outside his office, was another. George Trautman became an important cog after he took over at Columbus. Oliver French was a specialist in low-classification difficulties from his experience operating Cardinal farm clubs at St. Joe, Danville, and Greensboro and Asheville, North Carolina.

They, and later others, used to gather for talks at Country Life Acres in November of each year as Mrs. Rickey's house guests. Sometimes they came and went in such confusion she never knew how many she entertained until they had all left. Another one or two meant more silver and china and linen, too, if a bed was available. Often a divan had to suffice.

This warm and intimate open-house hospitality was a major factor in Rickey's baseball success, for it cemented relationships. "No other woman in the world but Jane would have put up with it more than once," he often said, and always with a sense of guilt.

The once poverty-stricken, now powerful St. Louis Cardinals accelerated Commissioner Landis' antipathy by openly challenging his prestige as titular head of organized baseball. Paradoxically, his employers, the sixteen owners of major-league teams, were following the Branch Rickey leadership as fast as they could.

Landis was openly rebuffed, because the philosophy of corporate-owned farm clubs was strengthened annually by the new minor-league administration and its legislation, and the sting went further when the major leagues incorporated the new rules into their own practices. His power of reprisal was limited to a single word, *control*. The Major League Agreement of 1921 stated that no club could control more than forty players.

For five years Landis studied every move of the minor-league farm-club growth, and intermittently issued warnings, decisions and opinions based on what he interpreted as violations of control. In so doing, moreover, he built up what amounted to a set of his own rules, reflected in letters, bulletins and stenographic reports of interviews. He then termed offenders against these rules that were his own invention "violators of the rules." He interlarded his bulletins with gamy terms like "illegal practice," "dishonest dealings," "cover up" and "secret."

The Commissioner's directives and decisions accumulated through the early 1930's and eventually hung over the owners' heads like a Damoclean sword. The baseball rules said they could. The Landis directives said they'd better not.

Branch Rickey obeyed the printed rules of baseball and so directed his field workers, a small regiment of dedicated men who beat the bushes in search of talent. They knew no office hours or season or union pay scale. They worked for Branch Rickey who "took care of them" — which meant he would do his best on salary for the next year.

They developed the "desk contract," an informal record that was card-indexed for future reference in tryout camps where, after satisfactory performance by hopeful ball players, the official contract was offered. The desk contract was the envy of less efficient organizations, and anathema to the Commissioner's office, but violated neither rule nor directive. It was one more manifestation of faith. Boys responded to the Cardinals' many opportunities to play baseball somewhere —anywhere. Bartelme's historic little wooden card-index box, taped and painted, was still used at this writing in the Cardinals' farm-club department.

Despite constant hard work, Rickey rarely avoided a chance for fun when it appeared, and no one in his organization was sacred enough to be spared. Once Blake Harper demanded a temperate manager to succeed the intemperate pilot he had fired. Rickey volunteered the man quickly. Met him that day. Who? Fred Hunter. Does he drink? Never drank a drop in his life. Played with Pittsburgh years ago. He was ideal for Harper, sight unseen.

That evening Hunter staggered into the meeting room, half fell across the threshold and caught his balance. He called for Harper in the unmistakable speech of a drunk, and said he was the new manager.

"Oh, no, Fred!" Rickey gasped. "You didn't!"

Harper jumped to his feet, grabbed Hunter's swaying shoulders, shook him indignantly, sniffed and pushed him away.

"This is a joke!" he said. "I wasn't sheriff of Sebastian County fifteen years without knowing a real drunk when I saw one."

Club presidents and managers in the Cardinal organization competed briskly, sometimes bargaining harder for players with each other than with outsiders to avoid the embarrassment of making a poor deal. During one convention

Giles sought the contract of a left-handed pitcher from Fred Ankenman. When asked $2500, Giles muttered, "You can keep him."

Ankenman later accepted $1500 for the boy's contract from Bob Bookwalter, of Danville, a Class B team, which couldn't afford as much as Rochester, Class AA. Papers for the sale were prepared and signed.

"We've had an interesting incident in our organization today," Rickey said at the evening gathering of Cardinal workers. "It would indicate that some officials of the lower-classification clubs have more sense than those of the higher." He turned to Bookwalter, "Bob, have you made any deals today?"

"Yes," said Bookwalter. "I bought a left-handed pitcher from Houston named Myers."

"Fine," said Rickey, nodding. "He'll make a good pitcher for your club. What did you pay Houston, Bob?"

"Fifteen hundred. But I don't own him any more. I sold him to Giles a while ago for twenty-five hundred."

The room grew tense, for it seemed to point up the Rochester-Houston rivalry too sharply. Giles's face reddened. Then Rickey demanded the papers, and destroyed them dramatically to end, he said, all possible internecine strife. Before the evening was over, they learned that he had promoted the maneuver as a hoax to rib all three executives.

21

In the spring of 1935, Branch Rickey's mother died of a stroke. It was not unexpected, but the cruel finality of the blow is never relieved by any amount of warning. In June a month later he was at Delaware with Jane, listening once more to graduation exercises in Gray Chapel. Proudly they watched their daughter and son march out with degrees.

Because of travel and his constant preoccupation with business, these milestones always took Branch Rickey by surprise. In December at Country Life Acres the family acknowledged his fifty-fourth birthday, but little more, because Jane and the girls were flying all over the place preparing for Mary's debut at a ball that was a highlight of the social season. Rickey was forced into serious contemplation of his daughter. She seemed the image of his Jennie Moulton at the same age. It was a shock to think Mary might marry soon and leave home.

"Those were hard days," Rickey said in tender reflection. "Mothers suffer, I know, but they live with the fear of losing their babies all their lives. It hits a busy father all at once, and right between the eyes.

"With five lovely daughters, I told myself for years that there weren't any boys in the acquaintance of the entire family who qualified for any one of them. Mary found a boy friend, or he found her, then a second, a third and a fourth. I found a lot of fault with the whole crowd.

"One evening at the dinner table the family chastised me, and my third daughter, Jane, pleaded the cause of her older sister. She asked, 'Just what kind of man *does* qualify?' Underneath my thinking, I suppose, was the belief that if I kept the standards high enough, I'd never lose a daughter. At the end of the week, I had boiled my qualifications down to three, as did Thomas Jefferson in selecting a candidate for government service.

"We had it out through another week of discussion, but I stayed by my guns and I said, 'Is he honest?' I wanted him to be respected in the community. Secondly I said, 'Is he industrious?' I thought that might mean grain, shelter, food and the respectability I had tried to provide. And my third one was, 'Is he infinitely kind?' It threw us into long discussions of health, wealth, wisdom and many things." He sighed. "Happily all five girls married young men who more than met the qualifications, which is what I really wanted, of course."

Branch Rickey's efforts to give his family a full and happy life were incessant. He encouraged all their plans for good times. The house was always full of friends and neighbors and, of course, business associates, because he brought them as close to him as possible. Pennant and World Series victory celebrations were particularly gay, but there were joyous occasions all year round.

The handsome home and beautiful surroundings Rickey had provided contributed greatly to his family's contentment. Thirty-three acres gave them all the wonderful feelings of freedom, spaciousness and privacy and plenty to do and talk about. The land was amply, if extraordinarily, "stocked" with an assortment of livestock and fowl that represented the individuality the family expressed in choosing pets. There were pheasants, turkeys raised on wire flooring, pigeons, plain and pouter; ducks and a goose on the small lake, a pea-cock, horses, ponies and about thirteen dogs. The number, naturally, varied from season to season. There was also a privileged goat, named, oddly enough, Goat. Goat had the run of the house, when he found an open door, and enjoyed himself immensely until the day he was caught on top of the piano munching a brocaded lambrequin. The girls were skilled at riding and jumping the several horses stabled in the care of Bill, the hired man. Bill was especially remembered for having all his remaining teeth extracted to escape the draft, only to learn that he was organically 4F.

22

FOR FIVE YEARS Branch Rickey's business calendar had been opened and closed by salary talks with Dizzy Dean. The 1936 discussion was the inevitable climax to the ones that preceded it. Moreover, it launched Rickey into the most eventful twelve-month of his life. Before the year was over he had expanded the farm system to a new and daring breadth by acquiring the Sacramento franchise in the Class AA Pacific Coast League. He had seen his two oldest children married, "lost" a key organization man, Warren Giles; heard flattering offers to take over three more major-league clubs, and received $25,000 for negotiating the sale of one; and he was almost killed in an automobile crash while hurrying to a tryout camp.

Rickey had a yardstick at contract time, not for spanking unsigned players, but for measuring salaries, especially of youngsters. Handling countless beginners with varying degrees of "potential," he by-passed evaluation of individual skill and, until the player became a standout, paid on the basis that "Players of like age and like experience receive like compensation."

Dizzy Dean flatly refused to permit his brother Paul to be signed on this basis. Along with Paul, ten others were to get bonuses of $450. Dizzy insisted that Paul had to have $600, or he wouldn't sign.

"Don't you realize," Rickey pleaded, "that if I give Paul

six hundred, I've got to give the others a hundred and fifty extra?"

"If you're that crazy, Mr. Rickey, go right ahead," said Dizzy.

Rickey paid Paul Dean $600, and raised each of the other contracts to the same amount.

"And I didn't have the fifteen hundred dollars, either," Rickey added in recollection. "It had to be borrowed from another item."

Another yardstick in baseball, more flexible, was based on a club's "ability to pay." A larger ball park, in the days before radio-television income became so important, permitted larger salaries. Though Rickey has operated from comparatively small ball parks, the record shows that he was neither the lowest nor the highest in club payroll, yet his teams were invariably among the youngest in the major leagues.

Over the years Rickey has bargained with thousands of players, many of them boys with great futures who promptly used their salaries to destroy their careers. He helped and rehabilitated them — the drunkards, the gamblers, the "roosters," the perennial divorcees — he came to know all types, and he heard every conceivable excuse for a raise or an advance against the future.

Rickey's final joust with Dizzy Dean occurred in January, 1936, when the pitcher, visiting Sportsman's Park for a salary talk, announced in the presence of sports writers that he would never again throw a baseball to catcher Virgil Davis in a ball game. He demanded Bill DeLancey, his battery mate of 1934, one of the greatest young catching prospects ever seen. He did not know that DeLancey's health had recently broken and that he had been voluntarily retired.

After pacing the floor at length and considering the shocking declaration, Branch Rickey wrote Dean a long letter of castigation for this reflection on his manager and team, and his disregard for his employers. The attitude could only "disturb and disrupt and disorganize the club of which you are a member."

If you agree that my position is a correct one [Rickey concluded], then you should write me an unqualified letter of assurance that you will be found this coming season with your shoulder to the wheel, supporting Mr. Frisch from the beginning to the end of the baseball season, and that you will wear your uniform constantly in the ranks, good soldier, well disciplined, pitching your head off when called upon regardless of who the catcher might be, black or white, young or old.

And I think you ought to retract the statement you made about Davis or any other derogatory statement to any player on our club.

For my part, I do not wish to discuss the terms of your contract until we have had a much better understanding about your intentions and purpose this coming year on the Cardinals team and, if we do not come to an understanding about it, then I prefer not to handle the negotiations of your contract at all. Someone else can do it.

If we do come to an understanding, it is my opinion that you and I will not have any great difficulty in arriving at satisfactory terms for your contract.

With all good wishes to you and Mrs. Dean, I am

Very truly yours,
BRANCH RICKEY
Vice-president

Within two weeks, Dean released Rickey's letter with his own reply that repeated his criticism of Davis, and cited his arm-taxing efforts on behalf of the club. He charged the Cardinals' loss of the pennant in 1935 (the Cubs closed with a surge of 21 straight victories) to the batting slumps of Medwick and Collins, and Rickey's trading Tex Carleton to the Cubs.

If you really feel that way [he began in reply to Rickey's letter] why wouldn't it be best for you to sell or trade me? I say this in all seriousness. You have been too good a friend to me, at least in the early days of my professional baseball career, for me to want to get into any row with you. And, furthermore, a row between us would cost us both money. As matters stand now [he had won 28 and lost 11 in 1935] I ought to bring a pretty good price if you would offer me for sale or trade; and I could undoubtedly get hooked up with a club that would at least feel that I was not preventing it from winning the pennant.

There was no comment from the Cardinals' office.

Dizzy Dean reached the Bradenton training camp unsigned and drove to the nice home he and his wife Pat had bought outside the city. Frisch had started workouts, and Sam Breadon, visiting, as was his custom, lived with the team.

Dean's salary for 1935 was $17,500, plus a bonus of $1000. His most lucrative single source of outside income came from General Foods, which paid him $15,000 a year to depict him in a comic strip to advertise cereal. This deal had resulted from a visit paid Rickey by his old Michigan Law School classmate, Clarence Eldridge, vice-president and advertising director of General Foods.

Within a week after reaching Bradenton, the Deans were impaled on the prongs of a dilemma. Eldridge arrived in March to say that he couldn't renew the contract with an unsigned player. Where was Branch Rickey? That was a routine question in the Cardinal organization. The anxious days rolled by. The Deans were eager to consummate the cereal deal. Eldridge was holding up a large advertising campaign, planned on the assumption that Dizzy would be signed and in uniform.

When finally reached by telephone, Rickey repeated his ultimatum, " . . . if we do not come to an understanding about it [the loyalty pledge], then I prefer not to handle the negotiations of your contract at all. Someone else can do it."

Eldridge took Rickey's figures, consulted Sam Breadon, drove out to Dean's house and presented a set of baseball contracts. Dizzy quickly signed for $27,500 in order to guarantee the renewal of the cereal deal. He wasn't permitted in uniform, however, until Rickey arrived ten days later and demanded the loyalty pledge. Dizzy complied with a brief hand-written note pledging cooperation and a willingness to throw at any catcher Frisch put behind the plate.

Rickey saw the Cardinals in a few ball games, held meetings on player distribution with Frisch and the coaches, and hurried to a tryout camp in Albany, Georgia. By coincidence, William DeWitt appeared with his bride. Rickey prevailed on DeWitt to drive him on to Columbus, Georgia, one hundred miles northwest.

They were spinning along through a drizzle when a loaded lumber truck suddenly swung out from the entrance to Fort Benning and onto the slithery highway in a slight skid. William couldn't avoid the monster and they collided almost head on. Rickey catapulted forward in the front seat. William's chest jammed against the steering wheel. He suffered lacerated knees and cut eyes. Rickey was unconscious from a head wound sustained when his forehead struck the rear-vision mirror. He was hospitalized for a short time, but he had double vision for several weeks after his release. The ailment wasn't too bad, he has said, because some of the players he watched were worth seeing double.

"The two views of the bad players really bothered me," he added wryly.

Most of the Rickeys gathered in Dayton, Ohio, in late June to see young Branch married to an Ohio Wesleyan classmate. The couple then started south to take over business management of a Class B club. Branch Rickey Jr. had completed a year of law at Michigan, but his father wasn't too hopeful of his plan to return. He had taken the boy on too many baseball trips. They were good companions, and they held each other in great respect as well as affection.

Father and son shared many experiences together and adventures like the following solidified their good relationship. They went on an alligator-hunting trip on the private lake of Otto Sens's estate near Houston. Fred Ankenman, John Crooker and Rickey took their sons in individual boats, with a boatman to pole for them. Alligators are hunted in the dark with a flashlight and rifle, and a sharp-pronged gig to haul in the quarry. After shooting two fair-sized 'gators, Rickey decided to gig one into submission while Branch, Jr., worked the flashlight.

The boatman poled apprehensively until Rickey found his 'gator. Unable to tell its size in the water, he made a perfect gig, but hoisted a massive reptile into the air.

"Keep him outa d'boat!" the poler shouted. "Keep him outa d'boat!"

The angered alligator writhed and whirled. Rickey fell back and had to drop his gig. The alligator landed in the darkness of the boat, visible only in the thin beam of Branch Jr.'s flashlight. While the boatman continued shouting the same warning, the alligator crawled toward the light. Rickey backed toward his son, grabbed him and was about to leap overboard. He paused. There was only one live alligator in the boat. The lake contained hundreds. The reptile waddled forward clumsily, mouth open and then stepped on one of the dead 'gators. With a lash of his tail and a snort, he bit into the small quarry, settling for a meal of his own kind instead of human flesh. Rickey jumped up, and in the beam of the flashlight gigged fast and effectively and killed the monster.

"Branch wasn't frightened at all," he always boasted.

"Trees in the petrified forest don't get frightened, either," young Branch replied. "I was so stiff and numb I wouldn't have felt the thing bite me."

Branch Jr. has sometimes cited an extraordinary reason for admiring his father:

"You had to respect a father who could high-jump to his top shirt button at the age of forty-seven. He cleared that height for years on Bartmer Avenue. I didn't realize that his shirt-button height remained the same. I gave up before I stopped growing."

Powel Crosley, Jr., assumed control of the Cincinnati Reds in June, 1936. Within two months Tom Conroy, club secretary, told Rickey that Larry MacPhail was through and that they wanted him as general manager to clean house and rebuild on his terms. Still in the midst of his own program, Rickey had to decline, but again he did suggest helpfully:

" . . . I think I have the man for you. Warren Giles at Rochester. He's my best. When Charlie Knapp died a few weeks ago, the International League agreed unanimously on Warren to succeed him as President. But that may not be an obstacle. He's thoroughly reliable."

Giles had recently signed an exciting new Cardinal contract to continue as president of the Rochester Red Wings for five years. In fact, he was celebrating the renewal the night the telephone calls began coming from Cincinnati, with Rickey hovering by, unwilling as always to reveal his part in initiating the interest. Strange as it sounds, and as much as Rickey liked or needed his men, he preferred to have them act independently. He and Giles were as close as friends could be, yet, as head of Cincinnati, Giles must have no ties or feeling of obligation to Rickey, a man with whom he would have to deal, or perhaps differ from, in the future. So, when Giles refused to answer the phone call at the party, Rickey took him to Country Life Acres for the night. Giles answered the Cincinnati call there.

"No, thank you, Mr. Conroy," he said. "I signed a five-year contract with Branch Rickey a few weeks ago. I'm very happy. I don't think I'll take the International League offer."

How do you tell a ten-year employee, and a friend, that he should leave you? Giles was only forty, with seventeen years of heavy baseball administration behind him. He could be of immeasurable help to baseball in the big leagues.

"You owe it to your family, Warren," Rickey said next day. "Cincinnati deserves a visit. I think you should see them."

Giles went to Cincinnati and paid a courtesy visit. When Rickey called a day later, he wasn't enthusiastic at all.

"Branch, you're just trying to get out of my contract," he accused.

"No, I'm not," Rickey argued, not daring to mention how badly he needed Giles at the time. "You should think of your future."

"I'll see them again," the reluctant executive sighed. "And, if I can make the right contract, I'll go."

Giles accepted terms that totaled twice his new Rochester salary, but still with reluctance. Working for and with Branch Rickey was, to many of his employees, a rich emotional experience. To leave his influence, guidance and companionship, even for a better job, was a difficult break to make. When Rickey told Breadon that Giles might go to Cincinnati, Breadon said, "He's not indispensable. Let him go. The only one indispensable to this organization, Branch, is you."

Shortly after Giles left, Larry MacPhail appeared unexpectedly at the Sportsman's Park office. Rickey was momentarily speechless. He presumed the redhead wanted a job, and there was none. But MacPhail had made the trip to express his thanks for all Rickey had done and tried to do for him, and to say he was returning to his family home in Grand Rapids, Michigan, where he would "rest for a year."

"Why a year?" Rickey asked. "Why not a day short of a year, or a year and a day. Better still, why put a time limit on it at all?"

The second offer to take over a rival National League club on his own terms came a few days later in mid-September. James Mulvey, vice-president of the Brooklyn Dodgers and representing his family's 25 per cent interest, called from four floors below in the Congress Hotel, Chicago, and asked Rickey to come down and see him. The job was a challenge similar to that from Cincinnati, but again Rickey declined, because of his contract with St. Louis and the unfinished job there. However, he told Mulvey he had the man for him, and he spent the rest of the meeting and all of another "selling" Larry MacPhail to him. A year later, after still another appeal by Mulvey, Rickey called MacPhail down from Michigan, and the redhead took over the Dodgers.

The third offer followed Rickey's sale of the St. Louis Browns for the widow of Phil Ball. He had healed the breach before Ball's death and, in appreciation of his salesmanship, Mrs. Ball sent him a check for $25,000 which he used to retire debts still remaining from the market crash. The purchaser, Donald Barnes, operator of a small loan banking system, wanted Rickey to take over as general manager. Rickey insisted that William DeWitt, who had developed the Barnes interest, was quite capable of running the club. And so the switchboard boy of 1916 headed a major-league operation.

On December 21 Branch Rickey made the first of his five marches down the aisle with a daughter on his arm in a wedding dress. At an improvised altar in a marquee built off the living room at Country Life Acres, he gave Mary away to a young law student. A very full year drew to a close on this happy note.

23

THE CHICAGO CUBS' need of a "stopper" on their pitching staff developed during the 1938 training season. Manager "Gabby" Hartnett so informed his boss, Philip Wrigley, who telephoned his assistant, Clarence Rowland, in the east, and said, "We have just held a meeting out here and decided that we need a 'stop pitcher.' The pitcher we want is Dizzy Dean."

"Do you know that Dean may have a sore arm?" Rowland asked.

"We discussed that, too," Wrigley said. "We still want him."

Rowland contacted Branch Rickey.

"Many people think of a 'stopper' in pitching," Rowland said in recalling the deal for Dizzy Dean, "in terms of a blazing fast ball or baffling curve. A stopper has good control. Alexander was a stopper long after losing his fast ball. Putting the ball where the batter doesn't like it is more than half the job of stopping him. We weren't sure about Dean's arm, but we knew him as one of the great control pitchers.

"I telephoned Branch Rickey to say we were interested in Dean. He said the pitcher was available, but the figure would be high, even though he had developed arm trouble. I said we were still interested if the terms were right. For straight cash, the deal would have been $250,000. We included in it two pitchers to bring the cash down to $200,000.

By adding an outfielder, we reduced the cash consideration to $185,000.

"That was all right with my people. Working out details as we drove somewhere in an automobile, I told Rickey we'd take Dean on a thirty-day trial. He flatly refused, and even wanted the arm-hazard written into the formal agreement. We settled for a written acknowledgment of the sore-arm possibility, which I gladly gave him, and closed the deal."

In the many thousands of words written of how "Rickey peddled a sore-arm pitcher to poor Wrigley," none concerned the fact that one of the pitchers Rickey got in the deal, Curt Davis, was a victim of stomach ulcers. Wrigley was pleased with the Dean purchase because the Cubs won the 1938 pennant, drew nearly a million paid admissions and reported a corporate profit. Dizzy Dean won seven games, lost only one, and walked only *eight* batters in seventy-five innings!

There was always a submerged element of shrewdness in Rickey's dealings with rival big-league clubs. It was curtained by good fellowship, laughter, "talking down" the player sought, and any device to provide time to analyze the dealer's ego or eagerness and discover what he wanted.

"I'll name two players — good players," he challenged William Benswanger, president of the Pittsburgh Pirates, "and you'll pick the wrong one for fifty thousand dollars."

Benswanger doubted that and asked to be shown.

Rickey named the two best hitters on his 1937 championship Columbus team. One was Enos Slaughter, batting champion at twenty-one. The other was Johnny Rizzo, whose .358 average put him third behind Slaughter and Jeff Heath. Both were outfielders. Rizzo was twenty-five and had seven seasons of solid .300 hitting in the minors. He seemed ready.

"I'll take Rizzo," Benswanger said.

"That's a deal," Rickey replied and shook hands. "And I think you picked the wrong one."

Rickey knew that the Pirates had too many left-handed batters. Benswanger had to choose the right-handed hitter, Rizzo, to balance his batting order. Thus, Rickey knew the "wrong" one would be picked. Rizzo was good, but Slaughter, in the little black book, had the greater future.

Commissioner Landis finally lowered the boom on the St. Louis Cardinal organization on March 23, 1938, by making free agents of seventy-four low-classification players who, he ruled, had been deprived of a chance to advance competitively because of "overlapping control." To the club, the action meant a numerical loss of players, and a waste of money in scouting expense and tryout camps. It was also a blow to the players, for at that level, none had specific playing value or any place to go. Only one caused Branch Rickey concern. Three years later he was National League batting champion: Pete Reiser.

Rickey wanted Breadon to take action, in civil court if necessary, to prove they had broken no baseball rule or law in owning the players. An action might have been very expensive and that consideration, added to the $200,000 represented by the loss of the seventy-four screened players, stayed Breadon's hand. Another factor was that the Commissioner had unlimited power in determining conduct "detrimental to baseball." As it stood, Landis had not punished or even denounced anyone. He simply freed the players. Actually Breadon saw his entire baseball structure in jeopardy. With his twenty-year accumulation of millions at stake, he refused to fight, or even take a positive stand, and a cleavage between the two partners began.

The next year the corporation reported an operating profit of $89,466. Sam Breadon declared a dividend of $101,520.

To Rickey's amazement, he then announced that all non-contract employees would take a salary reduction of 10 per cent.

"You can't do it, Sam," Rickey protested. "Those people have worked hard. I promised to take care of them."

Breadon pleaded a need for economy, but it had been rendered incongruous by the declaration of the dividend. Throughout the organization in the past, moves toward economy were humorously characterized by "Sam is turning the lights off!" But this new sweeping gesture was not humorous. It was a fork in the road to Rickey, because he knew Breadon meant it.

"Sam," Rickey pleaded earnestly, "I have made promises to certain people who trust me. I gave them my word on salary adjustments. I cannot go back on that."

"Who are they?" Breadon countered. "Maybe we can take care of a few and get you off the hook."

That was no answer. The irony was that the total sum saved by the pay cuts wouldn't equal the sale price of a second-string player's contract. Moreover, Sam hadn't been out in the field to see the sacrifices his salaried workers made to benefit his corporation . . . the long hours, the long trips, homes uprooted overnight by relocation. The loyalty of these people was held by Rickey's firm handshake and the simple phrase, "I'll take care of you."

Rickey tried again to have the pay cut rescinded. When he failed, he said quite simply and without rancor, but with unmistakable emphasis, "Sam, I will dig ditches at a dollar a day rather than work for you one minute beyond the expiration of my contract."

Being a man of his word, Rickey remained with the Cardinals until his contract had expired three years later. "His boys" worked along with him, despite another 10 per cent salary cut in 1940, to help attain the only goal they knew: a championship baseball organization.

Rickey's work after the "sewer digging" declaration is typified by an occasion which found him in the grandstand at Hollywood, Florida, in early 1941 with Barney Shotton, watching minor-league hopefuls.

"I told this boy to be sure and take batting practice," Shotton said, as a slender left-hander stood at the plate. "He's the pitcher who hurt his shoulder at Daytona Beach last fall playing the outfield."

After seeing twenty-year-old Stanley Musial swing a bat, both observers agreed his pitching could be forgotten. The question was, could he throw well enough to support his hitting? Regardless, Musial was henceforth an outfielder.

"Some kind of sixth sense warned me whenever Mr. Rickey was in the ball park," said Musial long after he had become a Cardinal immortal. "I always tried like the devil to impress him after he had pleaded with Springfield to take me on trial, to justify his faith in me. I think that's why I could 'hit over my head' against his teams after he left St. Louis. If he came to our games every day, I don't think they'd ever get me out."

Musial, "last of Rickey's Cardinals," hit .379 in 87 games after becoming an outfielder for Springfield, Missouri, in 1941. Moved to Rochester the same year, he hit .326 in 54 games. When the season ended there, he transferred to St. Louis in time to help the Cardinals' 1941 pennant fight by hitting .426 in 12 games.

Rickey's player transfers to the parent team after the close of minor-league seasons were always the scourge of pennant contenders, but never more so than in 1941. Eddie Dyer had managed Houston to its third straight Texas League championship. Burt Shotton led Columbus to the American

Association flag, took the playoffs and defeated Montreal in the Little World Series. Rochester didn't win, but delivered a half dozen major-league prospects who later helped make Cardinal history.

All baseball knew of the cleavage within the Cardinals front office, and marveled the more at Branch Rickey's continuing domination of National League baseball. Rickey-trained Giles had built a two-time pennant winner for Cincinnati in 1939–40. By 1941, the Rickey-trained MacPhail had built well enough to bring Brooklyn its first pennant since 1920, but a new team of young Cardinals chased the Dodgers to the wire.

Next year, Rickey's last in St. Louis, his team would win, and it would be good enough to win or contend strongly for many years. He left behind him the greatest collection of playing strength in the league's history. And fifteen years later, the outstanding St. Louis Cardinal, seeking his seventh batting championship and playing a record number of consecutive games for the league, is Stan Musial, "the last of Rickey's boys."

24

BRANCH RICKEY began a new life in 1942, his sixty-first year, by taking over the Brooklyn Dodgers as president and general manager. His energy and outlook, however, belied his age. He was active, virile, quick of step, and idealistic. He was overweight, but his figure had the square firmness of a former athlete, and there wasn't a strand of gray in his full crop of brown hair. His strong voice spoke of a positive program, based on youth and hope.

In this respect, he was a living contradiction of the times. America was fighting World War II. All available boys had been earmarked for military service. Other leaders in organized baseball huddled under a canopy of general retrenchment to wait out the manpower shortage. Rickey considered several offers, and boldly signed a five-year contract at $50,000 a year plus a liberal expense account and a bonus based on increased attendance above 600,000. Then he set out to earn it by building a new and better ball club. Before his contract expired, he had built another baseball dynasty.

His employers were three ownership factions, two with 25 per cent interests, owned by the heirs of Ed and Steve McKeever; and one with 50 per cent, this last held in trust for the heirs of Charles H. Ebbets by the Brooklyn Trust Company, of which George V. McLaughlin was president. The bank controlled policy. Rickey's first move toward putting his new ideas to work was to sound out McLaughlin, a former police commissioner of New York City and a power in state banking and politics. He asked McLaughlin to assemble the board members of the ball club as early as possible in 1943. Rickey said he would discuss the mass scouting of players.

"That might include a Negro player or two," he concluded.

McLaughlin eyed Rickey for an instant and said, "I don't see why not. You might come up with something. If you find the man who is better than the others, you'll beat it." As Rickey nodded, he added bluntly, "And if you don't, you're sunk!"

McLaughlin arranged a noon luncheon for five in a private dining room at the New York Athletic Club. Present in addition to Rickey were McLaughlin and George Barnewall, of the bank; Joe Gilleaudeau, of the Ebbets interest; and Jim Mulvey of the Steve McKeever interest. The food was good, but they had to digest an unpalatable analysis of their team. The Dodgers of 1941 had brought Brooklyn its first pennant in twenty years, but they had been overhauled by the Cardinals in 1942.

Rickey forecast a dismal future for the Dodgers, called most of them old and finished as big-leaguers. They couldn't possibly beat the strong and speedy team he had left in St. Louis. Despite the military draft, the Cardinals would still be better than any other National League team for many years. However, he had bold and costly plans for making Brooklyn supreme. While other clubs dismissed their scouts and sat out the war, he would hire more scouts and find players as young as sixteen — yes, fifteen.

Would he sign these boys?

"Yes, sir!" he declared. "And if the war continues past the two-and-a-half-year mark, we will lose them to the military at a cost of a hundred thousand dollars."

This was not the usual "line" of a new general manager. With the fact in mind that baseball, because of the war, might be discontinued, it was frightening.

"On the other hand," Rickey went on, "if the war ends within two or two and a half years, the Brooklyn Baseball Club will possess so large a complement of youth that our position for the future will be assured. By moving fast and carefully, we could be in an enviable position."

He revealed his plan to beat the bushes and sign whatever good players turned up, even if they happened to be Negroes. McLaughlin helpfully took up the cudgel and pinpointed the key factor, "Get the right ball player and the thing is a success." Rickey added that his scouts had been getting the right players for years. A man's color did not determine his batting power, running speed or fielding skill.

After a long and lively discussion, the directors approved all phases of Rickey's plans 100 per cent, although Gilleaudeau asked what the "real motive" was behind the scouting and signing of Negroes. All were pledged to utmost secrecy, and cautioned against mentioning the possibility even to their families. They agreed and Branch Rickey was "cut loose" to rebuild the Brooklyn Dodgers to his own specifications.

More important, he had cleared the first hurdle, or steppingstone, of six that comprised his program for introducing a Negro player to organized baseball. The six steps were:

1. The backing and sympathy of the Dodgers' directors and stockholders, whose investment and civic standing had to be considered and protected.
2. Picking a Negro who would be the right man on the field.
3. Picking a Negro who would be the right man off the field.

4. A good reaction from press and public.

5. Backing and thorough understanding from the Negro race, to avoid misrepresentation and abuse of the project.

6. Acceptance of the player by his teammates.

Many interpretations, hasty and wrong, have been advanced to analyze or impugn Branch Rickey's motive for scouting and signing Negro baseball players. Most of them fall short, because they are based on the assumption that his nature and thinking are deep and complex. Actually his erudition and easy command of a polysyllabic vocabulary cloak thinking that is, more often than not, simple and basic.

There was neither complexity nor a sense of crusading in Rickey's plan to sign Negro players. Legally trained, he thinks through to the rightness or wrongness of a problem without many tangents into doubt. His beliefs are thus unshakably firm, and immune to peripheral challenges. He found not a shred of law or reason to prevent Negroes from providing the playing skill which he needed desperately. Religious teaching had imparted the meaning of "In my Father's house are many mansions." He had found the words true when he taught two colored children without incident at the Turkey Creek school.

At Ohio Wesleyan he had learned that skin pigmentation does not affect athletic skill. Charlie Thomas had more than skill; he had shown great aptitude by changing from the outfield to the heavier responsibility of catching. Through Thomas, Rickey had learned how much racial discrimination could hurt. Whether he reacted against it from a sense of outraged justice, or compassion, he did react, and Dr. Thomas, now a dentist in New Mexico, says of those early years:

"From the very first day I entered Ohio Wesleyan, Branch Rickey took special interest in my welfare. As the first Negro player on any of its teams, some of the fellows didn't welcome me too kindly, though there was no open opposition. But I always felt that Branch set them straight. During the three years that I was at OWU, no man could have been treated better. When we went on our trips, Rickey was the first one to see if I was welcome in the hotel where we were to stop. On several occasions, he talked the management into allowing me to occupy a double room with him and his roommate, Barney Russell."

A most unforgettable scene took place at the Oliver Hotel in South Bend, Indiana, 1904, when a frightened supervisor halted the incoming baseball team in the lobby. The colored boy could not go upstairs. Rickey sent his student manager to the Y.M.C.A. to look for a vacancy.

"Maybe it would be better if I went back home," Thomas suggested.

"No, no," Rickey protested. "We'll be all right."

Rickey persuaded the hotel manager to let Thomas wait upstairs in his room. There the colored player broke down. His 220-pound body hunched over in a gesture that Rickey never forgot. As he rubbed hard from wrist to fingertips, tears from his grimacing face splashed against his large hands.

"Black skin . . . " he murmured in a half sob. "Black skin . . . Oh, if I could only make 'em white!"

Forty years later Rickey could easily ignore the charge of having ulterior motives in hiring Negroes, for he was well insulated by his simple premise, often stated, "I want players to help me win a pennant in Brooklyn." No one could question his desire to win, or to make victory paramount, or his right to win with any kind of eligible player. He never spoke of social consequences. He had firm beliefs about the equality of man, but they were never a factor in his decision. The sole issue was a colored player's ability to play organized baseball.

Scouting methods at the start were necessarily unique. Being orthodox invited risk of his secret leaking out. Two of his earliest searchers were professors with whom he confided in 1944 to obtain information from Mexico and the Caribbean countries. Besides players, he neded sociological information. Cuba still had a class system.

One of these emissaries was Dr. José Seda, of the University of Puerto Rico, who scouted his own country and Mexico. Another was an Ohio Wesleyan fraternity brother, Dr. Robert M. Haig, of the Columbia University faculty. Haig made a report on Cuban baseball after extended visits with university people on the Island.

A process of elimination at first, it was more of a survey than scouting, but it gave Rickey valuable information without revealing his goal. Pressure groups were forming fast to force racial issues from all avenues. Rickey deplored the thought of force as a factor in his objective.

Without a hint of his plan, Rickey discussed the Negro's right to play organized baseball, and openly espoused it. While speaking before the Brooklyn Rotary Club in 1944, he said, "The cause of prohibition, a most worthy one, was thrown back a hundred years by the Volstead Act. Very possibly the introduction of a Negro into baseball, even without force, might similarly throw back their cause of racial equality a quarter century or more."

Two of his family who knew of his plan were unable to encourage him. In understandable fear of inevitable controversy, Jane Rickey pleaded, "Why should you be the one to do it? Haven't you done enough for baseball? Can't someone else do something for a change?"

"It means we'll be cut out of scouting in the South,"

Branch Jr. said with a sigh. Much of his own hard-won results, started when he joined the Dodgers under MacPhail
in 1939, would be jeopardized and perhaps nullified.

"For a while, yes," the father replied, "not forever. Alexander Pope covers it mighty well in his *Essay on Man.*" He
paused to line up the words. "They don't want Negroes in
baseball, but when it happens, 'We first endure, then pity,
then embrace.'"

Rickey's opinion of organized baseball's failure to employ
Negro players rarely passed the point of regret at possibly
missing an outstanding performer. To him, all else was
secondary to that need in baseball. But he was outspoken
on the subject of the two segregated leagues, the Negro National and the Negro American. Because they were essentially fronts for a monopolistic game-booking enterprise,
controlled by 15-percenters in Chicago, Philadelphia and
New York, he termed them "in the zone of a racket." They
lacked uniform contracts and were loosely operated.

Major-league baseball participated in this exploitation of
Negro players by hiring out their ball parks for a high guarantee against a high percentage of the gate. Thus, it was
mere lip service in April, 1945, at Cleveland when the major
leagues appointed a two-man committee to "study" the
colored baseball situation with two Negro leaders of their
own choosing. Larry MacPhail, new president of the Yankees, and Branch Rickey headed the committee.

Feeling that little would be accomplished by such a committee, Rickey helped form and finance a third Negro circuit, called the United States League. It would have teams in
key cities, one of which would be Brooklyn, where the
"Brown Dodgers" would play at Ebbets Field. The team
also would serve as an ideal camouflage for open scouting
of Negro players. As soon as the new league met to organize,
Rickey turned several scouts loose — George Sisler, Wid

Matthews, Tom Greenwade and Clyde Sukeforth. They may have secretly suspected Rickey's true motive, but they did not know.

Meanwhile politicians were becoming increasingly Negro-conscious. There was a Fair Employment Practice Committee for national activity. New York State had an Ives-Quinn Law operating through a committee appointed by Governor Dewey. Mayor LaGuardia added a subcommittee for baseball to his Anti-Discrimination Committee. He persuaded MacPhail and Rickey to sidetrack their baseball-study assignment to become part of his ten-man subcommittee.

Rickey met these rising social-minded forces by accelerating his own activities. He had reports on Negro prospects, but his concern was the second and third condition of his six-point program — the right man on the field, and the right man off the field. Wendell Smith, a Pittsburgh *Courier* sports writer, had taken three colored ball players for tryouts with the Boston Red Sox. Rickey met Smith during a visit with Mrs. Ethel Vann, publisher of the Negro newspaper, and learned of the Boston candidates, Marvin Williams, Sam Jethroe and Jackie Robinson. He had these names, plus "Showboat" Thomas, Piper Davis, Satchel Paige, Silvio Garcia, Josh Gibson and many others. The name mentioned most often was Jackie Robinson. Rickey sent first one scout and then another to study him.

In late August, 1945, he summoned Clyde Sukeforth and said, "The Kansas City Monarchs are playing in Chicago next Friday night at Comiskey Park, Clyde. I want you to see that game and especially a shortstop named Robinson. There is some doubt as to whether he has a really good arm. Speak to him before the game and ask him to throw the ball overhand from 'the hole' in practice. We have good reports on this fellow."

Tom Greenwade called him the best bunter he ever saw.

Sisler said he could make it at second base, but not at short on account of his arm. Matthews said he protected the strike zone and was "one of the best two-strike hitters he had seen in a long time."

"If you like his arm, Clyde," Rickey continued, "and if his schedule will permit, bring him in. Get him away from his teammates so that nobody will know what you're talking about. I want absolute secrecy."

Sukeforth located Robinson, but the player had recently fallen on his shoulder and wasn't in the lineup. They met downtown after the game. The scout's record of the trip read in part:

> I asked him why he was discharged from the army and a number of other questions for information we may need. It seemed an old football ankle injury had brought about his discharge, but, as it proved, it did not bother him. I reasoned that, if he wasn't going to play for a week, this would be an ideal time to bring him in to Brooklyn. I had him make a few stretches into the hole to his right and come up throwing. His moves looked good. I wired the office.

Jackie Robinson remembers only patches of his three dramatic hours in the office of Branch Rickey on Tuesday morning, August 28, 1945. He recalls the illuminated goldfish tank and how much like a fish he felt. He remembers Rickey's bushy brows, and the large, gnarled fingers lighting a cigar, and the heavyset figure rocking back and forth in a large leather swivel chair behind a massive walnut desk. Rickey's voice, emphasis and the mounting tension in the opening seconds were overpowering. The interview began with salutations and inquiry about his game and whether or not he had a girl, then, "Are you under contract to the Kansas City Monarchs?"

"No, sir," Robinson replied quickly. "We don't have contracts."

"Do you have any agreements — written or oral — about how long you will play for them?"

"No, sir, none at all. I just work from payday to payday."

Rickey nodded and his bushy brows mashed into a scowl. He toyed with the ever-present cigar, seeking the right words. "Do you know why you were brought here?"

"Not exactly. I heard something about a colored team at Ebbets Field. That it?"

"No . . . that isn't it." Rickey studied the dark face, the half-open mouth, the widened and worried eyes. Then he said, "You were brought here, Jackie, to play for the Brooklyn organization. Perhaps on Montreal to start with — "

"Me? Play for Montreal?" the player gasped.

Rickey nodded. "If you can make it, yes. Later on — also if you can make it — you'll have a chance with the Brooklyn Dodgers."

Robinson could only nod at this point.

"I want to win pennants and we need ballplayers!" Rickey whacked the desk. He sketched the efforts and the scope of his two-year search for players of promise. "Do *you* think you can do it? Make good in organized baseball?"

Robinson shifted to relieve his mounting tension.

"If . . . if I got the chance," he stammered.

"There's more here than just *playing*, Jackie," Rickey warned. "I wish it meant only hits, runs and errors — things you can see in a box score . . ."

Rickey produced Papini's *Life of Christ* from the drawer of his desk. He often read the book himself as a guide to humility. It seemed appropriate to read aloud from it to a Negro baseball player who might become the first of his race to enter organized baseball.

"Can you do it? Can you do it?" Rickey asked over and over.

Shifting nervously, Robinson looked from Rickey to Sukeforth as they talked of his arms and legs and swing and courage. Did he have the guts to play the game no matter what happened? Rickey pointed out the enormity of the responsibility for all concerned: owners of the club, Rickey, Robinson and all baseball. The opposition would shout insults, come in spikes first, throw at his head.

"Mr. Rickey," Robinson said, "they've been throwing at my head for a long time."

Rickey's voice rose. "Suppose I'm a player . . . in the heat of an important ball game." He drew back as if to charge at Robinson. "Suppose I collide with you at second base. When I get up, I yell, 'You dirty, black son of a — ' " He finished the castigation and added calmly, "What do you do?"

Robinson blinked. He licked his lips and swallowed.

"Mr. Rickey," he murmured, "do you want a ballplayer who's afraid to fight back?"

"I want a ballplayer with guts enough *not* to fight back!" Rickey exclaimed almost savagely. He paced across the floor and returned with finger pointing. "You've got to do this job with base hits and stolen bases and fielding ground balls, Jackie. *Nothing else!*"

He moved behind his big desk again and faced the cornered Robinson. He posed as a cynical clerk in a southern hotel who not only refused him a room, but cursed him as he did so. What would Robinson do? He posed as a prejudiced sportswriter, ordered to turn in a twisted story, full of bias and racial animosity. How would Robinson answer the sportswriter? He ordered the player from imaginary dining rooms. He jostled him in imaginary hotel lobbies, railroad stations. What would Robinson do?

"Now I'm playing against you in a World Series!" Rickey stormed and removed his jacket for greater freedom. Robinson's hands clenched, trembled from the rising tension. "I'm a hotheaded player. I want to win that game, so I go into you spikes first, but you don't give ground. You stand there and you jab the ball into my ribs and the umpire yells, 'Out!' I flare up — all I see is your face — that black face right on top of me — "

Rickey's bespectacled face, glistening with sweat, was inches from Robinson's at this point. He yelled into the motionless mask, "So I haul off and punch you right in the cheek!"

An oversized fist swung through the air and barely missed Robinson's face. He blinked, but his head didn't move.

"What do you do?" Rickey roared.

"Mr. Rickey," he whispered, "I've got two cheeks. That it?"

At the end of three hours, the admonition, *You can't fight back!* had been established as the only foundation on which Robinson's move into organized baseball could be built. Before leaving, he signed a typewritten agreement of two paragraphs; the first set forth that Robinson would accept a bonus of $3500 and a salary of $600 a month for signing a contract with the Montreal Royals, which Rickey promised orally to offer on or before December 1. The second paragraph indemnified Rickey against any possible claim that Robinson was under oral or written contract to anybody.

"You'll have to tell about this," Rickey said, "or bust with the news. Tell your mother, or your girl, perhaps. No one else."

Rickey had planned to hold off announcing the signing of Robinson until after the football season. The news value of the announcement would increase during the winter and whet interest in the Dodgers' spring training. The sharpening focus of attention on the Negro, however, produced by the several and competing committees forced Rickey's hand.

Rickey resigned from the Mayor's Committee, for, with the secret signing of a Negro player, he felt that his position among the group was not a sincere one. The committee secretary, Dr. Dan Dodson, a tall Texan, and a New York University professor of sociology, had been a most helpful confidant in the Robinson matter. Now he became a barometer measuring surrounding pressures, chiefly political, for the cause of "Negro welfare" intensified as the November election drew near. Soon the question of the Negro in baseball was like a bone among dogs.

The Ives-Quinn Law Committee called upon the three major-league clubs in the New York area not to discriminate on the basis of race, color or creed in hiring or firing employees. A request for signed pledges from three club officials went begging.

Mayor LaGuardia publicized his anti-discrimination position on his Sunday radio broadcasts and hinted of his committee's effective work toward breaking down baseball barriers to the Negro. At this point an elderly committee member, Judge Edward Lazansky, confided to Rickey, "Branch, our committee's an election football!"

In mid-October the Mayor asked the committee to let him report by radio that "baseball would shortly begin signing Negro players, and that the fact resulted directly from the work of the Mayor's Committee on Anti-Discrimination." Rickey replied that he would like another week and asked the Mayor if he could postpone the broadcast. LaGuardia agreed to do so.

Rickey then wired Robinson to fly directly to Montreal. There, on October 23, 1945, Jackie Robinson signed a contract to play for the Montreal Royals. By releasing the news about Robinson before the Mayor's speech, Rickey's purpose would be clear to the nation: This record holder in track and field and college basketball, star of college football, lieutenant in the United States Army, had entered organized baseball solely on his merits as a great athlete.

25

THE SUDDEN and dramatic breach of organized baseball's invisible color line in 1945 drew excited comment throughout the hemisphere. No one was without an opinion. The nation's newspapers, in the main, were favorable. Countless editorials heralded Branch Rickey's historic move as the personification of democracy in action. Hasty outbursts of indignation and derision came from individuals defending selfish interests, or expressing fear of the "unknown" that so often hobbles change or progress. Among these was a premature claim of contract violation by the Kansas City Monarchs, soon withdrawn. Minor-league President Bramham emitted a colorful cry of "carpetbagger." Popular "Dixie" Walker, Brooklyn rightfielder, made a prophetic comment, "As long as he's not with the Dodgers, I'm not worried."

All the tumult and shouting, however, dwarfed a fact far more important to Branch Rickey than acquiring a ballplayer with dark skin. Jackie Robinson, though twenty-six, was part of his long-range gamble on youth and America's ability to win wars. Japan's surrender in August, 1945, ended hostilities and made Rickey's scheme a dazzling success. For two years his large staff of scouts had acquired teen-age baseball prodigies in a steady stream. With the war over, the "large complement of youth" put the Brooklyn Dodgers in the "enviable position" he had dared mention to the club directors in January, 1943.

These embryonic ball players first appeared in the war-time training camp at Bear Mountain, New York, in 1944. After being screened, the most promising of them were turned over to Jake Pitler, long a Dodger coach, but then manager of Newport News in the Piedmont League. There the harassed Pitler struggled with teen-age tempers and pouting as he taught baseball regimentation and field fundamentals.

"Actually I was little more than a glorified baby sitter," he laughed in recollection. "We carried a full supply of comic books and almost no shaving soap. I had to keep one sore-arm player who couldn't run, hit or throw, because he was the only one old enough to drive the bus. Once I fined Duke Snider for protesting a 'take' sign and kicking the water bucket in a rage, and he wired the Brooklyn office to please put him somewhere else."

Two fifteen-year-olds from Pitler's 1944 team never made the grade, but eight who later reached the big leagues were: Duke Snider, Bobby Morgan, Buddy Hicks, Clem Labine and Steve Lembo, all seventeen; Tommy Brown and Preston Ward, sixteen.

Throughout 1944 and 1945 operation of the parent Dodger team, managed by Leo Durocher, was devoted to the change-over from age to youth. And each change brought sharp reaction from loyal Brooklyn fans loath to lose heroes and familiar faces. They picked up derisive nicknames for Rickey from the press — "Mahatma" and "Deacon" and "hard-shelled Methodist." The hustling teen-age players were labeled "Mother Rickey's Chickens." Rickey was called the "Old Woman in the Shoe" and a violator of child-labor laws. One Brooklyn group burned him in effigy after he traded Dolph Camilli. When he tried to explain this and other moves, his erudite explanations were dismissed as double talk and his office was called "The Cave of the Winds."

Of Camilli, Rickey said he "can no longer pull to his power," meaning he couldn't get the bat around quickly enough to meet the ball at peak strength. "I'd rather trade a player a year too soon than a year too late," he continued; "the anesthetic player can ruin you." An anesthetic player was Rickey's unique term for the veteran whose brilliant past lulls the manager into thinking a position is adequately protected when, blind to the veteran's declining ability, he should be making a change.

The war's end found Rickey prepared in every way for full speed ahead. He not only had the young and green players; he had prepared places to put them and the returnees from the war. A purchase option on Montreal, top-classification club, was activated to make it the main incubator. Working agreements were drawn with St. Paul and with Edgar and Robert Allen after they transferred from Little Rock to Mobile in the Southern Association. When the Texas League, suspended by war, resumed operation, Rickey arranged a corporate purchase of the Dodgers' first wholly owned subsidiary. For $74,000 he got the Fort Worth franchise, ball park and twenty-two acres for parking space.

An enlarged staff to handle all this activity had gradually come to Branch from St. Louis and Columbus. Of greatest concern to Rickey during these years of planning and building was his younger brother. Frank had scouted effectively for seventeen years in St. Louis. He had a way with people and combined a little personal horse-trading with his scouting.

"I'm on the trail of a first baseman around here," he might begin with a baseball-minded farmer, and then he would ease into a discourse on the futility of working "a piece of ground like this with no mules."

"Mules! I couldn't afford mules."

"I'll send you a pair. Just take care of them and use them

all you want. I'll be around from time to time. Meanwhile, try and locate that young first baseman, will you?"

Frank had already bought the green mules and needed only a place to put them for a year or two, until they were properly broken. A team of well-fed and farm-broken mules was a gilt-edged investment. He had made a friend, developed an area scout or "bird dog," and soon would have a pair of seasoned mules.

At one time eight of the nine St. Louis Cardinals starting against the Yankees in a World Series were "Frank Rickey boys." Branch Rickey thought it best for Frank to scout for another organization when he took over in Brooklyn. Instead of a letter of recommendation, he prepared a list of seventy-seven players Frank had discovered or signed during his tenure with the Cardinals — Enos Slaughter, Martin Marion, Walter Alston, Bill DeLancey, Jimmy Brown, Max Lanier, Taft Wright, Preacher Roe, Burgess Whitehead and so on. Even more impressive was a list of twenty-five contracts sold from among "Frank's players." These sales, topped by $60,000 for Worthington and $52,500 for Johnny Mize, increased the Cardinals treasury by $428,500 in cash and fourteen new players.

Only an estimate of the total revenue from contract sales by Branch Rickey during his twenty-five years at St. Louis is possible. They insured economic survival when fluctuating gate receipts failed to offset the expense of a large scouting staff and the minor-league operations that at one time totaled thirty-one clubs of all classifications.

"Offhand, I'd say the total would be somewhere between two and a half and three million dollars," Rickey once guessed. "Up to the time I left. Sam made some sales later."

The number of administrative problems confronting Rickey during these years of reconstructing the Dodgers was unbelievable. The business schedule he carried, on slips of paper and old envelopes and in his head, was incredibly varied and full.

A call to Cleveland in April, 1945, was for a special meeting of major-league heads to elect a successor to the late Commissioner Landis. Landis' distinguished life had ended six months earlier, a few days after his seventy-eighth birthday. Before leaving, Rickey met privately with Horace Stoneham of the Giants, Robert Carpenter of the Phillies, and Lou Perini of the Braves. They agreed to back Ford Frick, the National League president, as first choice, and James A. Farley, Postmaster General in the first two Roosevelt administrations, as alternate. They could count on each other to hold a position on either candidate until the twelve votes necessary to elect were lined up.

Other club owners had similar ideas, for the chairman of the "weeding out" committee had been unable to present a suitably small number of candidates. When challenged, he offered more than a dozen, including Frick and Farley, Thomas E. Dewey, Justice Douglas, Frank J. Lausche, J. Edgar Hoover, Senator Albert B. Chandler, and Robert E. Hannegan, then Postmaster General.

Frick's anticipated candidacy was quickly talked down. Before Farley's backers could enlist strength, one club owner read a cruel dossier that questioned the man's fitness, depreciated him personally, socially and politically, and disparaged his integrity. While the others sat in amazed silence, two club owners protested quickly with, "That's not the Jim Farley I know!" and "Where did you get that thing?" The reader, admitting the paper had been prepared by professionals in Washington, D.C., "withdrew" the report, but a most effective job of hatchet work had been done.

Hannegan's strength now rose, but some were unfriendly to

the St. Louisan, whereupon the strength of a dark horse, Senator "Happy" Chandler, began to increase fast. Hannegan and Chandler ran even for two ballots. On the next vote, Chandler emerged with eight of the sixteen. Hannegan had five. Larry MacPhail then said, "Well, if you're going to elect Chandler, why waste time? Let's make it unanimous!"

From July through September of 1945, Rickey taxed his time and health to the limit with the most important negotiations of his career. When they ended, however, he owned 25 per cent of the Dodgers, which was pooled with quarter ownerships of his two associates, Walter O'Malley, an attorney; and John L. Smith, a Brooklyn chemical manufacturer, as a pledge against a note to the Brooklyn Trust Company, which financed the purchase. The long ordeal left Rickey weary and with less strength than he realized. He was also "flat broke," having sold his Air Reduction stock, the charred remains of Country Life Acres, half consumed by fire in late 1943, and pledged his life insurance. He was in debt for more than $300,000 but happy that his work and effort at last could go toward building something for himself.

December brought the minor-league convention in Columbus, Ohio, where he continued his heavy program, took on more problems and new and increasing tensions. Another major-minor agreement was discussed, as were the complicated matter of the new cash bonus rulings for free agents, keeping hands off high school players until graduation, the extent of the new commissioner's authority, and the reclassification of leagues.

Rickey rushed on to the major-league meetings at Chicago. Days and nights there were equally full with arguments, rulemaking, the nervous excitement of a hundred player trades never made, and then, suddenly, during a pause in the joint meeting of both leagues, the terrible strain exacted its toll.

Rickey leaned toward William DeWitt, who sat across the table.

"William," he whispered hoarsely, "I'm in terrible trouble. The room is going round. You're going round. If I get up, I'll fall and make a fool of myself. I've got to do something."

"What . . . what can I do, Mr. Rickey?"

Rickey blinked and shook his head, filled now with stark apprehension. His mother had suffered such a seizure, and his brother Orla a fatal one only recently.

"Just come around . . . to my side of the table . . . and stand close," he beckoned. William hurried over as directed. The others in the room had not noticed and continued their conversations. "When I get up, sort of help me, casually. I don't want to worry anybody. You hold me and be ready to take all my weight, because I don't know if I can make it."

He struggled and pushed himself up from his chair, and stood there unsteadily. As though he had entered a large whirling ball, everything — people, table, candelabra, floor — was circling in endless circumference. He took a step from the table. William clutched him tightly and bore the weight.

"Fine. Now point me toward the door and the elevators. I can't see clearly. Don't stop for anything or anybody. If you stay with me, I think I can make it. William, I'm sick!"

Chicago doctors disagreed on the cause of his trouble, but agreed that he needed rest and quiet.

Young Branch got him onto a train the next day. In the privacy of his drawing room, he battled dizziness and nausea. He suffered a second and more serious attack. On reaching New York, he was rushed by ambulance to the Jewish Hospital in Brooklyn and taken to the emergency room as "John Doe."

He was transferred the next day to the Peck Memorial Hospital. The family doctor, Dominick Rossi, called three specialists who, like himself, were unable to diagnose Rickey's ailment.

"I was never able to understand," Rickey said later, "why two weeks in the hospital were necessary — with continuous examinations, X-rays, cardiograms, and calls from one physician after another only to learn that no one seemed to identify the ailment. I was completely mystified and could not help insisting that I must have a brain tumor.

"Finally, Dr. Rossi brought in a great brain specialist and this proved to be Dr. Jefferson Browder. It was an immediate consolation to have him tell me the trouble and what to do about it. He kept me in the middle of the road. No longer did I think of any change in my work or plans. The whole experience was an upset, but a temporary one."

Rickey was host to a permanent, unwelcome guest, Ménière's disease. Happily dormant at times, it could strike him down without warning. The exact cause of the disease is unknown, but it is usually associated with deafness. Rickey was almost deaf in the left ear, indicating, he was told, a breakdown of the auditory branch of the eighth cranial nerve. Disintegration of the second branch, or vestibular segment, caused his imbalance and dizziness during sudden movements of head and body. The ailment was his boss. If he did not pursue a more peaceful, quiet and normal life, he would pay a stiff price in enforced confinement and worse discomfort.

Rickey couldn't afford that price. Yet, facing what he believed was the most important year of his life in the upcoming 1946, he tried, even in the hospital, to plan ahead. One day while there, he jotted down a list of forty-five "must" items, personal and professional chores and favors, to be tackled as soon as he could get out. So varied was the list that he seemed to be seeking the answer to his illness through restlessness.

Once on his feet, he played cat and mouse with his unwelcome guest, working at full speed between warnings. But it took over before the end of the year in the street near his office. The earth became a giant pinwheel. Faces, buildings and vehicles became a whirling mass of foggy shadows. He grabbed the nearest anchorage, a lamppost, and extended a trembling hand to the passing silhouettes.

"Help me," he pleaded, clutching and swaying. "Help me . . ." He asked politely until one presumptuous passerby growled, "Go on home where you belong, you drunken bum." That did it. This time he shouted, "Will somebody help me!" Jim Ferrante, of the Dodger office, was passing, heard the call and guided him to the sanctuary of a cigar store. Five minutes later, the ticket department telephoned his office for information. The *Daily News* had called to verify a tip that Rickey had suffered a serious heart attack.

Rickey's expectation of a tremendous year in 1946 was fulfilled. By February it was clear to the baseball world that he had put together another organization to rival the one he had left in St. Louis — right down to the Knothole Club. MacPhail had adopted the idea and Rickey expanded his work through civic and educational leaders. He had even initiated, with the Brooklyn *Daily Eagle,* a youth program called "Brooklyn Against the World." Newspapers in other cities sent teen-age stars to play sand-lot teams from Brooklyn and Long Island.

Eastern sports writers got their first close look at the Cardinal-type mass training at Daytona Beach and Sanford, Florida. In addition to many techniques of training that were peculiarly Rickey's, they also saw baseball's original pitching machine, brainchild of his St. Louis banking friend, Byron Moser. It employed the principle of the crossbow.

Electric power pulled back a pronged receptacle which held a baseball against a rubber strip. When released, it propelled the ball accurately to any desired spot 60 feet distant.

"The thing can throw twenty-five hundred baseballs a day," Rickey explained to the writers. "One pitcher averages one hundred twenty-five throws in a nine-inning game. This equals twenty pitchers working nine innings. And it takes only one man, who doesn't have to be a pitcher, to operate it."

Jackie Robinson, of the Montreal Royals, was at Sanford with his bride. The second Negro signed in organized baseball, John Wright, a pitcher, was also at Sanford. Wendell Smith, the Pittsburgh *Courier* sports writer, was on hand as guest of the Dodgers, as were most correspondents, to cover the camp. Rickey had followed the signing of Robinson and Wright with contracts for Don Newcombe, a pitcher; Roy Campanella, a catcher; and Roy Partlow, a pitcher. Those first five Negroes in organized baseball were paid a total of $13,500 in bonuses and monthly salaries aggregating $1800. Rickey could have signed all of them without bonuses, but he preferred to regard them in the same light as any other player.

It was never Branch Rickey's intention to flout laws in segregation states, use force of any kind or even embarrass municipalities. With this in mind, he had located the Robinsons with a private family in Sanford, and kept the address a secret to forestall off-field interviews. He understood Southern thinking and tradition in this respect, but felt that a baseball diamond would be excepted.

Some of Rickey's own workers with Southern backgrounds were subordinating their feelings to the welfare of his project and he appreciated it deeply. He wasn't quite prepared, however, for the reaction of his Montreal manager, Clay Hopper, a respected citizen of Greenwood, Mississippi. Sitting beside him at a practice game, Rickey jabbed Hopper's ribs when Robinson made a spectacular play and exclaimed that "no other human being could have made that play." Hopper turned and asked quite sincerely, "Mistuh Rickey, do you really think a nigguh's a human being?"

Only then did Rickey realize the priceless contribution that just one man would have to make in helping Robinson to succeed in organized baseball.

Testing Negro players under competitive conditions in the South was thwarted repeatedly by officials smarting under Rickey's unwitting affront to local segregation habits, if not laws. Clearance for Montreal to play Jersey City in Jacksonville supposedly had been obtained. But at game time, a city official cited by-laws against using public property for mixed competition. A game with Indianapolis at Deland was held up when Montreal arrived with Robinson and Wright, because the lights were being fixed. When asked what the lights had to do with a day game, authorities claimed the electricians were available only on that day. Games were quickly and voluntarily canceled on the way north at Savannah and Richmond.

"I didn't realize it was this bad," Rickey sighed. "We'll just have to train out of the country in the future."

On the day Montreal opened its regular season with a game against Jersey City, Rickey was asked, "If you knew that the presence of Robinson in Baltimore would produce bloodshed and perhaps end baseball in that city, would you let him play there?"

The question came from one of Rickey's oldest baseball friends. Frank Shaughnessy, now president of the International League of which both Montreal and Baltimore were members, pleaded in behalf of his clubs. When Rickey said he wouldn't, Shaughnessy added, "Then for God's sake, don't let him go, Branch, because that will happen. They're up in arms. Here are the stories."

Rickey scanned some lurid news clippings and replied, "But I don't think those awful things will happen, Frank. It's one more case of fearing 'trouble ahead . . . trouble ahead.' Robinson will go to Baltimore, provided he's good enough to be taken. Let's go over to Jersey City and see."

Robinson grounded out to short in his first time at bat. Then he muffed an easy throw for an error. In his second time at bat, with two Royals on base, he drove the ball into the leftfield bleachers for a home run. He beat out a bunt in the fifth inning, stole second, went to third on an infield out, tantalized the pitcher into committing a balk and scored. He singled cleanly to left in the seventh, stole second and scored on a single. He bunted safely in the ninth, went to third on a single and drew another balk to score again.

Jackie's work that day produced four runs scored, four batted in, two stolen bases and two balks. Most of the 25,000 spectators at Roosevelt Stadium stormed the field joyfully after the game. It took the player five minutes to reach the clubhouse.

Robinson played in Baltimore without incident six days later, and in Montreal after that. Signficant is that 66,551 fans paid to see the first three opening games in which Robinson played.

That summer with a team that was half old and half young, the Brooklyn Dodgers staged a seesaw race with the St. Louis Cardinals who were "half missing." Martin, Lanier and Klein, regulars who skipped to play in the "outlaw" Mexican League, couldn't be replaced. Brooklyn had lost a first-string catcher, Mickey Owen, and several minor-league prospects to the same competition. The Dodgers enjoyed a slim margin through much of the season, but both clubs had the press and the nation's fans near hysteria in the closing weeks of September. For the first time in baseball history, two major-league teams ended the full 154-game season in a tie.

Just before the playoffs began, two worried business executives came to Rickey's office, Herbert Kent, head of the P. Lorillard Company, and Ray Vir Den, of the advertising agency that handled Lorillard's radio sponsorship of Dodger games. They were prepared to be held up by Rickey, who had them tied to a broadcasting contract that did not include playoff games. Now another tobacco company had offered $50,000 to sponsor the playoffs.

"It's unfortunate," Rickey began, "that three big business-men weren't smart enough to provide for such a contingency, even though it has never happened in baseball before — "

"Come on, Branch," Vir Den said impatiently, "you have us over a barrel. We've got to have the games. What's the price?"

Rickey recalled the contract-signing and asked each man what he would have said, had the subject come up at the time. Both honestly felt that the playoffs would have been part of the regular season coverage. Rickey thought so too, and added, "If that thinking would have pertained then, it pertains now. Having no contract doesn't affect your sponsoring the playoff broadcasts — "

"You mean we don't have to pay anything extra?" Kent gasped.

"The broadcasting rights belong to you," Rickey said.

Leo Durocher won the toss and chose to play the first of the three playoff games in St. Louis, with the second — and third, if neither team won two straight — in Ebbets Field, leaving the winner in the east to meet the Red Sox in the World Series. The Dodgers lost in St. Louis. Returning to

Brooklyn on the day of the second game, Branch Rickey picked up an early edition of an afternoon paper and read in a sports column the startling accusation that he, Rickey, preferred to lose the playoffs. "This is one pennant Brother Rickey didn't want to win. It didn't fit into his long-range calculations . . ."

Rickey wept at his desk. The shock of such a charge by a writer of responsibility, on top of the season-long strain, the recurring dizzy spells — it was too much. For once he wanted to rush into the Dodger lockerroom and shout denial, but that was not his domain. After the Dodgers had lost the decisive game at Ebbets Field, he entered the hushed clubhouse. Again weeping openly, he said:

"The Williams column was a lie! I want none of you young men to leave here and go home with the idea that I don't want to win *every day,* every year. Because I do, with all my heart . . ."

In the visitors' clubhouse, the winning manager, Eddie Dyer, surrendering to tears of joy, gave a touching statement to the press when he said, "There is something I want you all to know. It was Branch Rickey who assembled this team. It was Branch Rickey who signed me as a pitcher back in 1922 and, when my arm went dead, persuaded me to continue as an executive and taught me every bit of baseball I know. If this is a good team, and it was today, then most of the credit is his. He got these ballplayers while he was still in St. Louis. If I am a successful manager, it's because he made me one."

It was heartening, Rickey admitted, and typical of "his Eddie," but it didn't ease the sting of the "didn't-want-to-win" accusation. It couldn't relieve the hurt of low-level journalism that had sashweighted him since spring, particularly the vilification by columnist Jimmy Powers, through his vicious "El Cheapo Rickey" campaign in the *Daily News*.

Powers had coined the term "El Cheapo" and linked it to the well-publicized raid by the Mexican League on contract players of organized baseball. He blamed Rickey's salary scale for wholesale desertions even while Rickey was working secretly through midwestern intermediaries for the return of the disillusioned players. From June through December, 1946, many of 180 "Powerhouse" columns disparaged Rickey and other owners, but 74 columns contained derogatory or insulting references to "El Cheapo" or "El Cheapo Rickey." They covered a wide range of fanatical aspersion, and reached something of a nadir in July with:

This column will welcome suggestions from Brooklyn fans: What shall we do with El Cheapo?

Shall we send him over Niagara Falls in a barrel?

Shall we maroon him on Bikini Atoll?

One reader suggests that all fans get together and each donate a $20 bill upon entrance to the park. A grocery store chain has kindly consented to donate 20 empty barrels.

If the fans will help fill these barrels with $20 bills perhaps Rickey's desire for milking money out of the franchise will be satisfied and he will pack his carpet bags and go away to another town and run his coolie payroll there.

Having visited Mexico, Powers boasted of how newspapers there had front-paged his "El Cheapo" label. He wrote that trucks were rolling off empty barrels at the *Daily News* in profusion for use in his campaign. He denounced Rickey's gift of still-scarce automobiles in behalf of a grateful organization as a tax burden to the players, and then claimed credit for "forcing El Cheapo to give" the cars, alleging that a phone call from the Dodger clubhouse had so advised him.

The temper of Rickey's office staff mounted. Workers in the field wanted something done. His family and close friends were humiliated when public ridicule assailed them at the ball park. His partners, Smith and O'Malley, thought it unfortunate, but they were helpless to do anything even when Powers wrote that Rickey had singlehandedly voted out part-owner Jim Mulvey as a director. Rickey appealed to the attorneys for the National League for civil action.

Suddenly the campaign lost its power to hurt. Rickey was surprised with a photostat copy of a letter on *Daily News* stationery that could be used in a move to silence his tormentor completely. It came voluntarily from an individual Rickey had never met. The sympathetic visitor said that others, suffering as Rickey had, had begged to use the letter and its ghastly un-American contents in reprisal. They were refused, but the "El Cheapo" campaign had gone too far. Now it should be used.

Branch Rickey read the letter and shook his head in dismay.

"I've never sunk low enough to do a thing like this, and I'm too old to start now," he said, tossing the letter across his desk. "I've never met this writer, but I thought he was a responsible person. We should never have taken him seriously. Now we can forget him."

26

THE DODGERS' TIE for the National League pennant and a record attendance at Ebbets Field in 1946 began a fabulous five-year period under Branch Rickey. A few figures of that first year offer graphic testimony to his genius at combining financial wizardry with success on the ball field that made him the envy, the model and often the scourge of rival baseball impresarios. He produced a net operating profit of $451,000 from tickets bought by 1,768,247 Brooklyn fans, the sale of radio rights, television revenue ($6000 in that pioneering year), concessions, and by selling surplus player contracts for $239,000 to competitors.

Not only had Rickey caught up to his talent-rich St. Louis team in four years; his minor-league clubs had passed the Cardinals at every level. Rochester, Columbus, and Houston, once his pride and joy, finished in the second division.

The Montreal Royals, after a runaway victory in the International League, had defeated Louisville to win the Little World Series. Modern baseball's first Negro, Jackie Robinson, had met the difficulties, hostility and near-tragedies Rickey had prophesied so dramatically a year before, but he had "fought back" only with base hits and stolen bases. He won the International League batting championship with an average of .349 and stole 40 bases. President Shaughnessy, grateful for a record attendance without riot or bloodshed, congratulated Rickey late in the year and suggested that

Robinson remain at Montreal a second year. Manager Hopper, a major factor in Robinson's success, volunteered assurance with, "You don't have to worry none about that boy, Mr. Rickey. He's the greatest competitor I ever saw and, what's more, he's a gentleman." Two other Negroes, Newcombe and Campanella, had helped the Dodger subsidiary at Nashua, New Hampshire, win a pennant in the Class B New England League.

Through the next ten years, Robinson, Newcombe and Campanella, three of the first five Negroes to enter organized baseball, became irrefutable substantiation of Branch Rickey's expressed reason for "breaking" baseball's invisible color line, "I want players to win pennants for Brooklyn." They were the backbone of Brooklyn offense and defense for a decade, during which period the Dodgers won six pennants and one World Series, finished second three times and third once. Robinson won honors as Rookie of the Year, National League batting champion and Most Valuable Player once each. Campanella was voted Most Valuable Player three times. Newcombe was Rookie of the Year and Most Valuable Player once each. Their presence dominated the National League lineups for the All Star Game from 1949 on. Campanella caught every inning of six classics from 1949 to 1953 inclusive.

The banner financial year of 1946 moved the club to buy a twin-engine Beechcraft to expedite Rickey's movements in the widening farm-club operation. The long-unpaid mortgage on Ebbets Field, $361,000, was satisfied. Another $250,000 was earmarked to buy the St. Paul franchise. But problems arose that Rickey couldn't solve with money.

The New York Yankees' president, Larry MacPhail, possibly from desperation or chagrin over his successor's phenomenal results, began a wholesale raid on the Dodger staff. He had taken scout Tom Greenwade. He had made repeated offers to Leo Durocher and had actually signed the Dodger coaches, John Corriden and Charlie Dressen. Because Dressen had agreed to remain in Brooklyn for two years at $15,000 a year, he was subsequently suspended by Commissioner Chandler for breaking his word. Rickey kept Durocher only by signing him to a one-year contract at $50,000, the highest salary ever paid a manager to that time.

One of the least understood aspects of Rickey's career is his steadfast refusal, in the face of widening criticism and name-calling, to lose faith in Leo Durocher as a man. He has been called stubborn, a "soul saver," with Durocher described lightly as his "favorite reclamation project." But this was more than a part of his thinking; it is the essence of his personal philosophy. He simply will not give up on a person who needs help of any kind.

But Rickey also believed in Durocher as a field manager. Forty years of study and experience had taught Rickey that the direction of a team in competition was a complex operation involving constantly changing values. To manage a winning team called for a specialized intellect, but one that could be developed in baseball without much formal education. It could exist in a mind deficient in many other channels of intelligence. It is reflected by an instantaneous reaction to the shifting complexities of the game, and by the ability to take split-second counteraction equal to intuition.

"Regarding your present ability as a manager," wrote Brooklyn Dodger coach Casey Stengel to John J. McGraw on the occasion of his resignation as Giant manager in June, 1932, "I can still safely say you are the fastest pulling the trigger before plays in baseball. Your brain has acted before other managers start thinking."

Leo Durocher was often compared with McGraw, but usually because of his volatile nature and trouble with umpires on the ball field. Actually, he had developed the quick-thinking baseball intellect to a degree that often confounded some of the smartest players under his direction. He commanded respect from stars on his teams who disliked him personally. He was a take-charge manager who, in every game, won respect and envy through quick and uninhibited decisions and, right or wrong, shouldering the blame.

In this respect, Durocher was even more like McGraw, for he anticipated forthcoming plays and usually gave signs for the next maneuver as the present play was being completed. He had already diagnosed the action, weighed the alternative, decided what should be done and readied the sign for his coach. When the pitch reached the catcher's glove, or the hitter's bat, Durocher was flashing his sign. By doing it as a form of "black art," he was one of the most deceptive sign-givers of the game.

Durocher may not have grown up with a dire need of help and understanding, but he reached St. Louis spiritually and financially impoverished in 1933, and never let go of Branch Rickey's guiding hand. Sidney Weil tried to relieve the personal and fiscal chaos the boy had brought to Cincinnati from his carefree years as a New York Yankee in the Ruth-Gehrig era. But Durocher only compounded his troubles under Weil. Rickey took full charge by giving the boy only $50 weekly from his salary and pro-rating the remainder to satisfy many debts and forestall threats of court action. By the end of the next year, Rickey had helped him to solvency and a worthy marriage. Three years later he was traded to Brooklyn.

In late summer of 1938 Rickey advised MacPhail, who was weeping in anger and frustration over Durocher, to saddle the shortstop with the responsibilities of managing the Dodgers, which MacPhail did. Four years later Rickey reached Brooklyn to find an odious situation developing around Durocher. The Dodger clubhouse reeked with gamblers, bookmakers, racing handicappers, fast "friends," and ticket scalpers. They had long enjoyed access to Ebbets Field and scurried from dugout to locker room like happy, squealing vermin in the rat runs of an aging barn. Club morale was dangerously low. Three civil suits had been threatened to collect horseracing debts. What to do? A summons to Chicago from Commissioner Landis ended Rickey's vacillation. Landis had all the facts and told Rickey to "clean house" at once or he would do the job himself.

The manager was nominally to blame, but the coaches had also neglected their responsibility and violated the trust placed in them. Rickey fired Charlie Dressen for his failure as a coach and for his open association with "Memphis" Engelberg, a professional handicapper, to whom he owed considerable money. He was re-hired eight months later. Durocher was ordered to keep the Dodger clubhouse and dugout free of bookmakers and handicappers — or else!

Within a year Rickey had to settle a player mutiny resulting from a clash between Durocher and sports writer Tim Cohane over the origin of a clubhouse story. He traded pitcher "Bobo" Newsom, the troublesome cause of the row and, at the end of the season, did not renew the contracts of either Durocher or Dressen. After considerable soul-searching and helpful consultation with Sid Weil, Rickey rehired them both for 1944. But again Durocher's companions played him false. During training at Bear Mountain, George Raft, the picture star, borrowed the key to Leo's Manhattan apartment, and presently a $12,000 loser in a dice game was hollering copper.

The next year, 1945, a man described as a foul-mouthed fan by corroborated testimony in open court, claimed he was ushered under the stands at Ebbets Field by patrolman Joe Moore and beaten by Durocher. Charged with felonious assault, Durocher pleaded not guilty. A year later he was cleared quickly by a Brooklyn jury. To forestall a second action for civil damages, which involved the Brooklyn club, Leo was advanced money from insurance coverage to effect an out-of-court settlement with the fan. This payment was quickly seized as an indication of Durocher's guilt. The end result was that still more individuals turned against the Dodger manager.

But some person or group of persons wanted him out of Brooklyn and really went after him in late 1946. No other explanation can be offered for a leak of confidential data from the offices of Brooklyn District Attorney Miles F. McDonald to newspaper columnist Westbrook Pegler. The information, relayed to Rickey by telephone from Pegler, was frightening! The telephone in Leo's Manhattan apartment was tapped. He had talked to racketeer Joe Adonis. Moreover, his signature had appeared on checks in the $800,000 Merganthaler swindle.

Rickey found both items true, and neither incriminating. The call from Adonis, traced to Leo's apartment, was not from the racketeer himself, but from a henchman, who had simply reminded Leo of his promise to send bats and baseballs to a New Jersey church. The check signature was among thousands impounded from a check-cashing firm at the time of the swindle. The mountain of drafts might have contained anybody's signature. Pegler, impressed by the distorted items, told Rickey of a forthcoming series he would write on the low estate to which professional sports had fallen. He would resurrect past Durocher stories to help emphasize his point.

With his manager already signed to a $50,000 contract, Rickey secretly asked Commissioner Chandler's help in convincing Durocher that he must, once and forever, sever all relations with unsavory characters, and move out of George Raft's home in Hollywood. Chandler met Leo shortly afterward on a golf course in Berkeley, California, and followed through on the request. Though he had a list of names in his jacket pocket, the Commissioner asked Leo to name his friends. "Keep talking, son," he said as Leo recited. With each name mentioned — Raft, Siegel, Engelberg, Adonis and others — Leo divested himself of "friends" and promised to avoid contact with so-called undesirables.

Here was a key episode of the winter-long concern over the rising threat of gamblers and crooks to many sports after the war. The situation was further highlighted at the Los Angeles baseball meetings, two weeks after the Chandler-Durocher meeting, when President Bramham blasted the "rottenness in minor-league baseball." The retiring president threw a wet blanket over the conventions by revealing crookedness in at least one smaller circuit, and pointed up the need of utmost vigilance. Branch Rickey felt that he had solved his own problem in this respect by meeting it head on.

But Rickey encountered still another problem during the meetings when George Trautman quietly withdrew as a candidate to succeed Bramham as president of the National Association. Trautman had moved from the Columbus, Ohio, ball club, to president of the American Association. After a year as general manager of the Detroit Tigers, he had resigned to seek the minor-league post, only to receive a call saying that a few baseball people with anti-Semitic leanings had "kicked his name around." Rather than be an "issue," Trautman pulled out. Within a few hours he found a handwritten note in his mailbox at the Ambassador Hotel:

George —
    If at all possible — I would like to see you — a few minutes.
Room 818 — Clark Hotel.

BRANCH

Trautman reported promptly to Rickey's room. They shook hands.

"I want you to answer two questions, George," Rickey began, motioning to a chair. "Then don't say a word. Just listen to me. Would you like to be president of the National Association?"

"I would."

"Do you think you can benefit baseball on the job?"

"Branch, I don't know of any place in baseball where I could do the game more good."

"Then why are you letting a few pettymongers and race-baiters chase you out the back door?" Rickey demanded almost angrily. "You are proud of your Jewish heritage, and I know you are. If you let these contemptible whisperers drive you back with a threat of racial smear, you are not the George Trautman I know, or that Lynn St. John knows, or that anybody worthwhile in this game knows. You have no right at all to pull out from the backing of people who like you, believe in you, need your leadership, and respect you for what you are, for what you've done — no right to back away from the oldest cry of derision we know . . ."

Rickey poured it on, but they were words Trautman wanted desperately to hear, and they came from the only man in Los Angeles, perhaps, who had the courage and the ever-lasting fairness to speak them. It was a challenge to roll up his sleeves and fight for the thing he wanted and believed in. Trautman isn't sure of what happened immediately after that.

"I had dinner with my wife," he said ten years later, "but I couldn't remember anything. My head was swimming and my feet were light. It took me most of the evening to come around to making a few telephone calls. I told some people emphatically that I was running for the job and would talk to anybody about it."

Trautman was elected almost without opposition.

Gambling and gamblers concerned club owners and rule-makers at the winter meetings in New York. National League president Ford Frick, in a major speech at the Baseball Writers Dinner, deplored player-association with gamblers and urged baseball leaders to "take every precaution by both rule and example to protect the player against himself and the public."

Leo Durocher had conformed to the Commissioner's warning in Berkeley, but he continued to make the headlines as a result of a whirlwind courtship of the actress Laraine Day. A condition of her California divorce was that she wait a year before remarrying. But Miss Day obtained a second divorce in Juárez, Mexico, crossed the Rio Grande and married Durocher in El Paso, Texas. They could live as man and wife anywhere in the world, except California, where both were denounced publicly by an affronted judiciary.

Rickey was not blind to the rising tide of protests. Letters from troubled spiritual leaders reached him. When he was petitioned in person by Reverend Vincent J. Powell, Brooklyn Diocesan Director of the Catholic Youth Organization, whose 50,000 members were part of the thriving Knothole Club, Rickey confidently turned the matter over to Walter O'Malley. Being of the same faith, O'Malley met Father Powell at least twice in Rickey's office, but the priest later withdrew the entire CYO from the Knothole Club in protest against Durocher as manager of the Dodgers.

Rickey then received a written plea to release Durocher, from Bishop Bermingham, of the Washington, D.C., archdiocese and Father Powell's predecessor as CYO director in Brooklyn. In reply, Rickey explained that Durocher had not violated his civil contract. Regardless, sweeping dirt under a rug did not make the house clean. He closed the letter by expressing surprise that "a man of your cloth or any cloth" would admit that one human soul was beyond redemption.

Quite unwittingly, Rickey brought the Durocher situation to a climax in Havana on March 8 when he saw two familiar figures in Larry MacPhail's official box during the first of two Dodger-Yankee exhibition games in Gran Stadium. Both qualified as "undesirable" under the standards emphasized by worried baseball leaders throughout the winter. One was handicapper Memphis Engelberg, the other Connie Immerman, manager of the Havana gambling casino, of which expatriate Lucky Luciano was part owner.

Rickey's anger exploded in the lobby of the Nacional Hotel after the game. He denounced MacPhail and the presence of the characters to two New York sports writers. He raised the question of one standard for managers and one for club presidents. The outburst was reported to the Associated Press.

At the next day's game another writer called Durocher's attention to Engleberg and Immerman, who were in the Yankees' official box again, and Durocher was quoted as asking, "Are there two sets of rules, one applying to managers and the other to club owners?" Recalling the Commissioner's admonition on the golf course that had made Engelberg a "former friend" of his, Leo added indignantly, "Where does MacPhail come off, flaunting his company with gamblers right in the players' faces? If I ever said 'hello' to one of those guys, I'd be called up before Commissioner Chandler and probably barred."

Within a week MacPhail had used the two protests to support a formal charge of "conduct detrimental to baseball" against Rickey and Durocher. He asked the Commissioner to call a hearing to determine the responsibility for and the truth of the statements.

Reaching Havana a week later, by way of Panama, where the Dodgers and Montreal had played an exhibition series, Rickey learned that Chandler had called a hearing for Monday, March 24, at Sarasota, Florida. He was not worried.

Defense consisted merely of identifying the guests in the Yankee box as known gamblers and submitting proof by ticket printing manifesto that they used Yankee tickets, and deposition as to who got them for free distribution. Ford Frick arrived on Saturday to weigh the National League's interest in a discussion with Rickey next day.

An ironic twist in the heightening situation came late Saturday night when Mrs. Rickey learned that her oldest brother, Frank, had died in Ohio. Rickey wired Chandler requesting a postponement of the hearing and now belatedly registered with the Commissioner a protest against the gamblers having been in the Havana ball park. He departed early next morning by plane in characteristic haste and confusion, leaving word that, if there was no postponement, the Dodger interests would be directed by O'Malley, who, at the moment, was having breakfast with Frick in the hotel dining room.

Later in the day at Sarasota, the Commissioner announced that the request for a postponement had been denied, that there might be two hearings and that newspapermen would be barred. Upon reaching Sarasota, President Frick announced that he had declined Chandler's invitation to the hearing. He gave no reason, other than that he did not wish to attend.

The next day's hearing was essentially a travesty on democratic procedure. It resulted in a black day for baseball. A permanent stain will remain if the stenographic transcript of the testimony is ever uncovered. Not a single word was spoken in defense of Durocher by the Brooklyn Dodgers or even by himself. Under questioning, Leo tried to say that his protest in Havana echoed the warning he had been given on the Berkeley golf course against unsavory associations, but Commissioner Chandler hushed him quickly.

The subject of gamblers in the ball park, so important during the winter, was carefully avoided. At the last minute, entry into the record was made of proof that (1) the two occupants of the Yankee box were undesirable to baseball, and (2) they received gratuitous tickets from the New York Yankee supply.

Rickey returned four days later to attend the second hearing, held in St. Petersburg, Florida, on March 28. He opened the long session with a detailed explanation of his outburst in the lobby of the Havana Hotel. He had not seen the sports writers' quotes, but would not deny them, since both writers were responsible reporters. What he had done, and wanted in the record, was protest the presence of Engelberg and Immerman as guests in the Yankee official box. Regardless of what may have been said in his behalf at the first hearing (a protective "general denial" had been entered), this was the reason for his outburst. And, if his manager, Leo Durocher, had protested similarly after the second game, he had done so with good cause, as the Commissioner well knew.

Chandler then sent for Arthur Patterson, traveling secretary of the Yankees, and questioned him about courtesy tickets to the Yankee-Dodger games of March 8 and 9 to see if he could deny that the gamblers had been guests of the Yankees. Patterson admitted handling the club's free tickets. He admitted knowing both Immerman and Engelberg. He admitted giving some of the tickets to MacPhail, who was in the hearing room but not questioned on this point. Asked if he had given free tickets to Immerman and Engelberg, Patterson replied, "I can't recall." When asked if, conceivably, he could have given them the tickets, he said, "Yes, conceivably I could have."

The Commissioner's face was a mask of imperturbability. He finally excused Patterson and then asked all to leave the room except O'Malley, Rickey and his assistant. When the door had closed, Chandler rose, went over to the Dodger table and said, "How much would it hurt you folks to have your fellow out of baseball?"

Branch Rickey emitted a gasp of amazement. His mouth flew open like a man hit in the solar plexus or lower. His gnarled fists went up into the air and came down against the table with an angry whack. Tears rolled down his sun-tanned cheeks. He exclaimed in a half-sobbing voice, "Happy, what on earth is the matter with you? Why, that boy has more character than the fellow you just sent out of the room!"

Ignoring the pointed reference to MacPhail, the Commissioner insisted he was trying to do his best; that he was under great pressure from "outside of baseball"; that he "had to do something"; and that he just wanted to know "how you all felt about it."

The sandbag landed two weeks later while Rickey was "working the blackboard" with his staff. The Commissioner's assistant, Walter Mulbry, telephoned to relay the decision on the hearings, one highlight of which was the fining of both Dodgers and Yankees $2000 each for "engaging in a controversy." The other was that Leo Durocher had been suspended from baseball for a year "as a result of the accumulation of unpleasant incidents in which he has been involved and which the Commissioner construes as detrimental to baseball."

The full decision, which Rickey obtained from a United Press reporter, showed a palpable perversion of the stenographic record of the hearings in at least one of the Commissioner's findings:

Evidence produced at the hearings shows that the alleged gamblers were not guests of MacPhail and did not sit in his box at Havana. [*Just the reverse was indicated by documentary evidence, photographs and Patterson's testimony.*]*

* The author attended both secret hearings as Assistant to Dodger President Branch Rickey and entered the documented evidence personally.

The lengthy decision closed with a firm admonition:

All parties to this controversy are silenced from the time this order is issued.

In the pandemonium that followed, Branch Rickey reflected on the bitter fact that, having lost his two coaches, he had now been deprived of his manager. The wholly unexpected blow caught him at the threshold of solving one of his greatest problems: Jackie Robinson.

Five steps of the six-stage program had been cleared. Robinson was undeniably the right man on and off the field. By April, Rickey was certain of a good reaction from the press and public, because both had challenged him to promote Robinson to the Dodgers or explain the delay. The player had qualified fully in spring training by batting .625 in exhibition games and making excellent use of the first baseman's mitt handed him in Panama.

Rickey had handled the fifth step, "the backing and thorough understanding of the Negro race to avoid misinterpretation and abuse of its meaning." On the night of February 5, 1947, Herbert T. Miller, Executive Secretary of the Carlton Branch of the Y.M.C.A. in Brooklyn, assembled more than thirty leading Negroes representing a cross section of civic responsibility. Rickey and three others were the only white people present.*

"I'm not going to tell you what you hope to hear," Rickey said after dinner. "Someone close to me said I didn't have the guts to tell you what I wanted to; that I didn't have the courage to give it and that you people wouldn't be able to take it. I believe all of us here tonight have the courage. I have a ballplayer named Jackie Robinson . . . on the Montreal team . . . he may stay there . . . he may be brought to Brook-

* Judge Lazansky, Dr. Dodson and the author.

lyn. But if Jackie Robinson *does* come up to the Dodgers, the biggest threat to his success — the *one* enemy most likely to ruin that success — is the Negro people themselves!"

The gathering was shocked into silence as though suddenly slapped.

"I say it as cruelly as I can to make you all realize and appreciate the weight of responsibility that is not only on me and my associates, but on Negroes everywhere. For on the day Robinson enters the big league — *if* he does — every one of you will go out and form parades and welcoming committees. You'll strut. You'll wear badges. You'll hold Jackie Robinson Days . . . and Jackie Robinson Nights. You'll get drunk. You'll fight. You'll be arrested. You'll wine and dine the player until he is fat and futile. You'll symbolize his importance into a national comedy . . . and an ultimate tragedy — yes, tragedy!

"For let me tell you this!" Rickey thundered, and his fist smashed against the table top. "If any individual, group or segment of Negro society uses the advancement of Jackie Robinson in baseball as a triumph of race over race, I will regret the day I ever signed him to a contract, and I will personally see that baseball is never so abused and misrepresented again!"

After deafening applause, a long discussion produced ways and means of helping. The group selected a master committee of five from their number to set up the policy of self-policing throughout Brooklyn and Harlem. The slogan "Don't Spoil Jackie's Chances" was used in pulpits, clubs and bars. By passing it on to other cities, the members made it possible for Robinson to be "let alone to play baseball and nothing else" during his first season in the big leagues.

The sixth and final step, "Acceptance of the player by his teammates," was also the most difficult and trying. Upon reaching Panama in mid-March to see Brooklyn and Montreal play exhibition games, Rickey learned that a petition had been organized by certain Brooklyn Dodgers to keep Robinson off the parent team. It was not a formal document, but a word-of-mouth and handshake agreement. He enlisted the help of his "glue man" on the team, Eddie Stanky, to dissipate the clubhouse end of it.

Rickey was not worried so much about those players easily led. His concern was for Southern boys whose upbringing made it impossible for them to recognize the justice of a Negro in organized baseball. The interviews in his Tivoli Hotel suite were heated, even though the petitioners had no valid defense for their actions. Rickey outdid Stentor at his best as he hurled some of his best verbiage into the tropical night. He cut the props from one player after another with telescoped lectures on Americanism. Several of the petitioners were ashamed and gave ground. One did not. He took the worst tongue-lashing of all. When Rickey finally thundered at him: "Do you want to play on the same team with Robinson?" he replied, "No, suh, Ah do not!"

"Would you like your contract transferred to another club?"

With his nose almost touching Rickey's, he replied, "Yes, suh, Ah would. But Ah don't want to be made the goat of a mess Ah didn't create!"

"Then I may accommodate you, sir!" the Dodger president exclaimed. "Good night!"

The boy left the room with flashing eyes and clenched fists. Rickey was visibly moved by the emotional strain of this last interview. His trembling hands had difficulty lighting a cigar. It was no moment for rage and reprisal against the player, Bobby Bragan, a third-string catcher, for Rickey recognized unusual courage. The player, he reasoned, had grandparents who fought the same way. Some day the boy would learn he was wrong. Meanwhile, he would remain a Dodger. (The next year, 1948, Bragan was appointed manager at Fort Worth, where he won the pennant and the playoffs, and won the pennant again in 1949.)

At Havana a few days later, Rickey was handed a letter from Dixie Walker, reflecting his comment of October, 1945, "As long as he isn't with the Dodgers, I'm not worried." Now obviously worried, Walker wrote:

> Recently the thought has occurred to me that a change of Ball clubs would benefit both the Brooklyn Baseball Club and myself. Therefore I would like to be traded as soon as a deal can be arranged. My association with you, the people of Brooklyn, the press and Radio has been very pleasant and one I can truthfully say I am sorry has to end. For reasons I don't care to go into I feel my decision is the best for all concerned.

With complete understanding and no little compassion, Branch Rickey viewed it as a plea from a player in grave emotional difficulty. A veteran of thirty-six and a Brooklyn hero, and a great managerial possibility, Rickey regretted that Walker was unprepared to recognize or accept the equality of mankind on the baseball field. Within three days Rickey had an offer for him. Pittsburgh agreed "to accept player Walker for $40,000 cash, Gionfriddo and Kalin."

Walker's transfer to Pittsburgh was set for the night of June 4, but Pete Reiser was hospitalized after running into a wall, and the deal canceled. At the end of the season, after Walker had hit .306 and played in the World Series, he was flown from Birmingham to St. Paul where Branch Rickey offered him the managing job of that farm club for $15,000 a year.

"I've got at least two more years of good play left," Dixie said, demurring. "I might get thirty thousand next year and maybe twenty after that. I think I'll play . . . somewhere."

"Fifteen thousand is actually more than we can afford to pay in St. Paul," Rickey said. "But I didn't want you to leave the organization without our best offer. I think I can help you get the money you want."

Rickey then asked for waivers on Walker for purposes of unconditional release, with the claimant of his contract to pay one dollar. Since Pittsburgh had finished last, it claimed first. Walker was awarded to the Pirates. Ordinarily that team would have paid $10,000 for his contract, but the dollar waiver permitted addition of the $10,000 to his $20,000 salary. Rather than announce that Walker was "traded for a dollar," Rickey added Dixie's name to a later multiple-player deal with Pittsburgh. Of course, Rickey was belabored in print for cruelly "peddling" the most popular player Brooklyn ever had.

On the day of Commissioner Chandler's shocking decision, April 9, 1947, the Walker difficulty was still in Rickey's mind, together with endless problems of player-transfer, team makeup, weeks of experimentation, and hoped-for, last-minute demand for Robinson's skill by "selfish" teammates who wanted to win. As a former player, Rickey understood this desire for the best on attack and defense in the lineup for maximum chance of victory. Having heard a few Dodger players murmuring praise of Robinson's work, he was confident that the demand would be made to clear the sixth and final step before the season opened.

But the turmoil and team upset that followed the loss of Durocher ended Rickey's chances of hearing the demand. Time, usually his ally, was now his enemy. With the start of a major-league schedule imminent, Rickey moved without actually clearing the sixth step. Almost certain that Robinson would succeed as a Dodger, he routed the player from bed on the morning of April 10, summoned him to Montague Street, and signed him to a Brooklyn contract. While the nation's fans were still in a furor of pro and con opinion over Durocher, they read:

The Brooklyn Dodgers today purchased the contract of Jackie Roosevelt Robinson from the Montreal Royals. He will report immediately.

BRANCH RICKEY

The notice was distributed to the press at Ebbets Field during the sixth inning of the Montreal-Brooklyn exhibition. The Negro entered the big leagues as a whisper in a whirlwind.

27

JOE MCCARTHY, one of three Yankee managers to resign under MacPhail in 1946, was Brooklyn's first choice to replace Leo Durocher. Others considered were Bill McKechnie, Rogers Hornsby, Bill Terry and Burt Shotton. Assigned to visit Buffalo and explain things to McCarthy, Durocher telephoned to "save time" and reported that McCarthy declined. While Rickey vacillated, Coach Sukeforth took over, finished the exhibition games and began the National League season with two victories over Boston. The three Dodger coaches finally decided, after an all-night discussion, that Burt Shotton should be their manager, and so informed Rickey. Later in Florida where he was scouting, Shotton pocketed a telegram and said to his wife, "Mary, Rick wants to see me in New York. I'll be right back."

Past sixty-two and white-haired, Shotton listened to Rickey through breakfast at LaGuardia Airport and most of the drive to Manhattan before learning the reason for his trip north. They were almost at the Union League Club when Rickey blurted out, "Barney, I need you to manage the Dodgers." At the club, Rickey got out, saying he would get a haircut and that Shotton could drive on. Slapping Barney's broad back, he exclaimed, "Well, boy, you know where the Polo Grounds is. Good luck."

Shotton hadn't seen the ball park in 25 years and was driving eastward in a westbound lane on the Triborough Bridge before a cop turned him around. He reached the Polo

Grounds too late for a meeting with his players and he lost the game to the Giants. Relating the experience to an amazed broadcaster, Red Barber, a few hours later, Shotton revealed that he had no contract, hadn't discussed terms and added, "Heck, I don't even have a hotel room for tonight."

The Dodgers' outward appearance of doing and saying nothing about the excessive punishment to Durocher may have rankled with MacPhail enough to make him violate the Commissioner's directive. He discussed and denounced the verdict for publication. Chandler was reminded of the defiance during a late-April appeal by the Dodger directors, O'Malley, New York Supreme Court Justice Henry L. Ughetta, Rickey and an aide. Refusing to review the case, Chandler cautioned the Dodgers, after repeated challenges, not to match MacPhail's violations and assured them that the offender had been summoned to hear a final warning against talking.

Sandwiched among administrative problems during the early months of the 1947 season were unresolved factors in the Durocher situation. Could Rickey pay salary to a suspended manager? Chandler didn't know. If not, what about the $21,000 Durocher had already borrowed against his $50,000 salary? Chandler didn't care. "Do as you please," he said. Rickey paid Durocher in full. When Laraine Day sought a hint of her husband's future in baseball by saying she "had to know in order to accept or reject an offer to make a film in Europe," Rickey said no more than that she should let nothing interfere with her film career. Approving Shotton, the CYO membership was reinstated in the Knothole Club.

To sports writers who badgered him with questions on whether Durocher's suspension was for a calendar year or baseball season, or if he would ever come back, Rickey said only, "It is not my decision to make. All I know is that

Durocher was suspended and I did not suspend him." He got away from the situation during a midsummer visit to the Dominican Republic to arrange training camps for Brooklyn and Montreal in 1948, but he was also caught cruelly incommunicado for several days. Reduced to begging newspapers at the gangplank of an arriving airliner, he obtained several just as his own private plane was about to leave.

Strapped in his cabin seat, he turned eagerly to the sports pages and learned that Shotton had put together a remarkable string of victories. Robinson was hitting well over .300. The Dodgers were pulling away. Staring out upon the nearby mountain peaks, he mused regretfully, "I just don't have a World Series pitching staff."

"It's only July, Branch," Mrs. Rickey reminded sagely. "Are you sure you have a pennant-winning staff?"

The two teams that had made headlines with off-field clashes all winter were now making them on the ball field. Under Bucky Harris, the Yankees were heading for their first pennant since 1943. The Dodgers, under the quiet, sardonic Shotton, had captured the imagination of the entire world, not only by nearing a pennant victory with a completely new manager and coaching staff, but with a symbol of democracy, Jackie Robinson, starring at first base.

The "symbol" himself did not have it easy. His home was besieged by both well-wishers and cranks, and he had to have police protection. Rickey had ordered every letter — flattering, threatening, derisive or insulting — answered by a special stenographer, read and signed by Robinson personally. Thousands of requests for photographs were satisfied. All offers of commercial exploitation of Jackie were refused, as were demands for personal appearances that flooded the office, with one excusable exception.

Rickey permitted response to a plea from a Connecticut sports writer that appeared in Dan Parker's New York *Daily Mirror* column. Assured that there would be no publicity or photographs, Robinson visited a badly burned colored boy in Middletown, Connecticut. Jackie gave the boy a baseball and saw tears of joy spill from his eyes. His reward, six weeks later, was a newspaper photo of the boy leaving the hospital on crutches. Scrawled at the bottom was, "Dear Jackie: We made it. Eddie Hamlin."

When the Philadelphia Phillies ownership called Rickey to report the threat of a player strike against Robinson's appearance, and that the games might be called, Rickey replied, "Trouble ahead . . . trouble ahead! Calling your three games only means that we win them by default, and we can sure use the victories." There was a rumbling promise of a strike by the Chicago Cubs, but it was never kept.

A more serious strike threat by the St. Louis Cardinals was uncovered by sports editor Stanley Woodward, of the New York *Herald Tribune*. He took the story to Ford Frick, who acted quickly. He warned the Cardinals through President Breadon that he would suspend any player or team that struck, that the press would desert them and that "the National League will go down the line with Robinson whatever the consequences."

In September, Larry MacPhail, smarting under the Commissioner's gag since May, cut loose with his most amazing tirade of all before three New York sports writers in Washington, D.C. Two wrote that he said:

It's a hundred to one that he [Durocher] won't be back in Brooklyn. Do you think Leo would have been suspended for a year if Rickey had not wanted him suspended? I'll buy anybody a suit of clothes if he can show me anything presented in Leo's hearing before the Commissioner which warranted such a suspension. I've got all the testimony in the case, two hundred and fifty pages of it, in my office and you all can come in and read it if you wish to.

For more than a year Rickey had been squeezing in trips when he could to his new 400-acre farm in Chestertown, on the eastern shore of Maryland. With a neighbor's cooperation, he had enough runway to accommodate the Beechcraft. Rickey was resting there from a recent attack of Ménière's disease, but the charge brought him flying into Brooklyn with a firm resolve.

"I've taken all I can stand," he murmured. "I'm telling the Commissioner it's either MacPhail or me. I'm suing MacPhail for a million dollars."

MacPhail was summoned to Cincinnati by Chandler. During a press conference a week later, the Yankee president denied that he was out "to get Chandler," but made no reference to the Ohio trip. On September 25 he announced his retirement from active direction of the Yankees, and that Wall Street had made offers for his stock. News of MacPhail's sudden stock activities was soon drowned by the delirious excitement over the astounding struggle between the Yankees and Dodgers.

The World Series of 1947 was dramatic, story-book stuff, thrill-packed from start to finish. When the Yankees finally won, four games to three, all fifty players and both managers had won the hearts of the baseball world.

In a passageway of Yankee Stadium after the final game, Rickey, walking alone, was taking galling defeat as hard as always when MacPhail appeared, draped an arm over his shoulder, grabbed his hand and murmured felicitations. It was too much for Rickey, not just the baseball defeat, but the overpowering recollection of bitter words and deceit and year-long chicanery. He abruptly ended a turbulent relationship that had survived seventeen eventful years.

"I am taking your hand," Rickey said, "only because people are watching us." Giving full expression to his bitter disappointment in MacPhail the man, he detailed his deep feeling of remorse and shame, and closed with a stern warning, "Don't you ever speak to me again!"

The 1947 World Series was over. The baseball year was at an end. MacPhail was out of baseball. Everybody asked, "Will Durocher return to the Dodgers?"

Rickey referred the questions to Commissioner Chandler, insisting that he must know the limitations of his own movements before deciding on Dodger management for 1948. When the Commissioner withheld direct reply, Rickey stormed, "If I cannot name my manager, or make a selection from several possibilities, I am not president of this baseball club!" He would not identify Durocher or anyone as a candidate, or discuss probabilities.

The final clash, most heated of all, came when Rickey visited Versailles, Kentucky, to enjoy the Commissioner's hospitality at a barbecue in late November. Sitting across from his host, Rickey stubbornly demanded that Chandler clarify Durocher's status in or out of baseball. The Commissioner stated with visible emotion that Rickey could "do as you damn well please" and that he did not care.

Rickey immediately brought Durocher from California to the Maryland farm. After agreeing to a few protective clauses, and getting his old job back through a renewal of the same contract, Leo returned to the coast. Though Rickey's movements were known to very few, his intent reached those who had persuaded the troubled priest, the Reverend Vincent J. Powell, to withdraw the CYO membership from the Knothole Club in February. Now there was a rush to save Father Powell the onus of withdrawing the reinstated membership after Durocher's return. Lou Niss, sports editor of the Brooklyn *Daily Eagle,* served as a last-minute intermediary. He pleaded on the day before the announcement for Rickey to make a token visit to a nearby office of a Supreme Court Justice. It was galling to those who knew that Durocher had already been re-engaged and that the visit was to compromise Rickey's independent position. They called it a "mousetrap."

"Everybody is welcome on this bandwagon!" Rickey replied almost angrily. He upbraided those who termed it a mousetrap for their own narrowness. "I'll willingly walk into a bear trap if it will keep fifty thousand youngsters in our ball park!"

Jamming on his fedora hat, he hurried across Borough Hall Park with Niss to relieve the priest's predicament through the formality of a brief meeting. Niss already had a story in type for a late edition, stating that the CYO ban on Durocher had been withdrawn, "clearing the path" for him to sign, "perhaps tomorrow," as manager of the Dodgers for 1948. With Durocher already signed, Rickey left immediately without comment for the baseball meetings in Miami. The formal announcement at the next morning's press conference reflected that Durocher, suspended from baseball without cause, needed no explanation for returning:

> The 1947 contract of Leo Durocher has been renewed for 1948 by the Brooklyn Baseball Club.
>
> BRANCH RICKEY

Despite six weeks of ideal training conditions, the Dodgers of 1948 failed to reach Ebbets Field as a welded team. Jackie Robinson's fire and dash were sorely missed when he reported thirty pounds overweight. Counted on to replace Stanky, traded to Boston, he did not reach top condition until mid-season. A barnstorming trip through the South broke records in precedence when Robinson and Campanella became the first of their race to compete with white players on a baseball field in segregated areas. Rickey could now train future teams in the United States.

Durocher, a strange mixture of caution and penitence for the first time in his life, vacillated on the vital matter of minor-league personnel for his team. Last-minute transfers were made, purchases recorded in the Trautman office, only to be canceled later when Leo changed his mind about their borderline abilities. Here Rickey was hurt by his insistence that the manager of the parent club control the make-up of his roster.

Rickey's efforts to help Durocher in this area troubled his minor-league department. Strong clubs were drawing crowds in Montreal, St. Paul and Fort Worth. When a staff member protested the transfer of questionable help for Durocher from "set" teams, Rickey exclaimed, "This is no time for a thumbs-down attitude!"

He had the further annoyance of falling attendance from the new record total of 1947. Durocher made the second western trip with only seven pitchers, one of whom was useless with a sore arm. On his return, the fans continued to shun Ebbets Field. Rickey met the impatience of the press by accepting personal responsibility for a poor and colorless team. Though he felt no outward criticism from his partners, O'Malley and Smith, he knew neither was happy with his arbitrary rehiring of Durocher who was called "box-office poison." He began to wonder how long his stubborn adherence to the manager could continue.

While he could hire and fire all personnel, Rickey was not completely free to pull the reins. His five-year contract had not been renewed — merely extended annually. His 25 per cent stock ownership was locked up in a ten-year pooling agreement that had seven more years to run. Two of the three votes within the pool controlled the 75 per cent ownership and, in turn, the club. He could quickly be outvoted. The agreement had paved the way for heavy financing. Rickey's large call loan with the Brooklyn Trust Company made his position vulnerable, which became apparent the day he tried to have part-owner Jim Mulvey reinstated as a Dodger director. Opposition was overwhelming, even with Commissioner Chandler in New York trying to help.

Anti-Durocher pressure mounted as fast as the team and attendance fell. Rickey postponed the decision, but finally made one at an informal staff meeting in his Brooklyn apartment. It was agreed that if or when the Dodgers hit the bottom, last place, Durocher should resign, or be asked to. Rickey then planned a two-week vacation with business friends in eastern Canada, his first in twenty years. On the very morning of departure by private plane, he was felled with a bladder infection that sent him to Peck Memorial Hospital.

By radio he listened carefully to the falling Dodgers as Dr. Rossi fought the rising fever and infection. Rossi succeeded but Durocher didn't. The Dodgers lost their sixth game in a row on July 2, and the next day, Saturday, they were in last place. On Sunday Rickey summoned traveling secretary Harold Parrott to the hospital bedside and confided:

"I'm under terrific pressure to do something about the team and I've got to have somebody handle it right away. Today. This afternoon. I have no alternative. It's got to be done."

Parrott sat in the Ebbets Field grandstand that afternoon, wondering how to handle his ugly chore, when Durocher was chased from the game in the fifth inning. Parrott rushed down to the manager's office just off the clubhouse and found Leo shaving.

"I've got some bad news," he said. "The boss wants you to quit."

Durocher turned. The razor was poised in mid-stroke.

"Why doesn't he tell me?"

"He's in the hospital. I was there this morning."

Durocher's lips tightened. "I won't quit," he declared. "He'll have to fire me. I'll call him and he'll have to fire me!"

The ball game with the Giants seesawed. Still shaving, Leo tried to talk down his rising anger and chagrin. Suddenly the door opened and a voice called, "Campanella just hit *another* homer!" Leo turned again, pointed a finger at Parrott, and barked: "I'll make it so tough for him he won't be able to fire me!"

Parrott's telephoned report to Rickey, who had returned to Maryland, produced one more example of Rickey's genius for indecision. Obviously he was delighted with Leo's courage and willingness to fight back. Perhaps he would arouse the team. Rickey seized this slender thread of hope and exclaimed, "Good! He's my manager as long as he wants to be!"

By the time Leo telephoned the hospital, Rickey had checked out. Desperate after failing to locate Branch Jr., he called columnist Bill Corum, of the New York *Journal American*. At breakfast the next morning he poured out his troubles. Corum wrote an open letter of suggestion to the Brooklyn co-owners, O'Malley and Smith, that they make up their minds, and chided them for putting pressure on Rickey.

On the afternoon of July 5, the Dodgers took the first of a holiday double-header from the Phillies in Philadelphia in ten innings. Durocher appeared over the visiting dugout, slapped it loudly and exclaimed, "We'll keep this up and see who gets fired!" The Dodgers kept it up, took the second game, and won the next day, 5–0, for their fifth straight victory. Returning to Ebbets Field, they beat the Braves in eleven innings for six in a row. Defeated the next night, they pulled back to sixth at the end of the home stand, July 11.

"I don't know what else might have happened to influence my decision," Rickey said, speaking of the ordeal for the first and only time. "But after I left the hospital, the thing that upset me about Durocher — that brought a climax, so to speak — was his failure to meet me in New York on the Saturday night before the All Star Game, which he was to manage because Shotton stepped aside. I had called him from Chestertown and made a special trip up there when I was not feeling too well and then, because of a social engagement, Leo did not meet me. It was an important subject and development I had in mind to take up with him. I was greatly disappointed.

"Then later in St. Louis, when Frank Shaughnessy told me about Horace Stoneham's intention to change managers — that Mel Ott was to be released shortly, if not immediately — that gave me the procedure. I happened to know with what high esteem Horace held Durocher as a manager. Only recently I had heard him say Durocher was the greatest manager in the world. So, I returned to Brooklyn as quickly as possible and got in touch with Horace."

The all-day maneuver began with a successful meeting of Rickey and Stoneham in Ford Frick's Rockefeller Center office at noon, July 15. Rerouting Durocher from a trip to scout the Montreal team, Rickey awaited the belated arrival at LaGuardia Airport with car and chauffeur. They sped to the Montague Street office. Eight hours had passed since the meeting with Stoneham. Now Rickey sat alone with the provocative kid who had come to him under violent protest fifteen years before. After hearing developments and possibilities of the unexpected change, Durocher said:

"Two questions. First, am I the manager of the Brooklyn Baseball Club as of this moment?" Assured that he definitely was, he continued, "Will I still be the manager tomorrow, the next day, next week, month?"

Rickey twisted the butt of a cigar in momentary silence. Then he explained that the question involved future, which gave him as much personal and financial concern as it did Leo. It was more than likely that Durocher's future lay with the New York Giants. Rickey then confessed his uncertainty — how long he himself could survive in Brooklyn. But for Leo, the Giants would offer challenge, opportunity and, for a while, security.

"That's all I wanted to know," Durocher said, rising. "I'll call you as soon as I arrange things with Mr. Stoneham."

The private telephone rang just before midnight. It was Leo. He and Stoneham had agreed on everything. Now they were going downtown for a bite to eat, and he'd see Rickey later.

"But, boy, you can't go anywhere with Mr. Stoneham," Rickey explained. "You haven't resigned from the club for the record. You must resign and your resignation must be accepted."

After a pause, Leo reported that they'd have to put it off, because Mr. Stoneham certainly wanted to see the resignation and —

"I didn't supervise Mr. Melvin Ott's resignation!" Rickey shouted. "As far as I'm concerned, the deal is off, and you're manager of the Brooklyn Club!"

He slammed the instrument into the cradle, rose with effort and said, "Come on, let's go home. We've done all we could."

An assistant moved to impede him in a stall for time. He had been going at such a pace all day, why not relax a couple of minutes? Within three minutes Garry Schumacher, Giants promotion director, called to say that he and Leo would be right over and meanwhile the resignation could be prepared.

Another hour passed before Schumacher arrived with Leo and Laraine Day, tight-lipped and cool. Leo began at once to copy the resignation in his frank and open penmanship. It was the simplest of documents . . . regrets and an expression of thanks. The acceptance was equally brief . . . regrets and an expression of thanks and good luck.

That was all, except for mutual agreement on releasing news of this hot potato. Time in Cincinnati, where the Dodgers waited to open the western trip, was an hour earlier than New York. The Giants, in Pittsburgh, wanted cooperation on an 11 A.M. break. Rickey agreed to have the Brooklyn front office withhold announcement until 11, and, of course, it broke in Wall Street on the news ticker at 10 o'clock the next morning. With the resignation and acceptance copied and signed, Rickey and Leo shook hands.

"Goodbye, Branch."

"Goodbye, boy."

28

Dodger traveling secretary Harold Parrott was routed from slumber in Cincinnati on the morning of July 16, 1948, by Branch Rickey's voice demanding an immediate press conference. To Parrott's query as to whether or not the writers should first have breakfast, Rickey replied, "When they hear what I've got to say, they won't be able to eat all day."

News of the Durocher transfer was a bombshell in Cincinnati, but its devastation had an atomic quality in Pittsburgh where stunned Giants correspondents heard Horace Stoneham introduce Leo as the new manager. The story, one of the biggest in sports, was both startling and dramatic across the nation. But incurable analysts soon dismissed it in terms of Branch Rickey "unloading his hot potato, Durocher."

Neither callous nor simple, it was an emotional wrench, and a bruise to Rickey's pride. His high regard for Durocher's ability was reflected minutes after the transfer when, asked about Leo's future chances, Rickey said, "Why, he'll fight back. He always does." After a pause, he nodded as though verifying it with an official source. "Yes, he'll fight back. Right to the top."

Some eight years later Durocher had led the Giants to two pennants and a World's Championship and was released. Rickey then said, "My estimate of Leo as a manager never changed. You deal out the cards. If they have a chance to win, he will make them win. I have often said that if I owned a ball club 100 per cent, I would not hesitate having Durocher as my manager. My reasons at the time I made the change, when other interests and feelings had to be considered, would not be the same today."

Barney Shotton rushed to Cincinnati and succeeded Durocher for the second time. Rickey flew back to Brooklyn where he picked up the reins of the professional football Dodgers, essentially a tax-loss subsidiary to keep the All America Football Conference alive. Rickey had high enough hopes for the new project to startle Lou Little, Columbia football coach, with an offer of a fortune to take over at Ebbets Field.

"When I refused $150,000 for five years," Little recalled with a shake of his head, "Branch pulled out a blank paper and pencil and said, 'You write the figure down, and whatever you write, it will be agreed.' I knew he meant it, but I just couldn't accept the challenge."

Shotton aroused the second-division Dodgers sufficiently to promise a first-division finish. Two of his problems were Billy Cox and Preacher Roe, obtained from Pittsburgh with $315,000 as part of a multiple player deal for which Rickey was soon criticized. Cox wasn't the infielder expected. Roe wanted to quit pitching. Rickey drew the reason from Roe and said, "Preach, if you'll give me one game in Boston, win or lose, we'll put you on a plane for Arkansas to stay home as long as you wish. You'll be paid just the same."

Roe defeated the Braves, went home and returned unexpectedly in a week. His wife didn't have tuberculosis after all. She was run down from worry and attending their store and the two boys. Roe pitched in and won eight games in the next six weeks.

The Dodgers couldn't finish better than third behind the Braves and the Cardinals in 1948, but Rickey realized the dream of a baseball lifetime. Hopper brought Montreal home first in the International League, and Walter Alston piloted St. Paul into the playoffs and won both rounds and the right to meet Montreal. The battle of two wholly owned subsidiaries for the highest minor-league honors had been seen but once before. Montreal won, four games to one, as was expected with a stronger pitching staff headed by Don Newcombe. Bobby Bragan led Fort Worth to a playoff victory and lost to Birmingham in the Little World Series.

With a write-off of $400,000 in football, the Dodger corporate operation still showed a profit after taxes of more than a half million. Rickey followed the banner 1947 player sales with $612,000 from surplus contracts. Four years of his stewardship, ending in 1948, produced total profits of $1,725,000. After paying the first stock dividend, $49,000 since 1943, the rest was plowed back.

Rickey then sought a third top-classification franchise by lining up Hollywood, of the Pacific Coast League, through the friendship of scout Wid Matthews and Fred Haney, a former big leaguer broadcasting the Hollywood games for owners Bob Cobb and Vic Collins. Cobb, head of the Brown Derby restaurants, objected to the Rickey association at first. His suspicions were intensified in New York during a taxi ride to Montague Street with Collins when the driver, learning they were to meet Rickey, laughed and said, "Hide your pocketbooks when you meet him!"

"That's enough!" Cobb roared. "I'm getting out!"

Collins pulled him back by the coattails and told the driver to shut up. After shaking Rickey's hand, Cobb quickly asked him why he signed Jackie Robinson, and why he sold Dizzy Dean. Detailing the facts of each case, Rickey studied Cobb's good features and cosmopolitan air, and said, "Bob, you're worried, and you shouldn't be. Branch and Clements told me the terms of the contract they offered you. It wasn't unusual and it wasn't perfect. I've been trying for perfection in working agreements for thirty years, and I've come to believe the imperfections are not in the terms of the contract, but in the people." Signing copies of a working agreement, he handed them across the desk, and said, "You fill in the details exactly the way you want them so our arrangement will be a pleasant one."

"Do you mean this?" Cobb asked, examining the blank spaces. When Rickey said he did, Cobb tore the papers and tossed them into a wastebasket. "If that's the way you feel, Mr. Rickey, I don't need a contract. Do it your way." Within a year, 1949, Hollywood had won its first Pacific Coast League championship since 1931.

Little more than a handshake signalized a deal that sent Pete Reiser to the Boston Braves a few weeks later when Rickey and Lou Perini used a torn scrap of the Minneapolis *Star-Tribune* for a memorandum reading:

Boston gives Brooklyn McCormick & 35000 for Reiser
Boston assigns Fernandez as directed for 10000.
                                        BR   L.R.P.

Throughout the Minneapolis meetings of 1948, and those that followed in Chicago, Rickey called his Brooklyn apartment almost nightly to ask about Grandma Moulton who had suffered a fractured pelvis. On Christmas Day, though bedridden at home, she was host to several grandchildren and great-grandchildren.

Branch Rickey sat at her bedside through much of the holiday afternoon, reading first lines from a Methodist Hymnal. She smiled in recognition and recited the rest of each verse. Before the visit was over, he heard the most welcome of words, a whispered expression of gratitude for making her long life a pleasant one. It ended the next day, within three months of her hundredth birthday. She was returned to Lucasville to rest beside Chandler Moulton.

"She was a benediction on my house," Rickey sighed.

During the winter Rickey became obsessed with the idea of incorporating into baseball a thesis from General Eisenhower's new book, *Crusade in Europe*. A whole team, he believed, could be taught to "take charge" on the ball field as they had for Eisenhower on the battlefield. Individuals, believing in a teammate's effort and willingness to help, could learn to coordinate aggressive thinking and winning spirit into a consolidation of will and determination to maintain team power and initiative at a constant maximum. Into an already crowded schedule, he squeezed flights for visits to convert individual players. Sports writers, of course, interpreted the thousands of traveling miles as "beating down the players' salary demands in person this year."

In an unprecedented move, the entire 1949 Brooklyn roster was submerged into a mass training camp at Vero Beach, Florida, and subjected to the last word in modern methods — mass cafeteria breakfasts, calisthenics, early-morning lectures, three practice diamonds, sprinting lanes, *three* pitching machines, additional pitching strings, sliding pits, lunch on the field, organized recreation periods, including amateur stage shows. This latest camp could process 450 players at a cost of $275,000. Trained as John Does, the Dodgers then moved to Miami for exhibition games.

After an unsteady start, the Dodgers began to climb in the National League race through balance and team-wide effort. Outstanding was Preacher Roe's pitching, and the third-base play of Billy Cox. As Roe headed for his biggest season of victories till then, and Cox displayed a dexterity equal to any ever seen at third base, the censured deal of 1948 became "Rickey's smartest maneuver," and, "He sure put one over on Pittsburgh!" Young Duke Snider and Hodges had "arrived" and Furillo, always great in the field, began to hit better than ever before.

Rickey made what he thought was a good trade in mid-May, sending Marvin Rackley to Pittsburgh for veteran Johnny Hopp and $90,000, but Rackley found a way to "outsmart" the club owners. He faked a sore arm in Pittsburgh and said he had suffered since spring training. Rickey canceled the deal and returned the money, put Rackley in the outfield where he not only played, but got a share of World Series money.

For three years Rickey had kept in secret contact with Mickey Owen and the Mexican League five-year suspension situation. Though most owners wanted to defy Chandler openly, Rickey preferred to operate secretly through an attorney friend, the late Arthur Curtis, of Springfield, Missouri. Owen made several secret visits to Brooklyn and worked closely with Rickey on solving the difficult problem. Commissioner Chandler finally reinstated the suspended players.

"I'm not sure of what was done by other owners," said Mickey Owen after his reinstatement, "but Branch Rickey worked in earnest during that winter of 1948–49. I think he did everything a man possibly could to end the suspension and bring us back."

The steps leading to Jackie Robinson's testimony before the House Un-American Activities Committee were many and secret. A Negro FBI agent, Alvin Stokes, sought help on December 31, 1947, to answer a charge of the Communist-minded that American Negroes would refuse to fight against Communist Russia. The Brooklyn Club consented, provided the eventual appearance be voluntary and free of political identification. When the date was finally set in early July, 1949, the plan leaked in Washington, D.C., and Robinson was surprised by a United Press reporter on the diamond at Ebbets Field. To a totally unexpected question, the player replied:

"I'd fight any aggressor. That includes *any* aggressor, as well as the Russians. I've been treated very well, and I'll fight anyone who tries to take away from me my American heritage. I want to fight for my child's right to live in this country, and for any other child's."

In the formal appearance later before the Committee, he read a paper that he, his wife, Rickey and Leslie Granger, executive secretary of the Urban League, prepared in Rickey's Brooklyn apartment. Essentially a combined effort, with Granger contributing heavily, it nevertheless reflected Robinson's extemporaneous statement on the ball field in uniform. The appearance highlighted his greatest year, in which he was spearhead, sparkplug and positive force, leading the Dodgers to one of the most exciting pennant victories of all. In August he limped on a very bad leg, and at least one sports writer wrote that he wouldn't play that night's game in Philadelphia.

"I didn't think I could play," Robinson said later. "I warmed up in front of the dugout where Shotton saw me limping, said nothing, and made out the lineup. I said to myself, 'If he can want me that much, I want to play.'"

Robinson ran out a leg-wracking slow bounder in the first inning, only to be thrown out by a half step. He played the full nine innings, and won the game in the ninth inning with a home run. Said manager Shotton later:

"Robinson on one leg was better than anything I could put in there. That's why I ignored his limp. If he didn't want to play, he could have asked out. But I knew his kind never begs off."

Robinson's hitting fell off in September, but he maintained his lead for the National League batting championship. Later the baseball writers voted him the Most Valuable Player, and Don Newcombe Rookie of the Year.

While the Yankees were winning the American League pennant on the final day in New York, the Dodgers struggled through ten innings in Philadelphia before they clinched the National League flag. The first three games of the World Series were close, but the Dodgers lost two of them. They were not in contention in the last two games.

A somewhat specious post-Series argument centered around whether the Dodgers or Yankees had the better farm system. Hollywood, Montreal, St. Paul and Fort Worth had won pennants or playoffs, while both Yankee top affiliations, Newark and Kansas City, were second-division teams. Then, while the Yankees were paying $265,000 for two Coast League players, Jensen and Martin, Branch Rickey was selling seven player contracts to five major-league clubs for $300,000 cash. Early that year he had occasion to check the sixteen big-league rosters and found that of the 640 players he had introduced or developed 140 of them.

Word quickly spread that the Dodger operation was as fabulous as the Cardinals. A New York broker appeared with an offer of $1,300,000 for Rickey's 25 per cent interest, the second in two years. Having referred one bid of $1,100,000 to O'Malley the year before, he turned over the new bidder to O'Malley, but again nothing came from the conference. Rickey was not eager to sell, and forgot the offers quickly, but they did establish that the policy of retiring mortgages and plowing back profits had appreciated his Brooklyn investment to more than a million dollars.

Through the winter he concentrated on improving the Vero Beach camp, signing his players and keeping them high in hope and spirit. The contracts were unmailed when Roy Campanella made a surprise visit in early 1950 to sign his contract. Rickey scolded him for sacrificing a bargaining position to go south to earn $500 refereeing basketball games. The catcher insisted he wasn't afraid of being treated unfairly, and could he please have his contract. Rickey sighed, tore off a slip of paper and handed it to him with a pencil, and said, "First, remember you're a good catcher — one of the best in the National League — and then write down the salary you ought to have."

Campanella stared, first at Rickey, then at the paper, grinned, cupped his hand and wrote a figure behind it.

"Now fold it," Rickey ordered. He took the folded paper, stuck it in the breast pocket of his jacket and said, "All right, boy, that's your salary for nineteen-fifty."

They shook hands. Campanella walked slowly to the door. He turned. "Mr. Rickey, please just peek at that figure? I wrote big."

Rickey laughed. "Whatever you put down, Roy, I got the biggest bargain in baseball. We'll sign the contract when you get back."

Like many Rickey teams, the Dodgers stumbled in the early weeks of the 1950 season as players were tried, found wanting and optioned to Alston at Montreal or Hopper at St. Paul. Rickey had switched his two AAA managers. Bragan continued at Fort Worth and Fred Haney at Hollywood. Rickey and Shotton agreed that pitching help was needed from outside the organization and that Howard Pollet, a twenty-game winner with the Cardinals in 1949, would insure a second pennant. Rickey contacted Fred Saigh, St. Louis president, to make the biggest cash offer, $400,000, for a player to that time. It remained the known peak until 1957 when the Boston Red Sox offered $1,000,000 for the contract of Cleveland's Herb Score.

"Actually the offer was $600,000," Saigh recalled in later years, "and Rickey wouldn't take my repeated refusals as final. The first bid was the $400,000, and he agreed to have a cashier's check flown west. Before giving up, he put in one of his young pitchers, and the 'throw-in pitcher' turned out to be one of the best in the league."

Rickey particularly wanted another Dodger pennant in what loomed as his final year in Brooklyn. He did not wish to leave. He wanted to remain, but circumstances were closing in on him. His situation became acute in mid-July when John L. Smith died, naming the Brooklyn Trust Company and his widow co-executors of his four-million-dollar estate. Mrs. Smith turned over administration of her baseball stock to the bank, and Walter O'Malley was a protégé of the bank. By representing his own stock and that of Mrs. Smith, O'Malley controlled two of the three votes within the pooling agreement and controlled the baseball club. Rickey was in a multi-million-dollar stock squeeze.

With no contract — merely an extension of one — Rickey had tried repeatedly and without success to have his new agreement, long since drawn by Lou Carroll, National League attorney, considered by the Board of Directors. What would happen on October 28, 1950, when he came to the end of his contract? Outvoted, he could demand nothing, nor could he go elsewhere in baseball without selling his stock. Certain conditions of the pooling agreement pertaining to "forced sale" provided for him to sell "at cost." His stock had at least trebled in value.

A fraternity brother, John Galbreath, Columbus, Ohio, real estate operator, learned of the predicament. He asked a New York real estate operator, William Zeckendorf, president of Webb and Knapp, about entering baseball. Learning that Rickey wished to get out, Zeckendorf wanted no part of it, saying, "Would you buy a racing stable, if they retired the best horse?"

But he agreed to a meeting. When Rickey promised to remain as a Dodger employee, Zeckendorf consented to examine the situation, and did the following day. It looked good at the price, $1,000,000. He agreed to buy. They shook hands. Only then did Rickey explain that the terms of his pooling agreement obliged him to make the same offer to his partners.

"Then you have no deal," Zeckendorf said. "You're using me to force a price. I can't tie up capital to be a 'put.'"

They sat down again and Zeckendorf, convinced that Rickey had not intended merely to "use" him, renewed the offer of a million, adding, "That's good for ninety days. If your partners meet it, you'll have to pay me fifty thousand for tying up my capital."

The deal was affirmed by handshakes. O'Malley declared immediately he would meet the offer. It was the only alternative to admitting new and aggressive ownership into the pooling agreement which would run until 1955. At that time, the new partner might be hostile enough to combine his "freed" 25 per cent with that of the Mulvey interests and create a stalemate.

Behind the façade of a tightening pennant race, with the Dodgers gaining on the Phillies, chagrin and tension mounted within the corporate operation. Except for salaries and an occasional dividend, no one had made any money from the Ebbets-McKeever holdings in a couple of generations.

Branch Rickey threatened to "walk out with a million." He was pictured variously as a holdup man, a double-crosser, and as selling his partners down the river for personal gain. His final report indicated otherwise. He met with the Directors for the last time in late October and summarized his accomplishments of eight years:

When he reached Brooklyn, Ebbets Field was the only property owned by the Ebbets-McKeever Exhibition Company, which rented the ball park to the Brooklyn National League Baseball Club for 10% of the gross income annually, not counting player sales, and was encumbered by a mortgage of $361,000. The mortgage had been paid and $650,000 spent on improvements. A few additional pieces of property had been added to the land already held, bringing total acreage to nine.

The Montreal park and franchise was now wholly-owned and worth conservatively $1,000,000.

The Fort Worth park, land and franchise was now wholly-owned and worth conservatively $400,000.

The St. Paul franchise, without land, was wholly-owned and worth conservatively $350,000.

A large and fully-equipped mass-training camp had been established at Vero Beach, Florida, under a long-term lease with the city. Bud Holman, of Vero Beach, was a member of the Dodger directorate.

In 1943 the Dodgers had 250 players under contract, of whom 150 were in the armed forces. In October, 1950, some 635 prime players were under contract and playing on 25 farm clubs.

From a debt-encumbered operation in 1943, the corporate holdings of 1950 consisted of a capital surplus of $100,000 and an earned surplus of $2,597,879. Cash on hand was listed as $899,509.81.

"I have tried repeatedly and without success," Rickey

read with concealed emotion, "to have my new contract introduced and considered by the Board."

When this statement was protested, Rickey simply verified it by a director present and continued. His last words to the group were to recommend for the record that Jim Mulvey be elected to replace him on the Board. He was succeeded by Harry H. C. Hickey, an executive of a bonding company. Eventually, however, Mulvey regained a place on the Board.

Instead of walking out happily "with a million," Rickey left his Brooklyn job with deepest regrets, for he would have stayed on at greatly reduced salary, had any offer been made. And once more he was in debt. Of the $1,025,000 purchase price, $50,000 went to Zeckendorf. Cash payments of $300,000 went to the Brooklyn Trust Company to help retire his debt and recapture his pledged life insurance. O'Malley was to pay the remainder of the stock purchase at the rate of $72,500 annually for ten years, with Commissioner Chandler's approval. Security was so arranged as to preclude violation of Rule 20 relating to ownership in the event Rickey was employed elsewhere in baseball. All Rickey had to do was live until age seventy-nine to collect in full.

His debt came from paying tax on the capital gains. The 25 per cent had cost $346,667, and he received a net of $975,000, making the gain about $600,000, or, after taxes, $450,000, to be collected in the future. He borrowed heavily in St. Louis to pay the tax and leave the annual payments free and clear for his estate.

And while the headlines screamed of the "sellout," Branch Rickey repaired to his Brooklyn apartment to consider offers for a job. They were several and all flattering.

29

WITH OMINOUS FRANKNESS, Branch Rickey asked John Galbreath whether or not he could afford to hire him as vice-president and general manager of the Pittsburgh Pirates. Heavy spending would be necessary for extra scouting personnel. Rickey also wanted to hire those who might lose Brooklyn jobs because of loyalty to him. Speaking in early November, 1950, Rickey neither threatened nor promised. He simply warned his friend and new employer that he wanted no part of another "rags to riches" operation. He would head the Pirates only if ample funds were available for his methods. He didn't know then, or ever, to the last dollar what he would need. He simply dreamed, schemed and went into debt sometimes, but plodded on until successful.

Assured that money was available, Rickey named the terms of a most liberal contract. For doing anything necessary to his operation of the club, he would receive an annual salary of $100,000 for five years. He would collect $50,000 annually for a second five years in whatever status he elected to assume — general management, advisory, or even retirement. Branch Jr. was to be his assistant and, if death prevented fulfillment of the contract, Jane would be liberally protected.

The team and organization that Rickey left in Brooklyn was as great, if not greater, than the Cardinal machine he had built and left in St. Louis eight years before. Keen executive skill was at every level. The minor-league teams had high-caliber managers. In that final Brooklyn year, his energetic scouting staff had beaten the bushes and produced some 125 free agents, about 20 per cent of whom were bonus players. The Dodgers would be contenders for many years.

Upon taking over at Pittsburgh, Rickey found that only 22 free agents had been signed for trials in 1951. None was a bonus player. Compared to nearly two dozen well-stocked Brooklyn teams, Pittsburgh's thirteen would need 119 new players to complete their schedules. Rickey had only 22.

"I had hoped to show definite progress within three years," Rickey explained, as the press hailed the forthcoming "Rickey touch" that would end Pittsburgh's pennant drought. "Certainly victory would come in five. But this meager supply for the D and C clubs meant the loss of a full year. Vacations were long since over. Boys had gone back to school, college or work. For several months we'd be unable to contact high school players — not until the day after graduation — June, 1951. It was the heaviest possible blow."

Rickey took on the "unwanted" from Brooklyn. Harold Roettger went to Pittsburgh. Clements resigned in California and joined Pittsburgh later. Burt Shotton, let out after losing the pennant to the Phillies in the tenth inning of the final game, went into semi-retirement in Florida, but his first lieutenant, Milton Stock, was taken on to help the Pittsburgh manager, Billy Meyer. Don Beach's long friendship with Rickey embarrassed the Dodger owners and he quickly transferred to Pittsburgh as auditor. George Sisler could have remained in Brooklyn, but he followed Rickey to head up the scouting department.

Perhaps the most outspoken "Rickey man" on the point of allegiance was Bob Cobb, the doubting Thomas of two years before. He flew from Hollywood to attend a farewell dinner tendered Rickey by the Brooklyn organization before the Pittsburgh signing.

"I'm ending my working agreement with the Dodgers," he announced from the dais, "and certainly not because of any dispute or reflection on Mr. O'Malley. I may be the loser from a baseball standpoint. I don't know Mr. Rickey's plans, or even if he's continuing in baseball, but I'm following him. If he goes into the laundry business, I'll fill the Hollywood park with washing machines and get a working agreement with him. I'm a Rickey man to the finish."

At age sixty-nine, Branch Rickey once more shifted his home. He sold the farm, stock and equipment at Chestertown, Maryland, where he had built duck blinds and pits for shooting wild geese. He bought one hundred acres in exclusive Fox Chapel township, across the Allegheny River from Pittsburgh, with a roomy colonial home and tenant house. He ordered a large stable barn built with the idea of breeding and raising ponies for his grandchildren.

Rickey's need of ballplayers in quantity forced him to take on a number of his old scouts and accelerate the spring talent hunt. They signed free agents and bonus players in a race against time. His "magic" in St. Louis had been locating the raw and zealous player with "the desire to win that dominates." His "legerdemain" in Brooklyn was the detection of high potential in teen-agers and signing them while other clubs waited out the war. Success in Brooklyn also came from secret scouting of Negroes and signing those of skill.

None of these methods was unique when Rickey reached Pittsburgh. All clubs were hunting for the desire to win that dominates. Because of the rule forbidding the signing of high school players until the day after graduation, scouts represented many or all big-league clubs at the nation's commencement exercises. The supply of Negro players was catalogued by all big-league clubs. An increasing number of owners, with nothing to fear now, had decided to follow Rickey's trail-blazing path. It was not until he had been in Pittsburgh three years, however, that Rickey introduced that city to its first Negro player, Curtis Roberts, a fair hitter, but a sure-handed fielder and play-maker.

For the first time in his long career, Branch Rickey was back on even terms with his competitors. He could work harder than they, but he couldn't surpass them in spending, though he came close to it. At one point in the dollar race for rookies an indignant Yankee official exclaimed, "Who do they think they're kidding? The Pittsburgh operation doesn't have that kind of dough to throw around!" By fall of 1951 Rickey and his scouts had spent $496,000 and not wisely enough. Desperate for young players, they had "lowered their sights" in appraising talent, and had paid high prices for mediocrity.

The spending, halted by a strained treasury, totaled more than the Pirates' four-year profit (1947–50) of $438,687. It invaded John Galbreath's private funds. Other stockholders, particularly the Johnson family interests and Bing Crosby, were unable or unwilling to advance loans. Now the club did not represent an attractive investment for additional private or banking capital.

Challenged as never before, Rickey studied his players at Pittsburgh's California training camp in 1952. He wrote Galbreath a letter citing twenty reasons why Ralph Kiner, one of baseball's great power hitters, and a Pittsburgh hero, could not help the Pirates. "This relates only to his baseball value," Rickey explained, "and certainly not to his personality. He is one of the nicest boys I ever met, but Ralph satisfies my requirements in only one respect — as a home run hitter. To me that isn't enough."

Rickey's hope of converting Kiner's value into operating

capital at once was thwarted by the player's off-field business relationships. One conflicting interest involved Pirate co-owners Galbreath and Johnson, and broadcaster Bob Prince. They held 26 per cent of the stock in an ultra-high-frequency television station, WENS, Pittsburgh, over which Johnson hoped one day to televise Pirate games. Nearly two years, and considerable scheming and negotiating, passed before Rickey sold Kiner's contract. Worth $200,000 at the time of Rickey's letter (the Braves had offered $150,000 and seven players), it finally brought $100,000 in cash from the Cubs.

What to do about Kiner's contract was only part of Rickey's reconstruction plans. Manager Billy Meyer was beset with personal and health problems. He would have to be relieved. Fred Haney had won the Pacific Coast League pennant at Hollywood for the second time in four years, and was stunned at learning that his contract wasn't to be renewed. Co-owner Bob Cobb had informed him with no little regret, because they were personal friends, when Haney asked for a salary increase from $16,000 to $20,000. Rickey planned to pry Walter Alston loose from Montreal, place him in Hollywood for 1953 and bring him to Pittsburgh a year later.

Immediately after that, the Dodgers dismissed another "Rickey man," John L. Reeves, president at Fort Worth. Bobby Bragan, managing in the Cuban Winter League, checked with Reeves, and then telephoned Brooklyn, "If you don't want Mr. Reeves, you don't want me. I'm a Reeves man and I'm a Rickey man. You have my resignation."

"Don't be hasty," pleaded Buzzie Bavasi. "There's a triple-A spot open for you in Toronto."

Bragan declined it curtly, and began telephoning Rickey to ask for the only other top job open, Hollywood. Rickey was in New York on his quest of Alston for Pittsburgh. He listened to Bragan and, when he failed to land Alston, signed Bobby.

Fred Haney, unemployed and attending the baseball meetings in Phoenix, Arizona, appeared in Rickey's room. Haney knew of the Meyer situation and that Pittsburgh needed a manager who could work with farm-club youngsters. Insisting he was that manager, Haney asked for the job, and persisted. Rickey listened to the insistent plea, and soon rationalized away his own objections. After all, Haney had managed in the major leagues, though for three disappointing years. He wasn't the right answer to Pittsburgh's problem, but who, besides Alston, was? So Haney received a contract, not at the $20,000 he had sought in vain from Cobb, but at $30,000. Rickey paid that figure rather than have it said he had cut Meyer loose to save $10,000. Meyer, in failing health, remained as Pirate farm-club trouble shooter.

The Kiner deal in June, 1953, tried the patience of the fans and sports writers, and Rickey moved to the hottest part of the griddle. *Press* sports editor Chet Smith had warned Rickey in reply to a confidential query about fan reaction to Kiner's departure, "You've got to win the pennant without Kiner, or contend for it with him."

Smith and less understanding critics of Rickey, who, they claimed, had "lost his touch," did not know that he had borrowed some $200,000 against future income to invest in the Pirates and help keep the foundering ship afloat. "My stock," Rickey said of the 12 per cent he had taken on, "isn't a good buy now. I've got to make it worth that."

In mid-season of 1953, Pittsburgh felt the pinch of losses to the military. Even bonus players were absorbed. Rickey was forced to field a young and inept team, one of the worst of his career. But he did not complain. "We get back what we give, and more," he said, "because the boys are stronger, better citizens. While none of the major-league clubs is spared, we in our situation are like the mite-giving widow St. Luke tell about. She cast in more than the others. We give players that we cannot spare."

The gravity of Rickey's many problems in Pittsburgh mounted during the second half of 1953. The declining income was ruinous. Sagging attendance at Forbes Field would dip under 600,000 for the first time in ten years. The corporate loss, with $677,263 for 1952, would total more than $1,100,000 for two years.

Rickey was not satisfied with Haney's work. In late summer he asked Walter O'Malley about the chances of getting Pee Wee Reese from the Dodgers as his playing manager. O'Malley discouraged this idea by indicating that Reese might succeed Charlie Dressen. Rickey's hope of landing Walter Alston was rising again when Harold Parrott, business manager at Brooklyn, visited Fox Chapel immediately after the 1953 World Series. With no more than coincidence as a guide, Rickey regarded the visit as both social and exploratory.

"I was delighted to see Harold," Rickey explained. "His conversation and questions were casual, and perhaps it was only my imagination feeding on desperation, but I chose to believe that Alston had become a strong candidate for the job of managing the Dodgers. It was a natural front-office decision, for Vice-president Bavasi and Walter had worked together successfully seven years before at Nashua. I talked freely about Alston, held back nothing in my appraisal of him as a big-league possibility. But when Parrott left my home, I felt certain that I now had neither Reese nor Alston."

Management and sundry worries were overshadowed temporarily in November. Rickey's younger brother, Frank, suffered a fatal heart attack while building a new home on the old Duck Run farm. The trip back to Rushtown took more out of Branch Rickey mentally and physically than any previous personal blow. Despite his own seventy-one years, he was wholly unprepared for death so close. Frank was only sixty-five.

Yet Rickey continued to neglect his own physical welfare while fighting to solve the desperate need of operating cash. Unable to hail a cab in midtown New York, he rode the subway with neither vest nor overcoat, got out at Wall Street and walked to an important financial meeting in a driving rain, arriving soaked to the skin. He was authorized to offer the Johnson family interests to a wealthy investor "at cost," provided the purchaser would match future loans to be made by Galbreath.

"We have the nucleus of a strong organization," he explained, "on the field and on my blackboard. It is future, of course, but good. The alternative to making this deal is . . . well, burning down the house to heat it! I will have to sell contracts I need to build around. Parting with them means a perennial eighth-place operation. But if I can keep them . . ."

The offer was declined after a few days of study. Within a month Danny O'Connell went to the Milwaukee Braves for six players and $200,000 in cash. Two weeks later Murry Dickson went to the Phillies for two players and $72,500. Rickey could now finance training at Fort Pierce, Florida, and minor-league camps at Brunswick, Georgia, and Huntsville, Texas.

Despite the last-place play of the parent team, Rickey had built one more bustling farm-club organization. And it had been done by scouts who were unable to compete financially with those of fifteen other clubs in the bonus field. They had assembled 344 minor-league players, not counting those on the Hollywood roster, and another 166 who were in the armed forces.

Just as the five players obtained in the Kiner deal failed to shore up the Pirates in 1953, so did the players obtained for O'Connell and Dickson fail to help in 1954. Pittsburgh had nine of thirteen minor-league teams in championship playoffs, but the parent team finished last for the third straight year. Forbes Field attendance dropped to a ruinous 475,000 and the books showed a net operating loss of $198,920.

Meanwhile, Bobby Bragan, winner of the 1953 Coast League championship with Hollywood, had tied San Diego for first honors in 1954. Could he replace Haney at Pittsburgh? It was a major topic of discussion at the Fort Myers, Florida, training camp.

"I am a weakling in such matters," Rickey says in trying to rationalize his dissatisfaction with Haney while still retaining him. "I procrastinate and hope. I wait for men around me to take the initiative, when I know in my heart they're counting on me. It's one of my glaring faults, and yet I hate to give up on anyone. I can fire a person for cause. But when I am responsible for many of a manager's troubles, or those of a scout or office worker, I leaven whatever shortcomings he shows with a conviction that it's not enough his fault for corrective action.

"Haney was not a disciplinarian. His failure to exact full measure of performance and team-first attitudes from older players influenced the work of some youngsters. He did not have a cohesive team, and it was my hope that he would develop one through the spring training. It was vital to us, because our over-all skill was admittedly low. With so much at stake, I felt certain Fred would realize this and take steps. Once he had a cohesive team, he would win more games, because his methods on the field were and are sound. And so, when we could have brought in Bragan, I prolonged the decision beyond the point for decisive, effective action."

The Pirates opened the season with six weeks of disappointing play, relieved only by a six-game winning streak. Another "meeting on Haney" was held at Rickey's home. Again the question of bringing in Bragan from Hollywood was posed. The staff decided such a move would be construed as "head hunting" to save Rickey in his fifth and pivotal year. Besides, the change couldn't help the team materially in 1955. Haney remained on.

As early as April, 1954, Rickey had forecast his "retirement at the end of my contract." Those of anti-Rickey sentiment saw great hope in the "retirement" prophecy, not knowing that he could name a new status, or remain as general manager. Through the closing weeks of 1955, they heralded his waning tenure with glee. The news that he could continue as direct or indirect head of the organization came as a shock. Would he retire or wouldn't he?

Actually Rickey held a position that could have been commanding, had he wished to be anything but cooperative. He owned more than 12 per cent of the club and had a firm contract calling for a salary of $250,000 over the next five years. Stock and contract represented a value of half a million dollars. More important to him than stock or salary were the key men who had followed him to Pittsburgh and worked under great handicaps. With his own status and future in doubt, he wanted them as secure in their jobs as conditions would permit, so he cleared the decks for new executive direction.

Fred Haney's contract contained a clause stating that failure to discuss the future by the last day of the season would automatically extend the contract another year. A week before the end of the season Rickey met with Haney. He explained that, because of the uncertain front office situation, he could not usurp the prerogative of the new general manager, whoever he might be, by hiring a field manager. Therefore the contract would simply not be extended. On Sunday, September 25, Rickey's secretary, Kenneth Blackburn, handed Haney a letter stating that his contract was not automatically renewed. Haney called Rickey at Fox Chapel to ask if this information was for release to the press. Rickey said no.

"What am I to tell the writers?" Haney asked.

"Nothing. It's simply a formality to cover the clause in your contract."

"But I've got to tell them something."

Rickey replied that he knew of nothing to tell them, and that no one could know anything until the ball club's board of directors met a month hence. But Haney showed the letter to sports writers, including those with the visiting Brooklyn team, and announced that he had been fired after three years of hard work and loyalty, and that he was out of a job.

Once again Rickey made the headlines as a hard-heart who had victimized a faithful employee with his own administrative ineptitude. During the World Series, Haney received all the pity and sympathy usually accorded a victim of major disaster.

A few days later John Quinn, general manager of Milwaukee, telephoned Fox Chapel to inquire about Haney's fitness, and the facts behind the "firing."

"I didn't fire him, John," Rickey said. "I was on the verge of replacing him a couple of time for his own sake as well as mine. In September it was a formality. He knew about it a week or ten days ahead of time. I've written to a couple of newspapermen correcting their misrepresentation." Quinn then asked if Haney would be a suitable "number one coach" under manager Charlie Grimm. "For your situation he'd be all right," Rickey replied. "You have a veteranized team. They know their way around. Fred can do the job. Do you want him to manage?"

"Charlie's contract has one more year to go," Quinn said.

"He'll serve your purpose, John," Rickey said. To intimates he confided later, "If Milwaukee gets off to a bad start next year, Haney will be the manager."

Not knowing that Rickey had cinched his appointment with the Braves, Haney and his many sports-writing friends continued to express chagrin that approximated bitterness.

Wid Matthews resigned from his job with the Cubs to make way for a front-office housecleaning in Chicago a few months later. Facing two attractive offers from National League clubs, he got in touch with his old boss immediately for counsel. Most of Rickey's former employees do.

Recommending Milwaukee, source of one offer, Rickey advised, "It's newer territory, boy, and perhaps more secure in some ways. You'll be with your old friend, Haney, and Fred can use your kind of help. You'll be happier and it'll work out fine for both of you. Good luck."

Branch Rickey's long-heralded retirement from the Pirates became a fact in late October, 1955. Named Chairman of the Board, he made himself available to his successor and the staff in an advisory capacity. He set up shop in a four-room office apartment at the north end of his tenant house at Fox Chapel. The occasional bellow of cattle replaced the anguished cry of Forbes Field fans. His personal secretary, Blackburn, was assigned to continue in the same capacity.

An operating loss of $601,846 for 1955 brought the five-year total to more than $2,000,000, a figure called, in corporate operation, "carryover loss." It can be recaptured from future profit years, if any. Pittsburgh figures were revealed with those of other clubs during the Congressional investigation of baseball as a business two years later.

Rickey's successor was thirty-seven-year-old Joe L. Brown, son of the famed comedian, who moved up from the ranks. Brown had served his apprenticeship in the front office at Pittsburgh, then at Waco, Texas. Appointed president of the New Orleans subsidiary, he built a thriving second-place club, so prosperous that Rickey was able to sell the franchise to a local group for $200,000 cash and $50,000 in New Orleans stock. That sale had provided him with capital to start the 1955 training season at Fort Myers.

With Brown promoted, all other personnel in the Pittsburgh operation remained essentially the same. Anti-Rickey feeling had been placated by the mere fact that he was "out" and that Brown, by Galbreath's assurance, was on his own as general manager.

Brown began his duties on November 1 by sifting applications for Fred Haney's old job. All were considered, but there was only one logical choice by any standard: Bobby Bragan. His place at Hollywood was filled by another old Rickey man, Clay Hopper, who transferred from Seattle. After a half century of Rickey influence, the appeal of his trade mark on a worker was inescapable.

Rickey's retirement brought countless columns of praise and paragraphs of regret throughout the nation. All of them delighted him, but none as much as an editorial in the St. Louis *Post Dispatch*. He had "made" those hallowed columns in the past, but rarely. He insisted that this last editorial would help "restore whatever good opinion my former friends had of me." It concluded:

> There are those — and they are not few — who would welcome Rickey back to St. Louis even if there are no baseball jobs open here. Like Red Smith, they remember him as "a player, manager, executive, lawyer, preacher, horse-trader, spellbinder, innovator, husband and father and grandfather, farmer, logician, obscurantist, reformer, financier, sociologist, crusader, sharper, father confessor, checker shark, friend and fighter.
>
> Judas Priest! What a character!

His table-desk in the office portion of his apartment was

soon piled as high as ever it had been in St. Louis, Brooklyn or Pittsburgh. His endless correspondence now contained even more invitations to speak, to write books and pamphlets, to help in church and charities. His telephone, still a direct line to almost all points in the baseball world, rang with such frequency that the switch in the main house was left open to route all calls directly to him. Soon he installed a special line with a private number, so that he wouldn't tie up the house phones.

Surrounded by walls covered from floor to ceiling with memorabilia from his career, such as cartoons from sports pages, college and law school diplomas and his nine honorary degrees, he sat at his desk in his first year of "retirement," contemplating trips to Mexico for ballplayers, to New York for preliminaries on deals, to Florida for fishing and kibitzing the team operation, to thirty-nine different cities for speaking engagements. He also undertook a month-long campaign in behalf of President Eisenhower's re-election, and a few advisory meetings with either Joe Brown or Branch Rickey, Jr., who lives nearby.

One high spot of his first "inactive" year came on June 1, 1956, when his six children and many of his grandchildren, now numbering sixteen, gathered at Fox Chapel. The telephone rang throughout the day. A steady stream of telegrams, enough to fill two large volumes, poured in. Friends dropped by. There were many tokens of remembrance, and congratulations for Branch and Jane, and Miss Mabel Moulton, too, for she was maid of honor in the wedding at Lucasville fifty years before.

Of the many invitations to speak, Branch Rickey favors those that provide an opportunity for him to discuss Negro integration. That subject occupied an increasingly large part of his thinking after he had relieved the spiritual perplexity created in him by the liberal-minded churchman. The prelate's casual statement that "nobody really believes in the divinity of Jesus any more" had moved Rickey to more intense Bible-reading which led him to a vivid parallel of his own dilemma. Zacchaeus, the rich and undersized tax collector of Jericho, was driven by curiosity and skepticism to climb the sycamore, overlook the crowd and see Jesus for himself. Rickey's reading and soul-searching convinced him that, being "up a tree," he was a kind of twentieth century Zacchaeus.

"Jesus saw him up there from the road," Rickey recounted in explaining his search for solution, "and said, 'Zacchaeus, make haste, and come down; for today I must abide in thy house.' That was good enough for me. I climbed down from my personal sycamore with the conclusion and assurance that He abides in my house, and that every man is therefore a cathedral unto himself. I was able to pray again, say grace and enter my church — enter any church — thoroughly clean in heart and spirit."

Within a year of Rickey's retirement, baseball began to feel and show the loss of his influence and leadership. He had vigorously protested the unwarranted annihilation of minor-league baseball that began with wholesale invasion of their territory by broadcasting in 1954. Equally ruinous network television followed. This devastating coverage resulted from the Supreme Court's ruling in November, 1953, that organized baseball was violating no existing antitrust law.

Four years later the minor leagues that Rickey had resuscitated almost singlehandedly in 1931 were gasping for survival. The nation's fans talked only big-league baseball as a result of daily saturation by radio and television. Lack of firm and assertive leadership within the big-league structure had permitted the runaway destruction. That lack also permitted a sudden rush to capitalize on the potential millions of television income in once-remote parts of the nation. Capricious financial maneuvers went unnoticed. Overlapping big-league financial interests were condoned. Chaotic uncertainty followed sudden pleas for drastic abandonment of still-lucrative and historic baseball areas and the fans responsible for both. All but forgotten was the importance of play on the field.

By this time, however, Branch Rickey's major concern was America's effort to solve her racial problems, particularly those relating to the inherent rights of the Negro. Buttressed by his own initiative and experience, his exhaustive study of all written material he could find on the subject, Rickey began to work as hard in this field as he ever did in developing baseball clubs.

"We will never think as a nation," he declared, "until the entire nation is permitted to think and act like one."

His effort in this direction is not without sacrifice, for at seventy-five he is far from his old and physically nimble self. He suffers from an arthritic left knee, a degree of hypertension that alarms examiners and, of course, his "permanent guest," Ménière's disease.

In late 1956 his "guest" took over while he was speaking in Washington, D.C. Faces in his large audience became a massive pinwheel and then disappeared as his vision failed. Fortunately he had gripped the sides of the lectern firmly. Letting go meant a loss of balance, collapse and another trip to the hospital. He held on desperately, silent, fighting to see again, fighting for just one glimpse of a word in his notes. Granted that, he would improvise.

What seemed an eternity of darkness lasted nearly three minutes before the paper slip whirled into focus. Finally he could make out the words. Still holding on for balance, but unable to see the audience, he spoke, first apologizing for the long and embarrassing silence. He explained his predicament. He assured them he was fine again. He wasn't, but he continued speaking to the end of his plea for integration without force, riot, bloodshed or further blots on the nation's history. He spoke with the authority of one who knew it was possible.

Since relinquishing his job as general manager of the Pirates, Rickey has evaded direct answers to questions about his so-called "failure" in Pittsburgh. He has never acknowledged the word as a factor of finality. It was always a temporary condition, a transient state, subject to improvement. So it was with his five-year tenure of rebuilding the Pirates. His plans, however grandiose, collapsed when the money ran out and he had to sell key players to keep the club in business. He refuses to blame anybody, and adds, laughing, "Why can't you just say the 'old man lost his touch'?"

But he will talk about another five-year venture that staggered and wheezed through to what might be called success. Always concerned about the danger of "bean balls" and the "dust off" pitch, he backed the idea of a Fiberglas cap for batters in late 1952. He set up a corporate operation, sold stock to a few friends, set aside some for his family and then began losing money. He sold bonds to the few stockholders and, when they became dicouraged, bought them back, poured in more money, bought up a few more discouraged stockholders and muddled along.

But in 1957 the batting helmet became standard equipment in the big leagues, and on many minor-league teams. Little Leaguers now wear them. Industrial baseball teams place large orders. Rickey was delighted to learn that his corporate effort would produce 300,000 helmets for the year, and even a profit after retiring many of the bonds. With the thing a success, he turned administration and the presidency of the American Baseball Cap Company over to his secretary, Kenneth Blackburn, looking forward to a month's fishing in Canada.

Branch Rickey's lifelong habit of looking forward leaves him no time to look backward. Today he looks forward with an optimism that mocks his seventy-five years. He expressed it best when an Ohio Wesleyan University alumnus, Dr. Norman Vincent Peale, once asked him what was the most exciting event of his long career.

"It hasn't happened yet," Rickey confided.

Droll though it sounds, the statement was an accurate reflection of Branch Rickey's unpredictable life. It was also prophetic, for the year 1957 produced an experience as exciting and challenging as anything in the seventy-five years of his past. Called to the White House in July, he was asked to contribute his knowledge and unique experience toward the success of the long-range program of Civil Rights. He consented and President Eisenhower appointed him Vice-Chairman of the seven-man President's Committee on Government Employment Policy.

The basic function of the Committee, which is now made up of three public members and four appointees from the Departments of Civil Service, Labor, Defense, and Defense Mobilization, has two major objectives. One is to provide simple and readily accessible channels of investigation and adjudication of any complaint of discrimination on account of race, color, religion or national origin made by any government employee or applicant for government employment. The other is to inaugurate a long-range program of education and persuasion designed to eliminate practices of discrimination and to invoke policies of equal treatment throughout the government. The Committee meets with and advises members of the President's Cabinet and serves the welfare of some 2,350,000 government workers.

Said a White House spokesman close to President Eisenhower:

"Of course, we are absolutely delighted to have Branch Rickey as one of the public members of this vital Committee. The President likes him and the record that Mr. Rickey established is one for American history on a large scale. Bringing him in as Vice-Chairman is a great boon to the government, and also a great honor and recognition of his leadership in the field of Civil Rights.

"Mr. Rickey will have an opportunity to express himself on a national scale, and even international, for this Committee will travel to all parts of the nation and could well reach into the outlying posts of the United States. It places on a presidential level a very important phase of Civil Rights, mainly the cleaning up of matters within the federal establishment — cleaning house — before asking the rest of the country, or the world, to do it. The Employment Policy group is a sister committee to the President's Committee on Government Contracts, of which Vice-President Nixon is Chairman; and it will coordinate its efforts with the work of the Civil Rights Commission, a third group, to be formed under the recently enacted legislation."

The unexpected midsummer development burdened Branch Rickey with a combination of great pride, deep humility and cruel frustration. He could handle the pride and humility, but the necessity of remaining silent about committee meetings, hearings, plans, discussions, when or if he met or dined with President Eisenhower, what was said, or hoped — his garrulous nature was challenged as never before.

"I just don't talk about any part of it," he sighed. "Besides, words alone won't solve the problems. It's got to be done by action."

Acknowledgment

BECAUSE a biographer owes more to his sources — libraries and people — than any other writer, a listing of my creditors would be longer than the index that follows. To name a few benefactors would unfairly qualify the assistance of others. Every story, letter and telephone call was a valued contribution. The Turkey Creek student, Class of '99, seen briefly in Spokane, Washington, helped as much as the librarian at Ohio Wesleyan University, where I was allowed to work at will and at length between trips to the files of the nearby Delaware *Gazette*. The man who showed me a receipt for 1911 office rent in Boise, Idaho, was no whit less important than the patient ladies at the St. Louis library who let me study the newspaper stacks for many weeks.

Nor does my failure to include thousands of precious contributions measure their value. A writer who can discard 75 per cent of his endless gleanings has the blessed assurance of little overlooked. My profound thanks to many individuals, privately expressed, runs the full gamut from Branch Rickey down, or up, to the editors whose protective pencils prevent authors from exposing themselves publicly as garrulous illiterates. I end up with little credit for the book itself. However, I can make one claim to accomplishment without help: Every error in this volume is my very own.

ARTHUR MANN

Index